Computational Science

Computational Science

Kunwar Singh Vaisla

ARCLER
PRESS

www.arclerpress.com

Computational Science

Kunwar Singh Vaisla

Arcler Press
224 Shoreacres Road
Burlington, ON L7L 2H2
Canada
www.arclerpress.com
Email: orders@arclereducation.com

ISBN: 978-1-77407-749-8 (Hardcover)

ABOUT THE AUTHOR

Dr. Kunwar Singh Vaisla is Ph. D. in Computer Science from Kumaun University, Nainital, MCA from University of Rajasthan, Jaipur, India and B. Sc. from Raj Rishi College, Alwar, Rajasthan, India. He is currently working as Professor at Department of Computer Science and Engineering at BT Kumaon Institute of Technology, India. He is editorial board member of many reputed international journals such as IJGCA, ITIST, IJIFR, CAIJ, ICACCE, IJWSC.

TABLE OF CONTENTS

LIST OF FIGURES

LIST OF ABBREVIATIONS

AFD	astrophysics fluid dynamics
AI	artificial intelligence
ALU	arithmetic logic unit
AM1	Austin model 1
CGI	computer-generated imagery
CNDO	complete neglect of differential overlap
CNS	compressible Navier-Stokes
CPU	central processing unit
CS	computer science
CSE	Computational Science and Engineering
CU	control unit
DFT	density functional theory
EMG	Estakhr's material geodesic
FIT	finite integration techniques
HF	Hartree-Fock
HMM	hidden Markov model
HPC	high-performance computing
IE	integral equations
ISM	interstellar medium
IT	information technologies
MCMC	Markov chain-Monte Carlo
MHD	techniques to magneto-hydrodynamics
MINDO	modified intermediate neglect of differential overlap
ML	machine learning
MM	molecular mechanics
MNDO	modified neglect of diatomic overlap
MOS	metal oxide semiconductor

MPI	message passing interface
OS	operating system
PCs	personal computers
PDEs	partial differential equations
PIC	particle-in-cell
PM	particle-mesh
PM3	Parametrization method 3
PPP	Pariser-Parr-Pople
PTD	physical theory of diffraction
RAM	random access memory
ROM	read only memory
SGM	semi-global matching
SPH	smooth-particle hydrodynamics
SVN	subversion

PREFACE

Computational science lies at the heart of most scientific processes. The field has witnessed an explosion in adoption over the recent few years, and is now applicable in various sectors such as healthcare, education, industry, entertainment, and so on. The discipline should also not be mistaken for computer science (CS), even though they sound similar.

Most computational science programs make use of considerable amounts of high-performance computing (HPC) resources. The general breakdown of the forms of computational science study areas includes smart devices, high-performance clusters, embedded components, and big data among others. Even though these applications may be used in different ways, their fundamental computational algorithms are quite similar to each other.

Additionally, the effective application of computational technologies needs abstract, methodological, technical, and scaling procedures. This allows for easy studying, monitoring, and prediction of objects. Consequently, different software libraries have nowadays been established in order to fill up particular computing needs, so that application developers don't need to waste their time re-developing supercomputing software to handle certain computing functions.

In this presentation, we are going to look at specific topics in computational science and their unique significance. Chapter 1 discusses introduction to computational science, Chapter 2 discusses about scientific visualization, Chapter 3 discusses about computational chemistry, Chapter 4 discusses about computational electromagnetic, Chapter 5 discusses about computational fluid dynamics, Chapter 6 discusses about computational ocean modeling, Chapter 7 discusses about computational structural mechanics, Chapter 8 discusses about computational biology, Chapter 9 discusses about computational astrophysics, and Chapter 10 discusses about computational finance.

The main task of a computational scientist is data analysis. Originally, just a few scientific fields dealt with large quantities of experimental data, for example, Astrophysics, but today that number has grown significantly and nearly every field can generate large quantities of data due to modern technology.

In most cases, their work involves analyzing the data, covering; clean up, reviewing systematic effects, fine tuning, understanding, and reducing the information to the perfect form for scientific research. The second stage in data analysis may also be done, which covers model fitting, that is, reviewing theoretical models and determining which one best suits the data apart from estimating their parameters using error bars, something that requires an understanding of statistics models.

Furthermore, computational science involves simulations, that is, generation of artificial data that are useful for understanding scientific models and seeking to recreate experimental data for purposes of characterizing the reaction of a scientific element.

To succeed as a computational scientist, you should have some background knowledge on coding systems and programming languages like Python, FORTRAN, C++ and C. Generally, it's crucial to have considerable experience with one or more programming language, however, Python is regarded as the safest choice since: it's well-grounded in many scientific fields, plus has simple to grasp syntax systems in comparison to other popular programming languages. Python also hosts the largest amount of scientific libraries.

Moreover, Python's performance is similar to C, C++ and Java when using optimized libraries such as scipy, numpy, and pandas, which feature Python front-ends to highly optimize C and Fortran codes; as such it's necessary for users to avoid loop explicit and learn how to develop a "vectorized" code, which allows whole data arrays and grids to be programmed in one step.

Chapter

1

Introduction to Computational Science

CONTENTS

1.1. INTRODUCTION

Computational science has recently been gaining popularity in the scientific community. It's a computer discipline that focuses on the design, application, and use of logical models to examine and solve scientific matters. Furthermore, the term may refer to the application of computers in doing simulations or mathematical exploration of a scientific method or program (Figure 1.1).

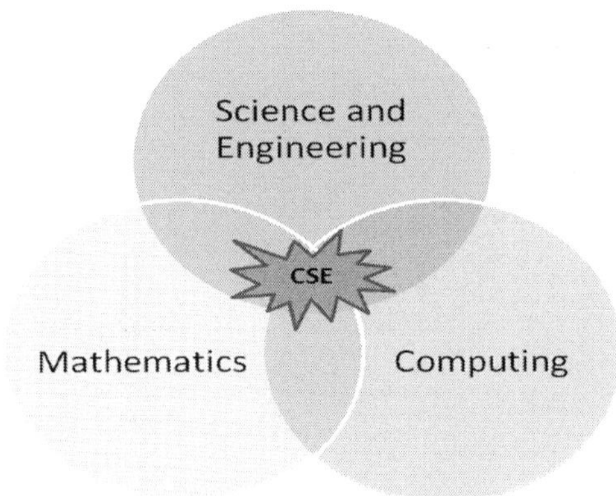

Figure 1.1. Computational science is driven by math, science, and computing models.

Source:*https://www.researchgate.net/figure/Three-pillars-of-Computational-Science-and-Engineering_fig1_220856954 (accessed on 3 April 2020).*

In previous years, there was observational, experimental, and theoretical science, but computational science is introducing the fourth dimension to science that's changing how researchers work and make discoveries. As a subject, computational science relies majorly on developments in computer hardware, including the enhancements in computer algorithms as well as arithmetic techniques.

Through computational science, operators can perform things which were previously way too hard to do because of the difficulty of the mathematics involved, massive amount of calculations involved, and even both. Besides, computational science further allows people to build models which allow them to make solid predictions, concerning what may occur in the laboratory, such that they can perhaps better organize to make solid observations or to comprehend better what they're seeing.

Additionally, computational techniques may be applied to perform experiments which may be too costly or too hazardous to perform in the laboratory. We may, for instance, use computational methods to predict exactly how a new medication may behave within the system. Consequently, this allows users to curb, though not eliminate, the total amount of animal tests which we may have performed before the emergence of computational pharmacology methods. Even though computational models can't possibly substitute the lab, still they have nowadays become an integral part of the general search for research knowledge.

Presently, there are different descriptions of computational science-many scholars describe the field as "a multipurpose approach to finding answers for complex problems which applies ideas and skills borrowed from the fields of science, computer (CS) science, and arithmetics." Of significance also is your grasp that computational science isn't CS, which is another field altogether-computational science, refers to a technique that allows for study of different phenomenon.

1.2. BASIC PRINCIPLES

In tech science, experimental data is often applied to develop and corroborate computational research; generally, computational research gives the theorists new guidelines and ideas to go with in their activities. Most of the basic questions in science (particularly those with possibly broad social, administrative, and scientific effect) are occasionally known as the "Grand Challenge" issues.

A majority of these so-called Grand Challenge issues are those which can just be addressed computationally. Definitely, chemistry problems are regarded by computational scientists as among the main Grand Challenge subgroups. As for the field of chemistry, among the main arguments proposed has been that we've known nearly all hypothetical mathematics needed to address every chemical problem since 1928 (Angela and Shiflet, 2014).

But it's only after the invention of computational science, during the late 50's, which led to the creation of tools and technologies required to solve these complicated mathematical equations derived from the theorists. Within this regard, computational science can be defined as a scientific application that's reinforced by the ideas and abilities of mathematics (algorithms) as well as CS (architecture).

Key to computational science issues is the research itself-what scientific occasion or problem carries the most interest? Other questions of concern are its possible boundaries, the components, or factors which are aspects of the system. When these key decisions are made, next the search engine looks for a convenient algorithm: which is a mathematical system that can be developed to represent the conduct defined by the problem parameters.

Oftentimes, it's necessary to use a few or multiple arithmetic "recipes" to commence the solution of the arithmetic model generated. Multiple arithmetical recipes are too complicated to calculate through hand and/or need repetitive calculations-iterations-for getting nearer to the answer. During this point, computational software tools can be applied for implementing an algorithm or arithmetical model, usually on well-sized computer through the computational software tool (Angela and Shiflet, 2014).

But true to say, the entire process is by itself "iterative"-meaning solutions to preliminary arithmetic methodologies to the problem produce a better algorithm, possibly with the requirement for improving computational power, as well as precision.

Possibly a basic problem is constructive. This issue is regarded as a good example of the computational approach because it's something which everybody will possibly understand. The implementation or problem which a computational scientist is seeking to solve also forms a big part of the equation.

1.3. REASONS TO STUDY THE SUBJECT

Present day scientists increasingly depend on computational modeling as well as data analysis for exploring and comprehending the natural world. Considering the popular use in science as well as its crucial significance to the direction that science and manufacturing takes, computational modeling contributes significantly to progress and scientific advances in the modern century.Additionally, this discipline seeks at educate the next generation concerning cross-disciplinary science where computational science applies, and possible values required to pose and resolve present and new scientific, technical, and societal issues (Holder and Eichholz, 2019).

1.3.1. A Multipronged Subject

Computational science is a special learning program that handles in a comprehensive manner computation, being the triple junction applicable to algorithm development plus analysis, top performance computing, as well as applications for scientific as well as engineering exhibition and data science. Generally, scientific computing concentrates on the creation of predictive computer prototypes of the globe around us. WHEN studies of physical matter evolved to address gradually complex systems, conventional experimentation is typically infeasible.

Additionally, computational modeling has grown to become a major tool for comprehending these systems; identical in stature, for just the appropriate questions, in order to analyze and experiment. Besides, the field of scientific computing covers the creation of new methods which make challenging problems compliant on modern computing systems, providing researchers and scientists with new windows reflecting the globe around us (Holder and Eichholz, 2019).

Data science concentrates on the creation of tools developed to identify trends within datasets which help researcher that are faced with massive hordes of data, for assessing main operations during those datasets.

These key connections provide features which allow scientists to detect models which, consequently, aid in the making of accurate estimates in complex structures. For instance, a main data science objective on the biological angle shall be improved care for patients (e.g., personalized medicine). Considering a patient's genetic pre-disposition, the accurate data-driven system would detect the most effectual treatment for the patient.

Merging machine learning (ML) and data analysis together with quantum calculations is an interesting topic, which may totally alter the future journey of computer simulations, plus how we examine physical systems within the least length scales (Holder and Eichholz, 2019).

1.4. MERGING INSIGHTS WITH STATISTICAL TOOLS AND COMPUTATIONAL ABILITIES

A significant goal of this subject is building your capacity to present and solve problems which combine insights from a few or several disciplines, ranging from natural sciences to mathematical tools and even computational skills. It offers a unique blend of applied as well as hypothetical knowledge and skills.

Basically, these attributes are priceless in the modern-day multi-disciplinary settings, both scholarly and professional. The key focus isn't on educating computer specialists, rather providing learners with an education that provides a solid understanding of the general science and an incorporated knowledge on ways of using essential processes from computational science (Langtangen, 2013).It needs an education which covers both the particular disciplines such as physics, geoscience, and mathematics, combined with a solid experience in computational science.

1.4.1. Application and Practicality

Computational science has been growing in bounds as a multidisciplinary subject that utilizes modern computing systems for understanding, as well as solving complex issues. Computational science combines three distinct factors which are:

- Algorithms (arithmetic and non-arithmetic) and demonstration and simulation software established to solve scientific, engineering, and humanities issues.
- Computing and informatics science which formulates and optimizes the high-capacity system firmware, software, networking, as well as data management elements required for solving computationally tasking problems.
- Computing infrastructure supports both scientific and engineering problem-solving, including the structural computer and informatics science.

Computational science is special since it emphasizes an interdisciplinary and teamwork approach, besides the subject is incorporated with a researching center to equip scholars with the skills for developing and applying modern modeling, simulation, and customization software for a wide range of real-life scientific examination, data-driven innovation, and product development solutions.Computational Science discipline provides wider exposure to applied math, scientific-computing, and engineering applications. Because of the broad scope of the interdisciplinary system, different concentration fields are available. The concentration areas permit for increased flexibility, and can evolve as required, to address academic and research aspects of national and universal interests (Langtangen, 2013).

The subject provides opportunities for considerable interaction with different faculty and scientists within the research fraternity. Most research topics in computational science are integrated with other general science-based subjects. Besides, the researchers are encouraged to participate in team-oriented focusing on real-life problems, plus the findings are prepared for adoption into the general public almost with immediate effect.

The primary research focus of Computational Science is meant to create leadership in vital technology areas that affect fields such as; environment, sustainable energy, health, and biological structures, progressive manufacturing, security as well as defense. In order to realize technological progress in some of these research fields, there's need for mutual inter-connected of computational science with other disciplines like physical and arithmetic modeling, grid generation and high-caliber computing.

On a more general note, oftentimes when you hear anything about computational-science and engineering (CSE), computerized models and simulations become a central aspect of the discipline, supplementing (or in some cases substituting) experimentation. Moving from simple application to enjoying computational results needs domain knowledge, mathematical modeling, arithmetical analysis, algorithm creation, software application, program implementation, examination, validation, and imagining of results (Langtangen, 2013).

CSE captures all of these attributes. The models are basically discrete estimations of continuous phenomena. The field addresses not just how to develop the model effectively under different restrictions (such as reduced computational power or computer-memory) but including how to decide whether the model plus its computational insight are accurate enough for reliability.

One common misconception about computational and analytical systems is that it isn't among the main pillars of science, there's also the perception that hypothetical models are equal to computational models having mesh size (Δt) and inclining to zero. Nevertheless, models of stability and constancy from mathematical analysis are required to solidify the connection; most logical-looking discretization may be revealed not to meet in the essential limits.

Besides, studying, and implementing these models to develop numerical approaches lies outside the dual supports of experimental information and theoretical models. As for experimental information it's usually patchy and noisy, plus occasionally inconsistent. Developing, analyzing, and corroborating computational approaches which handle these matters is another matter beyond the reaches of experimental data or theoretical models. Generally speaking, the main features of computational science are algorithms, computers, and information science, including the computing infrastructure (Langtangen, 2013).

1.5. SIGNIFICANCE OF COMPUTATIONAL SCIENCES

Modern advances in theoretical science and experiments depend a lot on developments in computational science. Take for instance the models of fluid dynamics, weather analysis, and radiations transport, whereby the prototypes are large-scale and flexible, thereby making computation science the "only real systematic method of progressing." Similarly, experimentation might not be feasible due to the issue of infeasibility (consider astrophysics of supernovae); inadequate composition for measuring (crash testing); and the more ordinary matters of ethics, safety, and cost in science inventions (Figure 1.2).

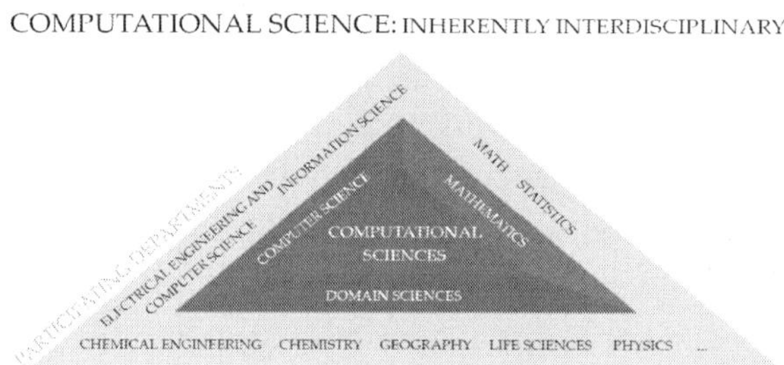

Figure 1.2. As an interdisciplinary subject, computational science is also used in geography, physics, and other fields.

Source: *https://sis.utk.edu/exploreprograms/masters/graduate-minor-in-computational-science.*

However, the idea of a third angle to research methods is definitely debatable. Some scholars contend that Science Has got Two Legs only, plus one can't possibly separate it since computational science has been deeply entrenched in both hypothesis and experiment. Additionally, "the concept in weather science applies a highly technical computational system." The only means to applying the theory is through computation. For example, the Condensed Muon Solenoid research at CERN's Great Hadron Collider produces up to 40 terabytes of fresh data per second, and this volume can't possibly be stored or processed by a few people. Managing such massive volumes of data needs advanced computation (Angela and Shiflet, 2014).

No matter what you believe concerning the amount of pillars that make up science, there's no worry that computational science forms the key to continual scientific progressions. There's constantly the important aspect of having the computations right, or else the models may fall on upon themselves. Other diverse examples emphasizing where computational science often plays a significant role in science breakthroughs are; climate modeling, web mapping, earthquake prediction and material discovery.

1.6. COMPUTATIONAL MODELS

The models of computing don't necessarily have to be quantitative. In fact, the metabolic pathways found in bio-chemistry present a well-known illustration for non-quantitative systems. Nevertheless, in the framework of computational science, almost all prototypes are quantitative, since they predict numbers which are comparable to the numbers derived from the real measurements.

Usually, the models which are most commonly deliberated within the perspective of scientific studies are those for objects in nature which we seek to understand. But, we similarly use physical prototypes to define the instruments which we normally apply to make observations, including non-material phenomenological models for accounting for the things we may not comprehend in detail (Eijkhout, 2013).

Among the widespread models for the latter group are statistical error prototypes, like the quite frequently (but often silently) made hypothesis that a perceived supposition is the "existent" value and an "experimental fault" defined by the probability distribution chart. Usually, computational studies that explore structures for naturally occurring systems are known as "simulations," these are typically performed on models assumed to be accurate, plus with the objective of obtaining data that's hard or difficult to acquire from mere observations.

Additionally, simulations covering a model for research instruments are typically categorized as "virtual experiments." The computational studies which apply statistical prototypes to the information are known as "data analysis" plus normally have the objective of deciding the group of model parameters which best define the data coming from live observations and simulation.

Most scientific models are formed in the context of a theory that describes the standard policies for a massive class of models. One example is the classical mechanics, referring to a model that defines the details of structures of point masses, and finite-size rigid bodies. In the context of classical mechanics, the model for a solid system may be described by just one function known as Hamiltonian (Eijkhout, 2013).

Hypothesis plays a significant role in many mature sectors of science (e.g., physics) though isn't essential for describing models. Much younger disciplines, for instance, systems biology, develop models in a rather ad hoc way without any clear underlying concept. Yet another method is the building of models obtained from diverse concepts in a multi-disciplinary structure, such as climate research.

- ***Computable Systems***: These are the science models which are of key importance to computational science. The computable model works as a reliable and solid system; whose results are comparable to information from observations. Given that validation needs the comparison of solid results with practical data, someone may presume that all quantitative prototypes in science work as computable models. Remarkably, this isn't actually the case. As a matter of fact, many mathematical models applied in science aren't computable.

Take, for instance, the definition of solar systems in regards to classical mechanics which dates back to the times of Isaac Newton and his laws of gravity and motion. In particular, the latter are variance equations for the locations and speeds of celestial objects. Alongside a set of benchmarks obtained from observations (for instance, the locations and velocities of different celestial bodies within a particular period in time), the equations define the specific positions and velocities within any period both in times past and the future (Eijkhout, 2013).

Nevertheless, they don't provide any solutions for computing the concrete numbers that can be evaluated to the observations. Another extra approximation is required to achieve a computable prototype.

For the basic case of a structure with just a pair of components, the analytical solution of a differential equation may be obtained. The solution covers transcendental functions, namely sines and cosines, which are quantifiable to any preferred precision. Nevertheless, when multiple bodies have been integrated into the model, then no analytical solution may be accessible and the differential comparisons should be approximated through finite variance equations.

The creation of computable estimations to the Newtonian system of celestial dynamics continues to be an active research topic. Generally speaking, one may consider the entire sector of numerical analysis to be dedicated towards the construction of computable estimates to non-computable arithmetic models.

It might seem surprising that many mathematical models applied in established domains of science don't actually deserve to be labeled "scientific," since they can't make sure predictions that are directly comparable to the witnessed data.

The definition is that computation systems were for many years regarded a menial duty not commendable of the attention that a notable mathematician or scientist will give, who must focus on mathematical as well as logical thinking systems (Eijkhout, 2013).

While nowadays, it's commonly believed by statisticians and logicians that computation plays a big role in understanding science models, many theoreticians in natural science subjects still regard computation to be an inferior method of exploring scientific models that can only be implemented from sheer necessity once other procedures have failed.

It's suspected that the lack of interest from "real theoreticians" concerning the computational features of science may have added to the challenges outlined above. It further explains why computational training now is still mostly lacking from many science-based curricula all over the world (Eijkhout, 2013).

Science-based models can be described in different ways: such as math equations, diagrams, and plain language among other factors.

This same model may be represented through different notations. Such as, by principle any math equation can be replaced through a verbal definition.

Besides, computable models may be shown in any particular Turing-complete official language, plus in particular whichever of the frequently used coding languages, therefore making them among the most accurate and definite scientific models.The exact fact that there can be a program which runs and generates results shows that the model description is holistic and unambiguous, supposing that the computing structure itself [firmware, operating (OS) system and compiler] function well plus that the coding language it's written in features clearly described semantics (which, regrettably, isn't the case for broadly used languages like C).

While the utilization of computation systems in the procedure of comprehending and detailing science models has been highlighted by scientists, still it's not extensively approved in the science community. One possible example from the engineering realm (the development of musical implements) has also been captured by some scientists. It's ideal for defining the geometrical systems which have been applied for many ages to develop string instruments. The notation is ideal for implementing a group of instructions meant for the computer, or accurate and definite definitions for human readers (Holder and Eichholz, 2019).

The final crucial point touching on computable systems is the significance of correctly detecting, understanding, and recording approximations. Researchers regularly make approximations concerning computational models without identifying them as such, plus therefore don't document these estimates in their publications.

One primary example is using finite-accuracy floating-point numerals in substitution to actual numbers. Many scientists may consider this to be a technical need in fulfilling of a model on the computer, plus therefore an execution feature of computational software. Nevertheless, floating-point figures have properties which differ considerably from actual numbers (for instance, adding, and multiplying are considered to be non-associative), plus the finite accuracy necessarily varies the outcomes of the computations (Holder and Eichholz, 2019).

To make these approximations obvious would also require the contemplation of alternatives, like using interval arithmetic. Generally, any adjustment to the computer program which modifies its results means estimation to the primary computational model. It also covers techniques like lossy condensing of output information, which consequently are regarded as application details.To put in into perspective, computational science covers handling computable scientific systems, which are either built from original principles or more commonly as estimates to non-computable prototypes. A publication defining the computational study must contain a whole definition of models which were really employed in the computations.

As for models put up as approximations, it means that the ultimate approximation must also be provided in order to fully document the procedure. Computable models may be expressed unambiguously through a Turing-full formal language. The ideal Turing-full language must be the ideal technique used for publishing prototypes.

1.7. COMPUTATIONAL SCIENCE TOOLS

Researchers use different tools to collect observational information, look into the model predictions, and do comparisons between the models. The word "tool" is generally used to mean physical objects (e.g., microscopes, and lasers) plus mathematical theories or procedures (e.g., calculus or algebra), though not arithmetic axioms and descriptions, which constitute.

The semantic of mathematics instead of its tool-box. Both PCs and software which are based on them are therefore considered tools. These tools are assessed based by how proficiently they can assist in really getting a project done, this leads to criteria like accuracy, performance, efficiency, expediency, and cost. In scientific journals, these tools are defined mostly in the "Methods" segment. A computational technique corresponds to operating one or several software tools having particular input parameters (Eijkhout, 2013).

Those using scientific tools, not just in science, form a mental model revealing how the tools operate and what they perform. Such mental models often are empirical, besides they are established from training and experience. They're personal and not official in any sense. There's no central difference in how people form cognitive models of a vehicle, microscope, and other objects such as a text editing tool running on the computer.

Usually, mental models get limited to the features of the tools which we need to know, plus they don't cover the tools' internal workings or construction particulars. For instance, to drive a vehicle, there's need for understanding acceleration, braking, and steering, though not the procedure of fuel combustion within the engine. Likewise, we can apply a microscope or even text-editor with far less understanding than it requires designing or building one. Nevertheless, the area of application including the accuracy that's expected from the outcomes form part of the cognitive models that researchers should have for their particular tools (Eijkhout, 2013).

Even though tools are necessary for conducting computational science projects, they aren't regarded to be part of the science outputs, which comprise of confirmed models. Editorials documenting scientific research define the tools and procedures that were applied in respective tests or computations, so as to allow readers to evaluate the relevance of the findings drawn from the respective outputs.

The creation of new tools can also be defined in scientific publications since these tools are significant items for the scientific researching procedure. However, these particular aspects (tools and results) must always be kept distinct. The deduction of a scientific research must always be free of any particular tool in order to merit the name "scientific." Yet another scientist must be able to achieve the same results utilizing different implements, this forms part of the need for reproducibility.

For computational science, the difference between prototypes and techniques isn't always perceptible, since both assume the model of algorithms. There are a few disciplines, like bioinformatics, which are quite methods-oriented plus rarely point back to the models. The bio-informatician is highly likely to suggest a "technique to forecast protein folding" compared to a "prototype for protein folding."

It's partly because of differences in research jargon among different disciplines, though it also highlights deeper issues regarding the function of computing systems in science. The universal basic of a knowledge-oriented prospect for proteins is visibly a technical model for a natural structure (Eijkhout, 2013).

This is even considered a computable model from the perspective of computability theory, whereby there are recognized algorithms which can define the universal minimum in finite period to any particular precision. Nevertheless, that finite period is so lengthy on today's computers, such that the universal minimum can't be calculated in practice.

Many bioinformaticians thus develop heuristic methods which find systems close to the universal minimum present in most cases. In case these heuristic techniques are deterministic, then they must be regarded approximations to the primary model. This isn't actually an option for the heuristic methods which cover random choices, since they don't create any special outcome for a particular input, and thus don't qualify as research models.

It's important to differentiate the application of casualness in heuristics coming from the application of probabilistic models, that is, models which predict noticeable quantities as medians over probability distributions. Besides, the latter are generally the universal-minimum example as highlighted above: the figures they predict are solidly defined and calculable, even though their calculation is often above the restrictions of today's computing innovations (Eijkhout, 2013).

In comparison, a system like k-simply means clustering, whereby the initialization stage needs a subjective random choice, produces a different outcome ever time it's applied, plus there's no reason for attributing any meaning towards the statistical dissemination of these results. As a matter of fact, the dissemination applied in the initialization stage is hardly ever filed since it's regarded to be irrelevant. The function of such heuristics for computational science continues to be studied.

1.8. FIELDS OF COMPUTATIONAL SCIENCE

1.8.1. Computational Engineering

Computational engineering is quite a new discipline which addresses the development and execution of computational systems and simulations, oftentimes combined with high-capacity computing, for solving complicated physical issues which come up regularly in engineering analysis, including design (computational engineering) and natural matter (computational science) (Earnshaw and Wiseman, 2012) (Figure 1.3).

Figure 1.3. Computational engineering provides more detail to mechanical concepts.

Source: *https://www.beuth-hochschule.de/en/b-ced.*

Computational science engineering (CSE) has been defined as the "3rd discovery mode" (close to hypothesis and trials). For many disciplines, computer simulation forms an integral and thus vital aspect of business and research. The computer simulation system offers the ability to enter fields which are either detached from conventional experimentation, or whereby performing traditional empirical investigations is restrictively costly.

CSE, however, must not be mistaken for plain CS, or computer engineering, even though it's a broad discipline that covers aspects like data structure, algorithms, and parallel programming among others. There are still some differences between the disciplines, besides some computer engineering problems can be modeled and solved using verifiable computational engineering techniques (Earnshaw and Wiseman, 2012).

- ***Methodologies***: Most computational science systems and frameworks consist of top performance computing and methods for gaining efficiency (via changes in computer architecture and parallel algorithms). Furthermore, it involves modeling and simulations. The algorithms for solving distinct and continuous problems is vital in this discipline. The analysis and conception of data also borrows from mathematical foundations, consisting of arithmetic and practical linear algebra, primary, and boundary value issues, Fourier analysis and optimization.

The data science needed for formulating methods and algorithms for handling and extracting knowledge from massive scientific data makes use of computing. Similarly, computing, computer-programming, and algorithms have a significant role in this field. The most extensively used coding language in science currently is FORTRAN, which borrows many of its concepts from computing.

Lately, C, and C++ programs have drastically improved in popularity more than FORTRAN. Because of the amount of legacy codes in FORTRAN plus its basic syntax elements, but still the scientific computing team has been rather slow in adopting C++ compared to lingua franca. Due to its largely natural way of conveying mathematical computations, as well as its integral visualization abilities, the trademarked language/environment commonly known as MATLAB is equally widely used, particularly for rapid application growth and model verification (Langtangen, 2013).

Additionally, Python together with other external libraries (like SciPy, Matplotlib, and NumPy) have gained considerable popularity as free and Copy-center substitutes to MATLAB. One numerical solution for the heat equivalence on the pump casing model is using a finite element method for computation.

Computational Science has different applications, such as in Aerospace Engineering or Mechanical Engineering, where combustion simulations, organizational dynamics, computational liquid dynamics, computational thermos-dynamics, and car crash simulations can be used to gain a more comprehensive understanding of the subject (Langtangen, 2013).

Additionally, astrophysical systems also rely on this technology. Battlefield simulations as well as military games, homeland security and emergency response. The fields of Biology and Medicine have also not been left behind, topics like bioinformatics, computational neurological molding, genomics, and biological systems modeling are all counted as part of computational science. For chemistry, calculating the arrangements and attributes of chemical elements/molecules and solids, plus molecular mechanics (MM) simulation and computational chemistry/cheminformatics are also components of the subject.

1.8.2. Bioinformatics

It's an interdisciplinary subject that involves development of computational systems and application programs, used for evaluating biological data. Being an interdisciplinary discipline of science, bioinformatics merges technologies from CS, statistics, as well as optimization for processing biological information.

The final goal of bio-informatics is discovering fresh biological insights via the scrutiny of biological data. Presently, a basic pipeline for addressing the science issue in bio-informatics follows the format mentioned below:

- Wet labs design tests and formulate samples;
- Huge amounts of biological information are produced;
- Current (or fresh) computational and statistical techniques are implemented (or established);
- Data analysis outcomes are further confirmed through wet lab testing methods; and
- Where necessary, the above processes are done all over again with improvements.

Nevertheless, the bio-informatics study normally reflects a double-sided concern. Scientists in (CS) computational science, including other similar fields only consider bio-informatics as one particular implementation of their models and techniques, because of the incapacity to offer accurate solutions to complicated molecular biology issues.Additionally, biologists focus on theory analysis of wet labs such that bioinformatics can act as an instrument for evaluating the biological data produced from their tests. It's not hard to notice that both angles have their unique limitations (Angela and Shiflet, 2014).Computational researchers must have a solid comprehension of biology as well as biomedical sciences, while biologists must better comprehend the structure of their data-analysis issue from an algorithmic viewpoint. Thus, the lack of assimilation of these two aspects doesn't just limit the growth of life-science studies, but further limits the creation of computational systems in bioinformatics.

- ***Beginnings of Bioinformatics*:** The bioinformatics field has grown to become a buzz-phrase in the post-genomic age. Nevertheless, the field isn't completely new. It was started almost 50-years ago by a group of 3 scientists, who made contributions that spurred the birth of modern-day bioinformatics, as a discipline that relies heavily on computational science. These three researchers were Richard Eck, Robert Ledley and Margaret Dayhoff.

While earlier it wasn't known as bioinformatics, still the implementation of computer technology in protein-sequence examination and tracing protein development became the basic aspect of modern bioinformatics. Out of all the scientists mentioned, Dayhoff's contributions particularly emerged the most, plus she's typically recognized as pioneer of bioinformatics due to her multiple contributions, including creating the original amino-acid substitution background for studying protein development.

- ***Bioinformatics Computing Languages***: The field of bioinformatics is mostly concerned with analyzing various tasks and processes that make up this field. For one to effectively manage different bioinformatics applications, it's necessary that various computer programs must be scripted by using different accessible computing languages.

Most of the languages applied to address bio-informatics issues and interrelated analysis are, for instance, the statistical programming languages and scripting languages like Python and Perl, including collective languages like C++, C, and Java. Besides, the R programming code is growing to become among the most commonly used software implements for bioinformatics. Mostly because of its flexibility, data management and modeling abilities (Langtangen, 2013).

The aim of computational science in bioinformatics is studying how regular cellular activities are transformed in multiple disease states, basically the biological data should be merged to develop an all-inclusive image of these activities. Thus, the sector of bioinformatics has transformed so that, even the most persistent task now includes the analysis and clarification of different forms of data.

It also includes nucleotide as well as amino acid structures, protein domains, or protein structures. Additionally, the real process of evaluating and inferring data is known as computational biology. Other sub-disciplines within the field of bio-informatics and computational biology also exist.

They may include, developing, and application of computer programs which allow for effective access to, supervision, and use of, different kinds of information. Including the development of modern algorithms (mathematical systems) and statistical measures which measure relationships existing between groups of massive data sets (Langtangen, 2013).

For instance, there are some techniques for locating genes present within a sequence, whereas others foretell protein structure plus/or function, apart from clustering protein chains into groups of related sequences. The key objective of bio-informatics is improving the comprehension of biological procedures. But what puts it separately from other techniques, nevertheless, is a focus on creating and applying computationally rigorous methods to realize this goal.

Some common examples being: data mining, pattern recognition, machine (ML) learning algorithms, as well as visualization. Some key research efforts for this field include; Chain alignment, gene detection, genome gathering, drug design and discovery, protein system alignment, protein arrangement prediction, gene expression estimation and protein-protein relations, genome-wide relation studies, the molding of evolution and tissue division/mitosis.

Additionally, bioinformatics now involves the development and creation of databases, algorithms, and computational and statistical methods, including theories for solving various formal and applied problems which may arise from the managing and examination of biological data (Langtangen, 2013).

Throughout the last few decades, quick advancements in genomic as well as other particle research technologies and progresses in information technologies (IT) have merged to create a tremendous quantity of information connected to molecular biology.

Some common actions in bioinformatics are mapping and evaluation of DNA and protein structures, matching DNA and protein structures to compare them, as well as developing and checking 3-D replicas of protein structures.

The bioinformatics field is the same as but different from biological computation, plus it's usually regarded as equal to computational biology. Furthermore, biological computation makes use of bioengineering systems and biology for creating biological computers, while bioinformatics utilizes computation to solidly understand biology.

As a computational science, the sector of bioinformatics underwent rapid growth beginning in the mid-90s, compelled mostly by the Person Genome Project including rapid progresses in DNA mapping technology. Examining biological data to create meaningful information comprises of writing and operating software systems which use algorithms from the graph model, artificial intelligence (AI), soft computing, information mining, photo processing, and computer recreation. These algorithms consequently rely on theoretical models like discrete math, control hypothesis, system theory, statistics, and information theory (Langtangen, 2013).

1.8.3. Computational Chemistry

For years, chemists have contributed significantly to the field of computational science, leading to quick advancements in the sector. Computational chemistry refers basically to implementation of chemical, arithmetical, and computing skills in finding solution to various unique chemical problems. The subject uses advanced computers to produce information like molecular properties or virtual experimental results. A few popular computer software that are useful for computational chemistry are; Spartan, GAMESS, MOPAC, and Sybyl among others (Wilson, 2013).

Computational chemistry is also becoming a practical way of examining materials which are too hard to find, or very costly to buy. It also assists chemists to make accurate predictions before operating actual experiments, such that they may be well prepared to make observations.

Moreover, the Schrödinger equation forms the foundation for many of the models that computational chemistry researchers use. It's since the Schrodinger equation defines the atoms and particles with mathematical equations. For example, it's possible to calculate factors such as; electronic structure definitions, geometrical optimizations, frequency measurements, and transition structures among other factors.

The word "computational chemistry" may be applied to mean various things. It may mean, for instance, the application of computers in analyzing information gotten from complex experiments. Nevertheless, more commonly this phrase means the application of computers in making chemical predictions (Wilson, 2013).

Occasionally, computational chemistry may be applied to predict fresh molecules or fresh reactions that are later examined experimentally. Sometimes, computational chemistry can also be used for supplementing experimental studies through presenting data which are difficult to examine experimentally (for instance, transition state arrangements, and energies). From its basic beginnings during the late 50's up to 60's, improvements in theoretical methods and computer-power have drastically improved the effectiveness and significance of computational chemistry.

Generally, there are 2 key aspects of computational chemistry: the first is classical mechanics, while the other one relies on quantum mechanics. Particles are considerably small items which, strictly speaking.

Policies of quantum mechanics should be applied to describe them. Nevertheless, under the appropriate conditions, it's still sometimes practical (and much quicker computationally) to evaluate the molecule through using classical mechanics. The technique is sometimes known as molecular (MM) mechanics, or the "force-field" technique (Spellmeyer, 2005).

Most MM approaches are empirical meaning that the strictures in the model may be obtained through fitting it to identified experimental data. Besides, quantum mechanical techniques can typically be grouped either as semi-empirical or ab initio. The latter label, ab initio, simply means "as of the start" and implies a technique that has no empirical parameters. The category covers Hartree-Fock (HF), structural interaction, multi-part perturbation theory and coupled-cluster model among other approaches. The methods, especially HF model, primarily focus on this approach. As for, semi-empirical, it comprises of methods that allow for serious estimates to the quantum mechanics laws, then apply some empirical parameters for (hopefully) patching up parts (Spellmeyer, 2005).

Techniques include the revised desertion of differential overlap, Austin Model I (AM1), among others. For density functional theory or (DFT), some of the approved techniques are quantum mechanical methods which are difficult to categorize like ab initio and semi-empirical. Besides, some DFT approaches are completely free from empirical markers, whereas others depend highly on fine-tuning with experiment.Presently, the trend for DFT researches is applying more amounts of empirical factors, thereby making new DFT methods semi-empirical. Among the assumptions of quantum-mechanics is that wave function comprises of all data that's known, or could be known concerning a molecule.Therefore, quantum mechanics methods present every possible information concerning a system, standardly at least. Practically, theoretical chemists must determine how to derive the property directly from the wave system, plus then they must write computer programs for doing the analysis. Nevertheless, it's now rather routine to calculate certain common molecular properties (Young, 2004).Presently, there are 2 main ways to review chemistry problems: which are through computational quantum chemistry as well as non-computational quantum chemistry. For computational quantum chemistry, the field is mainly concerned with the arithmetical computation of particle electronic structures through ab initio, as well as semi-empirical methods plus non-computational quantum chemistry further addresses the formulation of analytical systems for molecular properties, including their respective reactions. Previously mentioned words, ab initio, as well as semi-empirical arithmetical techniques are of great importance to the field of computational chemistry. Researchers typically use 3 different techniques to make calculations and these are:

Ab initio, (Latin meaning "from scratch") refers to a group of techniques whereby molecular structures may be calculated through applying the Schroedinger model, where values of certain fundamental constants, as well as the atomic figures of the atoms are factored (Atkins, 1991).

- Semi-empirical methods. They use estimates from empirical (experimental) information to offer mathematical model inputs.
- Molecular mechanics. These apply classical physics in explaining and understanding the conduct of molecules and atoms.
- ***Applications***: Computational chemistry may be applied for predicting photo-chemical reactions and designing photo sensitizers, which are useful for phototherapy on cancer cells. For instance, the action of photo sensitizers in DNA damage may be projected from the energy calculations of molecules. Generally, DNA damage is facilitated by these two processes: (i) photo-inspired electron transmission from DNA foundation to the photo-excitory photo sensitizer plus (ii) base modification through singlet oxygen production via photo-energy transfer directly from the photo sensitizer system to oxygen.

The DNA-destroying functions of photo sensitizers are also made possible through electron transfer, which is very much related to energy level produced by the molecule. It's been shown that the magnitude of DNA destruction photosensitized through xanthone analogues, more or less is relative to the energy-gap existing between the energy amounts of the photo sensitizer, including the one for guanine. Furthermore, computational chemistry may be applied to investigate the workings of the chemo-preventive influence on photo toxicity (Young, 2004).

Besides, the molecular orbital calculation can also be useful in designing a photosensitizer, whereby the process of singlet oxygen production is measured by DNA recognition. The Singlet oxygen has been identified as an essential reactive oxygen product to attack cancer.

Additionally, the management of singlet oxygen production by DNA is essential for achieving the ideal cancer photo-therapy solution. Various porphyrin photo sensitizers have furthermore been developed on the context of molecular orbital calculation, for purposes of controlling the process of singlet oxygen production.

Computational chemistry furthermore is useful in calculating vibrational spectra, including the standard vibrational systems for relatively basic molecules. Additionally, the computational cost of these calculations with bigger molecules quickly becomes restrictive, requiring empirical investigation methods (Wilson, 2013).

Luckily, certain functional clusters in organic molecules reliably generate IR and Raman groups in a unique frequency region. The characteristic bands are called group-frequencies. Relying on basic classical mechanical hypotheses, the basis of group frequencies can be defined. The linear grouped oscillator expands are defined and the result of altering this bond angle is provided.

The result of growing the chain length including hence the amount of coupled oscillators has been discussed by scientists, with the analogous model of bending vibrations further included. Depending on this simple framework, basic rules of thumb touching on some commonly encountered oscillator groupings are presented.

1.8.4. Computational Finance

In the modern financial markets, high volumes of inter-dependent assets are exchanged by a huge number of networked market participants in diverse sites and time zones. Plus, their action is of unparalleled complexity and the classification, plus measurement of risk characteristic of these exceedingly diverse groups of instruments is usually based on complex mathematical and computational simulations.

Solving these models precisely in closed form, up to the level of one instrument level, may normally not be possible, thus, we must look for effective numerical algorithms. It has become an urgent and complex matter lately, as the credit crunch has clearly shown the role of flowing effects going from one instrument through collections of single establishments to even the interrelated trading network. Comprehending this needs a multi-scale as well as holistic approaches where symbiotic risk factors like market, credit, and fluidity risk are modeled concurrently and at diverse interrelated scales (Angela and Shiflet, 2014).

Generally, computational finance operates as a group of applied computational science which deals with issues of practical finance interest. A few slightly different descriptions are the research on data and algorithms presently used in finance, plus the arithmetic of computational programs that recognize financial copies or systems.

Plus, computational finance highlights practical numerical techniques rather than scientific proofs and concentrates on methods that factor directly to financial analyses. It's an interdisciplinary subject between arithmetical finance and numerical procedures. Two major aspects are efficient and precise computation of equal values of fiscal securities and the molding of stochastic cost series.

- ***Background*:** The conception of computational-finance as a subject can be traced back to Harry Markowitz, who invented it during early 50s. Markowitz perceived the portfolio choosing problem as an activity in mean-variation optimization. This needed more computer power compared to what was accessible at the time; therefore he worked on practical algorithms for estimate solutions.

Mathematical finance started in the same manner, but diverged through making brief assumptions to reveal relations in basic closed forms which didn't need complex CS to assess (Angela and Shiflet, 2014).

During the 60s, hedge fund directors pioneered the application of computers in modern arbitrage trading. For academics, refined computer processing was required by researchers like Eugene Fama to assess large quantities of financial data-supporting the efficient-market theory.

In the 70s, the primary emphasis of computational finance moved to options valuing and evaluating mortgage securitizations. By the late 70s up to early 80s, a team of new quantitative specialists who were called "rocket scientists" came to Wall Street and carried along personal computers (PCs). These actions led to an eruption of both quantity and diversity of computational finance systems.

Most of the new methods arrived from signal processing plus speech recognition instead of conventional branches of computational economics, such as optimization and time sequence analysis.

By the 80s, the end of Cold War produced a massive group of disenfranchised physicists and practical mathematicians, most from working behind the curtains, into mainstream finance. These individuals become referred to as "financial engineers" (while "quant" is a word that covers rocket scientists, financial engineers, and quantitative portfolio directors) (Miller, 2007).

Ultimately, this caused a second main extension on the variety of computational techniques used in finance, plus a shift away from personal (PCs) computers to mainframes as well as supercomputers. During this time also, computational finance grew to become as a unique academic subfield. In fact, the first degree courses in computational finance got provided by the Carnegie-Mellon University back in 1994.Throughout the past 20 years, the sector of computational-finance has grown into almost every aspect of finance, plus the demand for specialists has grown radically. Besides, many specialized businesses have emerged that supply computational finance products and services.

1.8.5. Computational Science Career

The computational scientist basically is a scientist who has solid skills in the scientific computing process, plus is mostly concerned with developing software.

Typically, there are two key areas, in most fields of computational science and these are:

- ***Data Analysis:*** Traditionally, just a few disciplines of science got to deal with huge amounts of experimental data, for example. But astrophysics, nowadays also apply its concepts including many other fields that produce significant quantities of data because of modern technology. The objective of computational scientists is basically to analyze the incoming data, which is, clean-up, checking systematic effects, calibration, understanding, and condensing it to a form that's ideal for scientific exploitation. Usually, a second stage of data analysis entails model fitting, meaning, checking which theoretical systems best fit the information and approximate their parameters using error bars, this needs understanding of Statistics as well as Bayesian methods, such as the Markov Chain-Monte Carlo (MCMC) model.
- ***Simulations***: Generation of artificial data applied for their personal good in the comprehension of scientific systems, or by seeking to recreate experimental data for characterizing the reaction of a scientific appliance.

1.8.5.1. Necessary Skills

Beginning your career in computational scientist today is rather easy; having a background in whichever field of science notwithstanding, it's possible to enhance your computational skills taking advantage to various learning resources that are available, such as, online tutorials, free digital video courses, publications on Data Analysis and Software Carpentry workshops that conduct boot-camps for researchers to enhance their computational skills (Langtangen, 2013) (Figure 1.4).

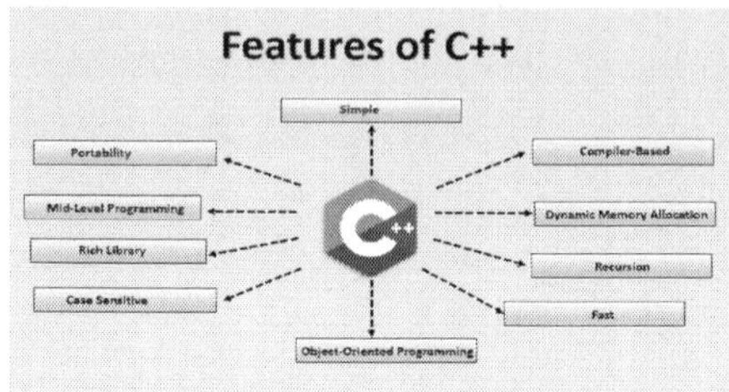

Figure 1.4. C++ is a basic programming language that's essential to understanding computational science.

Source: *https://www.educba.com/features-of-c-plus-plus/.*

The syntax is simpler to learn compared to other shared programming languages. Besides, it boasts the biggest number of science-based libraries. This system is equally simple to interface together with other languages, that is, one can re-use the legacy code applied in C, C++ or FORTRAN formats. This program may be used equally when building something uncommon for computational scientists, such as web development application "Django" or interfacing with firmware "Pyserial."The Python performance can be compared to C/C++/Java, especially when utilizing optimized libraries such as numpy, pandas or scipy which feature Python frontends that have been greatly optimized to either C or Fortran programs; thus is necessary for avoiding explicit for loops plus learning to script the "vectorized" code, which allows for complete arrays and code matrices to get processed in a single step. A few significant Python tools you can learn to help with your computational science career are; emcee, ipython, h5py, scipy, and numpy among others (Langtangen, 2013).

As for parallel programming, ipython parallel can be applied to distribute large quantities of serial and self-running jobs on the cluster. Similarly, PyTrilionos is a computational science system that's useful for operating distributed linear algebras (top level operations using data spread across nodes, and programmed MPI communication). Python may also be used to learn more about shell-scripting using "bash" which for basic automation duties is well suited, plus is fundamental in learning version control using git or mercurial systems.

Python computational science code is simple to use, and can learned through books and digital tutorials. Even without any formal training in Computer (CS) Science, still the most complex concept to learn is

Object Oriented coding which is rather easy to understand. Your job as a computational scientist would analyze huge quantities of data, implementing software systems or data processing.

Regrettably, in science there's typically a push towards finding quick and convenient solutions to computational problems. Instead, there's need for learning how to create easily-maintainable libraries which can be re-used for the future. It involves learning more progressive Python, version management, unit-testing, and much more (Langtangen, 2013).

You can learn some of these tools through passing through tutorials and documentation available on the web, plus you get all the answers you need on technology-based websites and blog posts. Besides, it's also helpful to become a member of core development programs such as "healpy," which is a useful Python package used for 'pixel' sky maps processing.

Computational science skills can get you hired at Supercomputer Centers, where your main duty will be helping with data processing and analysis. Programs like python or parallel coding are essential in managing big data. Operators may be required to partner with research teams in any discipline of Science, while helping them to arrange and optimize digital applications on super-computers.After an advanced course such as PhD, computational scientists who have gained experience in data review or simulation, particularly if the expertise involves parallel programming, will quite simply find a position like PostDoc suitable for them, besides many research teams have large amounts of data, plus require software development skills for their everyday operations (Eijkhout, 2013).

Nevertheless, faculty jobs in computational science mostly favor scientists owning the best research publications, plus software development typically isn't renowned as a top priority scientific product. Many interesting opportunities exist in Academia, such as Research Scientist posts in research centers, for instance Lawrence Berkeley Labs as well as NASA Jet Propulsion Lab, or super-computer centers. The careers are mostly permanent spots, unless the organization operates on funding, and permit for working 100% on research.Yet another prospect is working as a Research Scientist within a particular research group within the University, though it's less mutual, and relies on the accessibility of long-term funding. However, the overall number of accessible positions present in Academia isn't quite high, thus it's essential to also lay open the prospect of a career in Industry. Luckily, nowadays many skills of computational scientists are quite well understood in Industry, therefore, it's recommended to be selective, whenever possible, plus learn and utilize tools which are widely applied also outside traditional Academia, for instance, Python, Git version control, unit testing, shell scripting, databases, parallel programming, multi-core programming and GPU coding (Langtangen, 2013).

1.9. COMPUTATIONAL METHODS

For the most part, it's mathematical and algorithm methods which are applied in computational science systems. Some commonly applied techniques are; computer algebra, comprising symbolic computation in sectors like statistics, algebra, equation solving, geometry, linear algebra, calculus, and tensor analysis among others. Integration methods on the uniform mesh follow a rectangle rule (commonly known as the midpoint rule), as well as trapezoid rule and Simpson's rule.

Both historically and presently, the "Fortran" method remains very popular in many applications involving scientific computing. The other programming languages as well as computer algebra systems widely used for mathematical concepts of scientific computing programs are Julia, Maple, GNU Octave, Haskell, MATLAB, Python (on 3rd party SciPy library) as well as Perl (on 3rd party PDL library). Other more computationally rigorous features of scientific computing shall often employ some variant of C-code or Fortran, plus optimized algebra libraries like BLAS or LAPACK (Eijkhout, 2013).

The computational science (CS) application systems typically model real-life changing conditions, like, climate, plane airflow, vehicle body disruptions in a crash, or explosive devices. These programs may develop a 'logical mesh' within the computer memory, whereby each item relates to an aspect in space plus contains data concerning that space which is appropriate for the model. For instance, in weather prototypes, every item may be just a square kilometer; where land elevation, present wind direction, humidity-content, temperature, and pressure play a significant role. Additionally, the program can calculate the potential next state depending on the present-state of an object, solving equations which define how the program operates; and then replicating the procedure to estimate the next state (Eijkhout, 2013).

1.9.1. Learning Programs

There are many colleges that are devoted to the development, study, and implementation of computer-based prototypes of natural as well as engineered systems. Students are thoroughly prepared for computing science careers in large industry, state, and academia. Some of the program is even offered through the option of taking up portions at a time, or for some cases, doing the entire coursework off-campus through Tech-based Professional Education.

The syllabus may be structured in such a way to provide students with a strong CSE basic knowledge and skills, plus include comprise of specialization courses which enhance a learner's domain knowledge. Advanced elective programs will allow learners to concentrate in a specific domain and technical field that focuses on their specific interests. Besides, an optional thesis aspect of the program needs fulfillment of the cross disciplinary research project (Holder and Eichholz, 2019).

1.9.2. Admissions Requirements for Computational Science

For master programs, often students joining graduate training courses will have to obtain a bachelor's certificate in a technical subject, for example, math, CS, and science or engineering subjects.

Additionally, students must have registered to some undergraduate calculus programs. Some CSE subjects will need extra coursework in topics like linear algebra and differential equations. Furthermore, a working understanding of probability as well as statistics can be helpful in various fundamental courses and specializations.

Learners should also have taken one course at minimum, but ideally two and have established some expertise in programming at high-level language codes like C, Java, or FORTRAN. Pupils who are deficient in a few or many of these areas might still gain admission, though can expect to register to some supplementary coursework to cover for the deficit (Holder and Eichholz, 2019).

In addition, there are home unit, where every student who's approved for the computational science program would be admitted to one particular "home unit." There are home units which may also have extra requirements surpassing those mentioned here. The student handbook available in most colleges where this subject is offered provides information about these requirements and others that applicants must achieve.

Furthermore, financial aid and lab space usually are determined based on the rules and individual aspects of a home unit. Some home unit subjects that can qualify for credit in computational science studies are Computational Science and Engineering, Aerospace Engineering, School of Mathematics and Biomedical Engineering (Holder and Eichholz, 2019).

Chapter 2 Scientific Visualization

CONTENTS

2.1. INTRODUCTION

As the world technology is advancing with each passing day, the data to be processed is also increasing tremendously. Therefore, new, and faster ways of processing data in a blink of an eye need to be invented. Many technological experts have opted for the use of visualization technology so as to present data in an image format. The image is designed in such a way that it represents all the components of the required data. Viewers of this kind of raw data represented in images need to be keen and perfect in their evaluation techniques for them to be able to understand the information being presented to them. This ensures that it takes the shortest time possible to convey information in different technological areas. The technique of the presentation of information using images is referred to as scientific visualization (Figure 2.1).

Figure 2.1. Scientific visualization is as a result of the scientific computing which deals with the innovation of newer and more advanced computing technologies which aid in the understanding and solving of complex problems in our era.

Source: *http://agencia.fapesp.br/cinema-promotes-advances-in-scientific-visualization/20106/ (accessed on 3 April 2020).*

2.2. SCIENTIFIC COMPUTING

A computer is an electronic machine which can be instructed with the aid of special codes which are in a language it best understands, the machine language, for it to produce the required results after being fed with the appropriate input information. The concept of instructing computers with codes is referred to as computer programming. The current computer devices have been programmed with the help of installed programs which enable them to perform a variety of computing tasks.

A computer system consists of all the components that help the computer to function perfectly at its level best.

The components include the hardware, (the tangible components of a computer), the software, (the seen but not tangible components of a computer), and the user of the computer. The term computer systems can also be used to refer to the interconnection of different computers to form a network (Vladimir, 2013).

Generally, computers can be used to perform a variety of task. Some may be used in industrial plants to control different components of the industry plant or different activities being conducted. In factories, they may control devices such as industrial robots.

Could also be used in computer aided designs to come up with the best designs for different products to be manufactures. They may also be used for general purposes in devices such as the personal digital assistants and hand-held electronic devices such as the current smartphones.

The Internet is basically an interconnection of several devices some of which have been connected using physical media and others using wireless connection. The interconnection allows computers to communicate by sharing different resources.

Early computers were only constructed to be used for calculation purposes. Simple devices which carried out their operations manually like the abacus computers were used to help the population in the first technological age in performing different calculation tasks.

In the earliest technological ages, some mechanical devices were constructed to enable the execution of some tedious and repetitive tasks to be automatic. More complex electrical machines were used to carry out specialized old calculations.

The first computer like electronic device used for calculation purposes was developed in the eve of the second technological era which saw the development of the first computer like device, the analytical engine, constructed by Charles Babbage (Liseikin, 2009) (Figure 2.2).

Figure 2.2. The rates of processing information in computers have been advancing with each passing year ever since the first digital like device was developed.

Source: *https://www.slideshare.net/JofredMartinez/computers-and-information-processing (accessed on 3 April 2020).*

The current computers are mostly made up of only one processing component, the Central Processing Unit (CPU) which is in the form of a metal oxide semiconductor (MOS) which basically has a small microprocessor, along with some type of computer memory used to store information either temporarily or permanently in the computer. The processing component of the computer conducts some arithmetic and logical operations with the help of the Arithmetic and Logic Unit, which is a component of the CPU, and the scheduling of activities by the control component of the computer help in changing the order in which instructions will be processed. Peripheral devices (devices connecter externally to the computer and make use of interface cables to transmit data and information to and from the computer), include input devices such as the keyboards, mice, joystick, among other; output devices such as the monitor screens, printers, among others; and the input/output devices that perform both functions such as the touch screen devices among others. The peripheral devices allow information to be retrieved from an external source and they enable the result of operations to be saved and retrieved later (Liseikin, 2009).

2.3. HISTORY OF COMPUTERS

Computers must have existed since the existence of human beings. This is because the human race has always had a way of making their tasks easier. Even if the machines the humans invented were not computerized, they did at least have some characteristics similar to the modern computers.

The abacus machine was the first machine to be recognized as one of the first computer like instrument, though we cannot really affirm if it was the first, for we do not hoe many more machines were invented before it. It was initially used for arithmetic tasks, more so for addition and subtraction calculations. Since the discovery and the invention of the abacus machine, many other forms of reckoning boards or tables purely for calculation purposes have been invented.The Antikythera mechanism believed to be the earliest mechanical analog computer was designed to calculate astronomical positions of different space components.

Many mechanical devices were mainly constructed to be used for calculation and measurement purposes in both the astronomical and navigation areas as many scientists were eager to learn more about the space. The sector, a calculating instrument used for solving problems in proportion, trigonometry, multiplication, and division, and for various functions, such as squares and cube roots, was developed in the late 16th century and found application in gunnery, surveying, and navigation areas (Holder and Eichholz, 2019).

2.4. COMPUTER COMPONENTS

A general purpose computer has four main components which include the arithmetic logic unit (ALU), the control unit (CU), the memory, and the input and output devices. These parts are interconnected by buses, which are pathways for electrical signals which are often made of groups of wires.

1. ***Input Devices*:** These are devices which accept data and send it to the CPU for further processing before the required results are displayed to the user. Once the input device accepts data, the data is converted into a format which the computer understands, the machine language. Input devices include the following:

- *Computer Keyboard*: It is used to input data into the computer through the keying mechanism.
- *Digital Camera*: It is used to capture data in photographic format.
- *Digital Video*: It is used to capture information in motion pictures incorporating the voice or the sound associated with the pictures.
- *Graphics Tablet*: Used mainly by designers to aid in the drawing of different designs of various objects. The drawings on the graphic tablet are done using a special pen, the stylus, which taps on the screen to come up with a certain shape.

- *Image Scanner*: It is used to capture data from an object and convert it into a digital format.
- *Joystick*: It is used to play computer games.
- *Microphone*: Used to directly capture data input in voice format.
- *Mouse*: Used to enter data in the computer by controlling a pointer on the computer screen.

2. ***Output Devices***: These are used to give out the desired results after the data input into the computer is processed in the processor. They are divided into two categories.

The first category is the softcopy output devices used to display results to the end user in an intangible format which can be seen but cannot be touched. They include the:

- *Computer Monitor*: Used to display information in the form of text, pictures, and video enabling the user to monitor what is going on in the computer.
- *Sound Output Devices*: Used to display processed data in sound formats such as regular beeps of machines, audios, and videos.

The second category is the hardcopy output devices which present processed information to the end user in a tangible format. They include:

- *Printers*: Produce the result of a processing activity on a piece of paper.
- *Plotters*: They also produce processed information on a piece of paper but they specifically deal with large sizes of hardcopy output.

3. ***Central Processing Unit (CPU)***: The CPU is the most important component of the computer. It is basically a tiny chip etched into a silicon chip mounted on the motherboard of a computer. Its main function is that of executing instructions hence its name, The Brain of the computer, for all processing activities are carried out inside it.

The CPU is further divided into several categorized based on various functions it conducts as the one and only processing component of the computer.

4. ***The Control Unit***: The CU is a component of the computer mostly categorized under the CPU. Its main function is to coordinate all processing activities in the CPU using a System Clock (a program which controls the timing assigned to different

processing operations) which sends electrical signals informing that it is either time for the next instruction to be processed or that the current processing activity has been completed. CU also determines which instruction is to be processed next by fetching the raw data from the main memory and places it in the right order in the processor. It is also responsible for sending back the end results of a processing activity back into the main memory for it to be displayed later to the end user.

5. ***The Arithmetic and Logic Unit (ALU):*** The ALU performs all arithmetic and logic operations in a computer. The arithmetic operations are based on the ability of the computer to carry addition, subtraction, multiplication, and division operations while the logical operations are based on the ability of the computer to compare two or more values using the greater than (>), less than (<), equal to (=), not equal to (=!) operators among others.

6. ***The Main Memory*:** It is a type of storage that is directly accessible by the processor for it provides a storage location for data and instructions which are mostly accessed by the CU category of the CPU. Main memory is further classified into several categories.

7. ***Random Access Memory (RAM)*:** The RAM is a storage location used to hold data and instructions needed by the currently running applications. The information stored in them is continually read, changed, and removed hence they are only used for temporary storage purposes. They are referred to as random access because their content can be read directly regardless of the sequence in which it is stored.

8. ***Read Only Memory (ROM)*:** The ROM is a storage location is a storage location used for the storage of already processed data (that is now useful to the end user) permanently or semis permanently. It basically stores information that is not frequently accessed or the type of information which takes long periods of time before being altered.

9. ***Buffers*:** These are temporary storage locations which are used to temporarily hold data while it is being moved from one place to another in the processing cycle of the CPU.

10. ***Registers*:** These are high speed temporary memory locations within the CPU which are used to hold data and instructions just before and after processing in the Arithmetic Logic Unit.

11. ***Secondary Storage Devices*:** These are commonly referred to as the backing storage or the auxiliary storage media are mainly used for backing up purposes in a computer. They basically provide an alternative long term storage space for information in the computer. They are of great importance for in case of any damage to the original storage locations of computer information, they can be used to retrieve all the lost information.

2.5. THE HISTORY OF SCIENTIFIC VISUALIZATION

The three dimensional visualization techniques were among the earliest examples of the Maxwell's thermodynamic surface, manufactured in clay in the year 1874 by James Clerk. This led to the modern scientific visualization techniques that use computer graphics concepts (Perotto and Formaggia, 2015).The early two dimensional equipment examples include the flow map of Napoleon March from Moscow designed by Charles in the year 1869, the "coxcombs" used by Florence Nightingale in 1857 as part of a campaign to improve sanitary conditions in the British army and the dot map used by John Snow in 1855 to visualize the cholera outbreak which affected Britain broadly.

2.6. VISUALIZATION METHODS FOR THE TWO DIMENSIONAL REPRESENTATIONS

Scientific visualization which uses computer graphics gained its popularity as the most advanced graphics matured technology. Primary applications back then were their use in the scalar fields which only have direction components and vector fields which had both direction and magnitude from computer simulations and also measured data. The visualization of two dimensional scalar fields used methods such as the color mapping technique which is basically adding color to two dimensional fields so that they would appear to be more real and drawing of contour lines which help in specifying their exact shapes.

2.7. APPLICATIONS AREAS OF SCIENTIFIC VISUALIZATION

Scientific visualization is used in business to organize, identify, and communicate information about the ever-changing trends in the market and the customer data that are too minute to see without amplification with the help of special techniques.

Scientific visualization is also used in astronomy to observe objects which are known to exist but cannot be viewed clearly from the earth's surface such as black holes, gravitational waves, collisions of neutron stars, unknown objects among others. This kind of information is of great use to astronauts for they are able to gain more knowledge about space without having to incur cost in the physical exploration of space (Perotto and Formaggia, 2015).

Scientific visualization is also used in the medicine sector to observe cell growth, guide specialists in conducting medical diagnosis, and prepare surgeons for operations. The surgeons use technological images representing information about the functioning of different body organs for them to be able to understand how they are supposed to carry out their surgical operations.

Scientific visualization is mostly applied in the field of weather forecasting to help in visualizing the results obtained from weather forecasting, placement, illumination, and texture for use in television weather programs. The coloring technique enhances the interpretation of different visuals.

Two most famously know visualization techniques are the representation of ash plumes information from volcanic eruptions in visuals and the representations of Visible Man from microtome traversal and computed tomography scans in visuals which are of great use to geographers for they use such visuals to understand different geographic events (Bærentzen et al., 2012) (Figure 2.3).

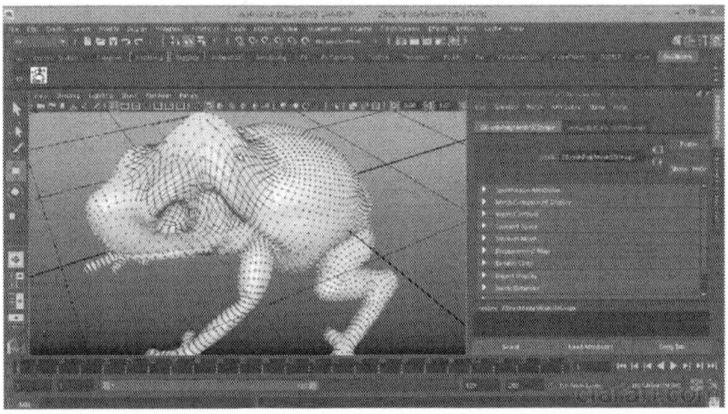

Figure 2.3. Scientific visualization has already been of great importance to the scientific world for it simplifies the analysis of the results from complex computer experiments and does help the scientist to gain more information about the unknown aspects of scientific problems.

Source: https://www.youtube.com/watch?v=h3O4FCsd_-I (accessed on 3 April 2020).

Different datasets are growing at a faster rate as researchers explore science in greater detail. Visualization experts are doing their best to ensure that the representation of information using visuals is enhanced by trying to increase the number of picture elements used in every visual. The modern research being conducted about the visualization technology is focusing on coming up with ways of combining different data sets so and filtering the most important information from the combined information. The filtered information is later to be incorporated in visual format for it to be shared across various platforms which will support visual information. The developers are also planning on coming up with specialized search engines to be used to search only visual information (Vladimir, 2013).

2.7.1. Computer Animation

Computer animation is the art, the technique, and science of creating moving images with the help of computers. The three dimensional techniques are mostly being used in the development of visuals. This has not rendered the two dimensional technology useless for it also being used because of its ability to support low bandwidth information, its unique styling techniques among other advantage. Sometimes the target of the animation is the computer itself to guide it in the carrying out of different activities most of which require visual guidance for them to be executed but sometimes the target is another medium, such as film. It is also referred to as CGI (Computer-generated imagery or computer-generated imaging), especially in situations when it is used in films. Applications of computer animation include its use in the medical sector which is most commonly utilized as an instructional guide for medical professionals to help them in perfecting their knowledge on different aspects of medical procedures or their patients to help them in understanding what really causes the conditions they might be in (Vladimir, 2013).

2.7.2. Computer Simulation

Computer simulation is a computer program, or a set of interconnected computers, that attempts to automate the activities of a sample model of a particular system and come up with a computerized way of conducting different activities. Computer simulations have become a useful part of mathematical modeling of many natural systems in areas such as physics, and computational physics, chemistry, and biology; human systems in economics, psychology, and social science; and in the process of engineering and new technology, to gain more knowledge and understanding of how the operation of those systems is conducted, or to observe their behavior. The continuous visualization and simulation of a system is called visualization (Liseikin, 2009).Computer simulations are different from one computer program to another for in some they are designed to run for only a few minutes, in other applications they are used to aid in the interconnection of different nodes which are programmed to run for hours, to ongoing simulations that run for months. The number of different interconnections of nodes which has incorporated automation of their activities is tremendously increasing with each passing day.

2.7.3. Information Visualization

Information visualization is the study of the representation of a large collection of information, be it numerical or non-numerical in visual formats all at once. It is mainly focusing on the creation of new and better ways which are more advanced than the previous ones of representing only the most important contents of an entire set of information. The key difference between scientific visualization and information visualization is that information visualization is often applied to data that is not generated using the modern computing techniques. Some examples are graphical representations of data for business, government, news, and social media.

2.7.4. Interface Technology and Perception

Interface technology basically deals with the interaction of the user with modern computing techniques and perception simply allows users to have different opinions of the information they access. The combination of both interface technology and perception allows people to have a better understanding of underlying information being communicated enabling the scientific visualization community to grow.

2.7.5. Surface Rendering

Rendering is the process of generating an image from a model, by means of computer programs. The model is basically a description of three-dimensional objects in a well-defined way using a specific language or data structure containing only the information to be used. It would contain geometry, viewpoint, texture, lighting, and shading information. The image is either a digital image or a raster graphics image. The term surface rendering may also be defined differently depending in the understanding of the information they are trying to convey to their audience in general. Rendering can also use to describe the process of calculating effects in a video-editing file so as to help in the production of the final video output.

2.7.6. Volume Regeneration

Volume rendering is a technique used to display a two dimensional sample which has been extracted from a three-dimensional sample data set. A three-dimensional data set is basically a combination of multiple two dimensional data sets which have been acquired through scanning process. The scanned samples of three-dimensional data sets have more clarity because of the quality of picture elements used. Volume visualization strictly scrutinizes the different mathematical techniques to be used in creating the final visual used in the representation of multiple set of information. It has become a very important technique in the medical sector for it does help in the visualizing of possible analysis of results obtained from a patient's medical test. It can also be used to visualize clouds and understand what they really mean and the effect they have on the weather in general. Volume regeneration does help in the study of water flows, molecular, and biological structures among others. The continued development of hardware and software components of the computer is helping in the perfection of volume visualization. Developments of web-based technologies, and the use of browser software's have allowed simple volume visualization techniques to be used in the calculation of the total amount of data the web browser can support per unit time (Liseikin, 2009).

2.8. SOFTWARE TOOLS USED IN SCIENTIFIC VISUALIZATION

Computer Software's are a set of instructions that direct a computer on what to do. They are divided into two main categories.

The system software's are used to manage the operations of the computer itself and make sure that the computer works efficiently. The system software's are further divided into two main categories. The operating system (OP) which basically governs the interaction of the user with the hardware components of a computer. The utility software's which help in the smooth running of computer operations.

The application software's are designed to help the end user perform specific task. They are further divide into two main categories. The general purpose application software's are basically used to perform a set of operations in the computer. They are developed with no major specific task to be conducted. The second category is the specific purpose application software's which are developed with only a specific user need in mind (Hansen and Johnson, 2011).

Since scientific visualization basically deals with images, software tools are required to aid in the designing of these images. Visualization images are complex and require real different software tools to be used so as to come up with a perfect image communicating all the required information without having to leave anything outside.

Bespoke softwares which are under the category of application software's built specifically for handling certain classes of step by step procedures for the generation of a certain object. The bespoke software's are uniquely designed and tailored based on the specifications of the user. They are not available in shops and once developed they may not address the needs of other users. The main advantage of bespoke software's is that they are easy to user for they are manufactured with the help of the user since the user is the one who really knows specifically what needs need to be met and how they will be met.General purpose visualization systems are part of the software tools required for scientific visualization for they support a variety of techniques and handles a wide variety and range of data types. They are mostly needed because of their capability to handle different types of data. This is because the information to be incorporated in an image is composed from different data types and a system which is able to understand all this types of data will be of help.

Graphical software tools are used to enhance various features of the graphics used in scientific visualization. They include self-organizing maps which automatically guide on various locations more so visually, charts which summarize information to be incorporated in visuals, graphs, scatter plots, zoom feature which helps in the enlargement of the visuals to be used, sort, overview/detail, hierarchies among others.

Presentation graphics are different form scientific visualization techniques for they are primarily concerned with the communication of information and results in ways that are easily understood. They are different because in scientific visualization, one seeks to understand the data being communicated better with the help of visuals.

There are two underlying approaches which are used in the transformation of data into visual representations. They include the graphical primitives and data sampling.

Graphical primitives approach involves filtering data to extract the most useful information and maps these data using geometric primitives such as points, lines, or polygons.

The second approach is that of data sampling which involves moving data into structured grid fields of different types which might be uniform, rectilinear, and irregular among other types using interpolation and extrapolation techniques.

2.9. ADVANTAGES OF SCIENTIFIC VISUALIZATION

It reduces the size of large volumes of information by summarizing them just a few pictures. This saves on the storage space in devices where this kind of information is stored. Compression does speed up the transmission rates of such types of information (Liseikin, 2009).

Scientific visualization can be used to inform more about the relationship between different measurements in terms of space and time for it combines different components to so as to come up with a final copy data to be presented in visuals.

It can create different structures a new and give them unique features beside the ones which are already known from previous displays. This is because it has to completely change a visual representation for it to be able to present information using that visual.

Scientific visualization allows users to access only a certain section of a whole set of information for the data presented visually has been filtered from a large group of data components and interactively for the end user is able to associate with the visual representations in real time (Liseikin, 2009).

The observation of the movements of various structures allows one to acquire a better understanding of the ever changing aspects of visuals.

Scientific visualizations is very useful for it allows one to change the different arguments in visual representation interactively and be able to observe change with immediate effect through a process known as computational steering.

2.10. DISADVANTAGES OF SCIENTIFIC VISUALIZATION

Oversimplification of data leads to conclusions which do not represent a complete summary of information to the end user. The combination of different swaths of data so as to filter the most useful parts of the entire information and represent it visually in a simpler and more basic way leads to omission of some important parts which would be of great use to the end user.

The step by step techniques which are followed in the creation of a final visual representation are limited to human inputs. This is because humans are prone to make errors, and in the technological world, more so while dealing with the computers, the concept of garbage in garbage out does apply. Any error made during the procedural creation of the algorithm will lead to production of wrong results during the compilation of the final visual representation (Liseikin, 2009).Overreliance on use of visuals to understand data is becoming a limitation to the end user more than it is to the developer of the visuals. This is because visual representation is simple and easy to understand as compared to other means of data representation. The user ends up gaining information which is not complete for not all times will visuals display to you the most important components of the information required.

With scientific visualization, not all viewers are able to interpret the information being displayed by use of visuals.

Viewers of information represented visually might interpret the information differently. Wrong interpretation of visuals leads to the bias of the general knowledge the user will have in the end.

Scientific visualization world is rapidly growing. To most people, this information might be great news, but with further scrutiny, it is a limitation. This is because more companies are coming up with different software's to be used in the creation of visual summaries of information. The software's do not have a standard protocol to follow, leading to the confusion of which software will really summarize information perfectly and present it in visual formats in the most suitable way.

Chapter 3

Computational Chemistry

CONTENTS

3.1. INTRODUCTION

Computational chemistry involves the use of computer simulations with the main purpose of being able to solve chemical problems. It deals with the use of well-incorporated theoretical chemistry methods in computer programs that are efficient, for the calculation of properties and structures of solids and molecules.

These methods are necessary because it is not possible to analytically solve problems involving quantum many-body problems, especially when they are in closed form. Not only do results achieved from computational chemistry complement the data that is gotten from the chemical experiments, but also they can help in predicting chemical phenomena that has not yet been observed. These methods are highly used when it comes to designing new drugs and materials.

The manner in which we understand how the world works are due to the daily work that computational chemists do, when it comes to their influence in helping manufacturers come up with processes that are much more efficient and productive. It also helps in the extraction of helpful and important knowledge from a lot of compiled data. It is also in computational chemistry that we get to study and understand the important properties of chemical reactions, molecules, and atoms, though the use of thermodynamics and quantum mechanics (Wilson, 2013) (Figure 3.1).

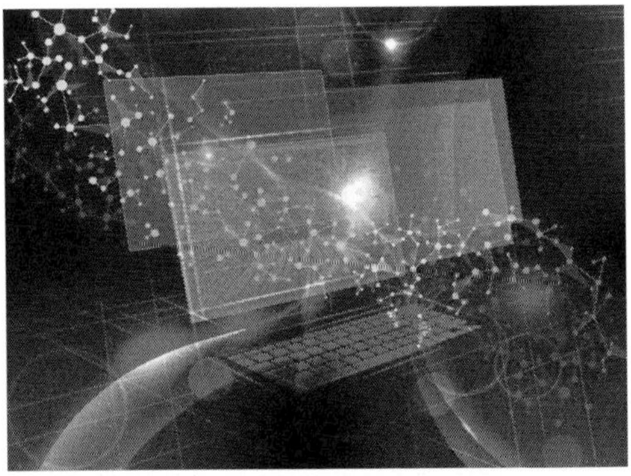

Figure 3.1. Regardless of how fast the computer power is growing, computational chemistry has still been considered compromising when it comes to the ability to get an answer that is accurate, and one that is quick.

Source: https://www.chemistryworld.com/opinion/computational-chemistry-a-virtual-reality/3007719.article (accessed on 3 April 2020).

Computational chemists normally utilize large databases, statistics, and algorithms for the integration of chemical modeling and theory with observations that are experimental. There are some chemists who are able to ensure the creation of simulations and models of physical processes, and there are also others that utilize techniques for data analysis and statistics for the extraction of the required data from large amounts of data. Computer chemists have been able to provide readily understandable forms of complex analyses due to the advances in the capabilities of computer visualization. They are the. Able to utilize these forms for better designing experiments and new materials, in addition to ensuring that the results are valid (Wilson, 2013).

In computational chemistry, the chemists may utilize simulations so as to make different identifications of sites on protein molecules that have the highest chance binding new drug molecules, or they may also be able to work on the creation of synthesis reaction models for the demonstration of kinetic and thermodynamic effects on the kinds and amount of products being used. They are also able to make explorations on the main physical processes that are found in certain different phenomena such as phase changes, corrosion, energy storage, or superconductivity.

One of the greatest employers of computational chemist is the pharmaceutical industry, and this industry has for a long time focused on discovering and designing new small molecular therapeutics. However, in the past few years, there has been a need for the application of chem-informatics, which is a combination of Information science methods, chemical modeling, and laboratory data; and computational chemistry, for the development of processes, Biologics (using or extracting from biological sources to manufacture medicinal products), and analytical chemistry (Wilson, 2013).

These problems can be solved using high-performance computing (HPC) such as computing clusters and super computers, and these can also help in the creation of simulations that need a large amount of data. Some of the tools that are used in computational chemistry are: full statistical analysis, quantitative structure activity relationships, molecular dynamics simulation, electronica structure methods, and chem-informatics.

It may not be correct to say that computational chemistry is similar to, or is the same as, computer science (CS), despite the fact that professionals in both of the fields are able to have multiple collaborations. Computer scientists normally spend most of the time in the development and validation of computer algorithms, database visualization capabilities, and software and hardware products. On the other hand, computational chemists normally deal with theoretical and laboratory scientist for the application of these capabilities to simulation and modeling, visualization, and data analysis for supporting the efforts of their research (Spellmeyer, 2005).

Many of the computational chemists normally work to promote the development and application of algorithms and computer codes; however, it is possible for computational chemists who are practicing to have careers that are highly rewarding without having to work on code development. Some of the skills that are required when it comes to programming include: working within a Linux, MacOS, or Windows environment; performance of statistical analysis with the use of SPSS or R; performance of shell scripting with perl, python, Tcl/Tk, or bash; and even compiling C code or FORTRAN.

As the development of computational modeling platforms and chem-informatics tools occurs, it is now much easier for scientists to make definitions of workflow tasks through workbench environments that are graphically based (Spellmeyer, 2005).

One of the most commonly used trends these days when it comes to reduced-order modeling and other methods that are similar is the ability to enable computational tools that are fairly powerful to undergo implementation on devices that are portable such as smart phones and tablets. This makes it possible for researchers to perform what-if calculations in addition to trying out different scenarios when they are either out in the field or even in the plant.

The present and future is influenced greatly by the past; for example, being able to simplify approximations and assumptions that are important in the era of pre-computing in computational chemistry has remained an important and relevant aspect up to today when it comes to allowing simulations of systems that are much larger with an amount of computer time that is considered reasonable. Through being able to highlight significant milestones in the work that has been put in when it comes to simulation and theoretical tasks, all aiming at comprehending the nature of a chemical bond, we are able to trace the evolution and development of electronic structure calculation methods that have been used all through the years (Wilson, 2013).

As a guide, the ability to use temporal relationships between methods through being able to place the different methods within a timeline that can divide these methods into three main era, with each era being explained through its specific computing power for problem-solving, experiment data, approximations, and relative reliance on theory. To be much more specific, the theoretical models that were constructed for ensuring explanation of spectroscopic emission spectra came to help in laying the foundation of the computational chemistry field when there was lag behind in the experiment of the theory.

During the period in which the Schrödinger equation was promulgated-which helps in describing total system properties and energy from the perspective of quantum mechanics-it led to a shift of focus of the field to the development of methods that would help to solve the equation. There was however, a major difficulty with came to solving the Schrödinger equation during the era of pre-computing, which led to the entire field looking for ways to create methods that are increasingly refined so as to make sure that they were able to obtain solutions that were approximate.

To be much more specific, so as to supply parameter values that cannot be accessed through direct calculations through the first principles, semi-empirical methods normally depend on experiment data. This is different from approximate methods that utilize simplification so as to get rid of the necessity to calculate cross interacting terms (Wilson, 2013) (Figure 3.2).

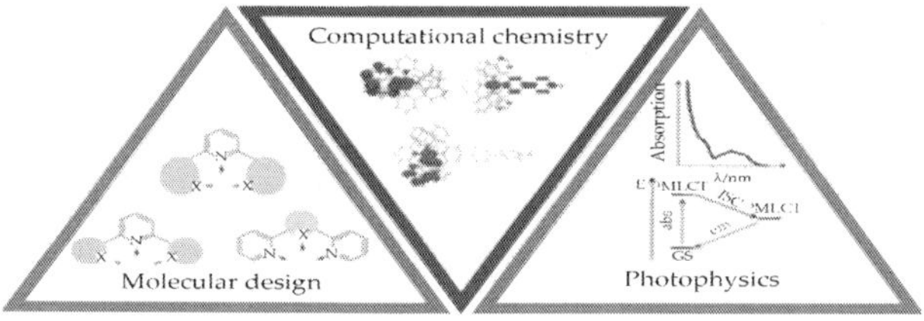

Figure 3.2. There is a need to find a balance between speed and accuracy in computational chemistry, and it all depends on the size of the system. With an increase in system size should come an introduction of approximations that trade accuracy for speed.

Source*:* *https://www.sciencedirect.com/science/article/pii/S0010854515001162 (accessed on 3 April 2020).*

Due to the fact that there was an increase in the availability of large amounts of computing power that are not expensive, there was development of the ab initio simulation methods (first principles) which were able to calculate the electronics structure properties of systems that are large, such as Long chain biomolecules, with very little to no simplification assumptions and at highly fine scales. This however, was still difficult because high-power computational resources were not easy to access outside institutes that are created for research. Therefore, contemporary research deals with the development of high resolution simulation methods, which are referred to as coarse-graining, that are only used for solving problems that have a high importance aspect, and leaving the other aspects of defining the problem to techniques that are coarser.

This being said, coarse-graining normally helps in facilitating the ability to probe system sizes that are realistic for solutions in sync with reality. Due to the fact that the thread is chronologically delineated, it is also makes it possible to ask examining questions that are counterfactual, and therefore from a historic point of view, has led to the relative roles of theoretical intuition and computing power when it comes to the evolution of computational chemistry (Young, 2004).

In contrast to the notions that have been spread globally, that any advances in computational chemistry were mainly due to increasing the computer power, there is an argument that has shown that the relation between computing power and theoretical imagination is much more to blame for the advancement of computational chemistry, especially due to the fact that the two exact influences that differ at different main junctures in the evolution of computational chemistry.

3.2. MAIN PRINCIPLES TO UNDERSTAND

3.2.1. Energy

In science, energy is considered one of the most useful concepts. The ability to analyze energetics can help in predicting what molecular processes are likely to happen or are also able to happen. Energy is defined in all computational chemistry techniques, such as, the most stable system is that with the lowest energy. This means that being able to find the shape of a molecule is in correspondence with the ability to find the shape that has the lowest amount of energy (Wilson, 2013).

Generally, there are two forms of energy that are used to break down the amount of energy in the system. These are: potential energy and kinetic energy. It is possible to further separate kinetic energy into rotational, translational, and vibrational motion. It is also possible to make a distinction between the different forms of kinetic energy through that which is due to nuclear motion and that which is due to electron motion. Coulomb's law can help in purely expressing potential energy, and it is also possible to break it down into hydrogen bonds, conformational energy, bond bending, and bond stretching, and so on.

Bond stretching or reactions are chemical processes that can be divided into diabatic and adiabatic processes. Adiabatic processes are processes whereby there is no change in state within the system throughout the process. Diabatic processes are processes that normally have the electronic states changing as part of the process. These normally follow the lowest path of energy and normally change in state when the necessity occurs (Wilson, 2013).It is important to define a reference system that has the definition of having zero energy during the formulation of a mathematical representation of molecules. There is a difference in this zero of energy from one approximation to the other. For density functional theory (DFT) and ab initio methods, which work by modeling all the system's electrons, zero energy corresponds to having all electrons and nuclei at a distance that is infinite from one another.

Most semi-empirical methods normally utilize a valance energy that correlates with the ability to have the removal of the valence electrons, as well as the resulting ions at an infinite distance. As zero energy, there are few methods in molecular mechanics (MM) that utilize chemical standard states, however, most of them normally utilize a strain-less molecule instead. The zero of energy is completely arbitrary in some MM' methods (Spellmeyer, 2005).

The total energy values in relation to the zero of energy that is being used in a certain method, are mostly quite inaccurate in any particular approximation. Most of the times, the reason for this inaccuracy is systematic error. Due to this, it is most likely to find that the most accurate values as relative energies that are achieved through the subtraction of total energies from calculations that are separate. This is why it is easy to accurately compute the difference in energy between bond dissociation energies and conformers.

3.2.2. Atomic Units

This system was mainly created for the simplification of mathematical equations through being able to set many important constants equal to one. This is a way for scientists to save records with the use of a pencil, and therefore there are many more errors. Atomic units also help in lowering the level of computer time that is required for the performance of chemical competitions, which can be quite a lot. Another advantage of these units is that there are no effects that occur on the theoretical results with changes in the measured values of physical constant. There are some scientists that entirely use atomic units within the work; however, there are many researchers that normally ensure conversion of the results that are provided by the scientists into unit systems that are much more familiar.

3.2.3. Thermodynamics

One of the most well developed mathematical descriptions within chemistry is thermodynamics. Many of the concepts of energy, entropy, and free energy are defined by the field of thermodynamics. It is not possible to consider thermodynamics as a subject that requires extensive amount of research due to two main reasons which are: there is a general inability for the provision of insight that is well detailed into chemical processes and there is a completeness of existing and/or previous work.

Most of the time, it is much easier to use a pen and paper work for thermodynamic treatment, due to the fact that most of the aspects of chemistry have been described so accurately with very simple expressions in mathematics. It is possible to relate computational results to thermodynamics. The result of computations might be free energies, internal energies, etc. all depending on whatever computation has been done. In the same manner, it is possible to make a computation of different contributions to the entropy. One of the main issues that can frustrate a scientist is that, the software's that are used for computation do not make it evident on the energy that is being listed, because of the different terminologies that are used in thermodynamics and computational chemistry (Spellmeyer, 2005).

3.2.4. Quantum Mechanics

This refers to the correct mathematical description of how electrons behave, and therefore of chemistry. In theory, it is possible to use quantum mechanics for the prediction of any property or any molecule or atom exactly. When it comes to practice, the equations that are used in quantum mechanics have only been exactly solved for one electron systems. There are many different collections of methods that have been created for making approximations on the solutions that are provided for many different electron systems. The usefulness of this approximation is very high, however, they require for one to have a certain amount of sophistication, especially on the scientists, part so as to know the validity of each approximation and whether the results are as accurate as they should be after using the approximation (Figure 3.3).

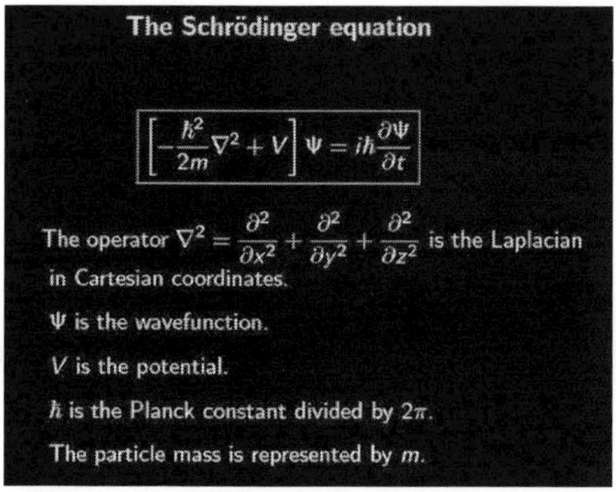

Figure 3.3. A visualization of the Schrödinger equation well explained.

Source: *https://www.quora.com/What-is-the-detailed-proof-of-the-Schr%C3%B6dinger-wave-equation (accessed on 3 April 2020).*

This equation is a linear partial differential equation that helps in describing the state functions or the wave function of a quantum mechanics system. The discovery of this equation was an important landmark in developing this subject of quantum mechanics where it is a key result. It was named after Erwin Schrödinger. In 1926, he was able to publish the equation, which was postulated in 1935, which was what led to him receiving the 1933 Nobel Prize in Physics.

This equation is not considered the only way for the studying of quantum mechanical systems as well as for making predictions within the systems. There are other quantum mechanics formulations that include path integral formulation and matrix mechanics. The Schrödinger equation and matrix mechanics was incorporated into a single equation by Paul Dirac.

3.2.5. Statistical Mechanics

This is the manner in which thermodynamic properties of bulk materials are calculated in mathematical means, from describing the materials in a molecular manner. Most of statistical mechanics have remained at the stage of theory that involves paper and pencil. Due to the fact that it is not yet possible for quantum mechanicians to solve the Schrödinger equation yet, mechanicians in statistical mechanics do not have a foundation for treating this field. Regardless, there have been some very important and useful results that have been achieved from bulk materials.

Most of the time, you find that computations in statistical mechanics have been tacked onto the end of vibrational frequency calculations that are found in ab initio methods, for gas phase properties that are at a lower pressure. In the situation of condensed phase properties, it is necessary to use either Monte Carlo calculations or molecular dynamics so as to obtain statistical data.

3.3. NUMERICAL TECHNIQUES USED IN COMPUTATIONAL CHEMISTRY

The commonly used numerical techniques in computational chemistry are MM, semi-empirical, and ab-initio. It is important to understand the definitions of each of these terms so as to fully understand how computational techniques are used in computational chemistry.

- ***Ab-Initio:*** This term is Latin for the word scratch. It is used to refer to a combination of methods that can be used in the calculation of molecular structures with the use of nothing else other than the Schrödinger equation, the atomic numbers of the atoms that are present, and the values of the fundamental constants.
- ***Semi-Empirical Techniques*:** These techniques normally utilize approximations that are found from experimental data for the provision of inputs into the mathematical models.
- ***Molecular Mechanics*:** These mechanics normally utilize semi-empirical or empirical force fields and classical physics for the explanation and interpretation of how molecules and atoms behave.

3.3.1. Ab-Initio

These are computational chemistry methods that are based on quantum chemistry. This term was introduced to this field by Robert Parr, David Craig and other co-workers. Robert Parr helped in describing the background of ab-initio. It means "from the beginning," used to imply that the only aspects that are inputted into a calculation in this method are constants that are physical. This quantum chemistry method normally aims at solving the electronic Schrödinger equation, once one is given the nuclei positions as well as the election number so as to be able to find information that is deemed useful such as the energies, densities, and other properties of the electron systems. Being able to use this calculation has made it possible for theoretical chemists to find solutions too many different problems, as well as having the importance of these calculations being highlighted through Walter Kohn and John Pople receiving the Noble prize (Lewars, 2010).

3.3.1.1. Hartree-Fock Method

The Hartree-Fock (HF) calculation is the most commonly used ab-initio calculation. In this calculation, the primary approximation is referred to as the mean field approximation. This means that in this calculation we do not take into account the Columbic electron-electron repulsion, however, in the calculation, there is inclusion of the average effect. This calculation is variational and this means that the calculated approximate energies are either all the same as or higher than the exact energy. The calculation's accuracy is all dependent on the size used on the basis set, however, due to the main field approximation, the calculations that are derived from the HF methods to obtain the energies are always much higher than the tent and the exact energy, with a base size that is increasing, to a limit value that is referred to as the Hartree-Fock limit (Lewars, 2010) (Figure 3.4).

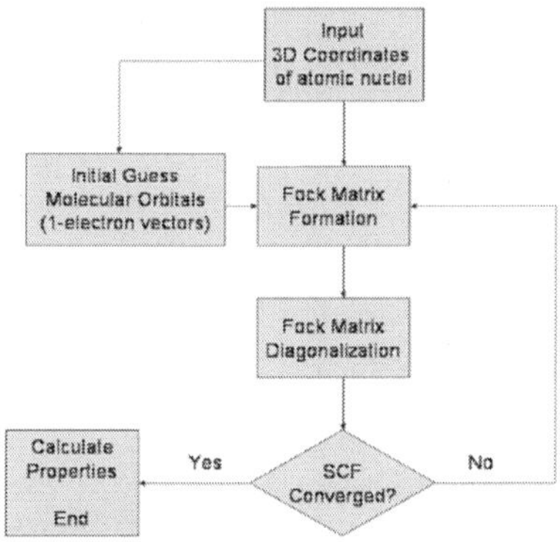

Figure 3.4. This method normally forms a matrix that is irregular. There are many algorithms that have been implemented to make this method much more accurate; however, obtaining a numerical consistency has proven to be difficult.

Source: *https://en.wikipedia.org/wiki/Hartree%E2%80%93Fock_method (accessed on 3 April 2020).*

One of the other issues that may come up when it comes to the accuracy of the results that have been completed, is the form that has been picked for the business functions. It is of course not possible to know the actual form of the single electronic molecular wave function. For the basic functions, the forms that are used can help in providing either a worse or a much better approximation to the actual Hartree-Fock equation's numerical single electron solution.

Most of the times, the basic functions that are utilized are a combination of Gaussian type orbital's or Slater type orbital's. Linear combinations of atomic orbitals are what make up molecular orbitals. This linear combination of atomic orbital are nothing more than basis functions that have been combined in a linear manner with coefficients that have been provided from efficient and appropriate atomic Hartree-Fock calculations. Due to the fact that this approximation has been used, most of the HF calculations give a greater computed energy in comparison to what should be the maximum energy provided by the HF limit (Wilson, 2013).

The steps in this calculation are normally begin with initially guessing, with the help of the semi empirical method, for the orbital coefficients. This function is normal utilized for the calculation of a new set of orbital coefficient as well as energy, all which can thereafter be utilized for obtaining a newer set, and so on. This is referred to as the calculation converge. This however, does not have the ability to guarantee that there will be a convergence of the calculation. In some situations, where the calculation does not converge, there is a need for technical expertise for fixing the problem. This procedure is referred to as self-consistent field procedure. There are some researchers who normally use these calculations as reference for making distinctions from earlier methods that were created by Hartree, however, the HF method is more widely used (Wilson, 2013).

Orbital's are constructed to reflect unpaired or pairs electrons through variations of the Hartree-Fock procedure. It is possible to use the same orbital spatial function in a situation where the molecule has a singlet spin, and for each pair, both the a and b Spin electrons can be used. This is referred to as the restricted HF method.

For the construction of HF wave functions of molecules that have electrons that are unpaired, there are two main techniques. The first technique is through the utilization of two sets of orbitals that a completely separate for the a and b electrons. This is referred to as the unrestricted Hartree-Fock wave e function. In this method, these electrons that have been paired will not have the same special distribution. This therefore leads to the introduction of a calculation error that is referred to as the spin contamination. That might be a very insignificant error that is introduced by the spin contamination, however, the error could be huge enough to affect the results and make them unusable in accordance to the involved chemical system. These calculations are popular due to the fact that they are much easier to implement and they run in an efficient manner (Wilson, 2013).

The second way in which the wave functions could be constructed for open shell molecules is the restricted open shell HF method. Unlike the previous method, in this one, the electrons that have been paired will be able to share the same spatial orbital. This means that there will be no spin contamination. The only downside of this method is that it is much more difficult when it comes to implementation, in comparison to the previous method, and it may need much more central processing unit (CPU) time for its execution. In situations where the spin contamination is too large when using the unrestricted HF wave e function, it is advisable to use the restricted open shell HF method.

At the equilibrium geometry, when it comes to singlet molecules, the wave functions of both the Unrestricted HF wave functions and the Restricted HF wave functions are always quite similar. It is advisable to use the Restricted HF wave functions with functions for singlets due to the fact that the calculations that are done normally take up less CPU time. There are some situations, however, they are rare, where a sig let molecule has structures of bi-radical resonance, and the Unrestricted HF wave functions will help in providing a better molecule description. The results of the restricted HF wave functions end up ensuring that the electrons remain paired. In this situation, there will be a failure in the calculations to make rejection of cases in which the electrons should have uncoupled. For example, some calculations that are done using the restricted HF wave functions for H2 with bond lengths that are successively longer will provide results showing that there is dissociation of the H2 molecule into H– and H+ instead of two H atoms. It is important to consider this limitation especially when there is modeling of processes involving unpairing and pairing of electrons. This limitation has shown to be responsible for specific areas that are systematic in the results, for example atomic charges that are too large and dipole moments, vibrational frequencies that are too high, bond length that are slightly too short, and activation energies that are too high. The dissociation that is found in unrestricted HF wave functions is normally correct (Spellmeyer, 2005).

3.3.1.2. Accuracy

These methods normally aim at calculating the many different functions of the electron which is considered to be the answer to the electronic Schrödinger equation.

The main function of an electron can be defined as the linear combination of various functions that are much simpler, with the HF function being the main function. There is then the approximation of each of these simple functions by only using one-electron functions. There is then the expansion of the one-electron functions as a linear combination of basis set functions that have been grouped in a finite way.

The main advantage of this approach is that it is possible to make it converge to the specific solution, when there is tending of the basis sets towards the complete set limits and where there is inclusion of all possible configurations.

This advantage may also bring a limitation, in that it is very demanding computationally converge to the limit in addition to most of the calculations that are needed being quite far from the limit. Despite this limitation, there have been many important conclusions that have been achieved from these classifications that are much more limited (Spellmeyer, 2005).

The computational costs of these methods are one thing that needs to be considered during the determination of whether they are necessary for the problem that needs to be solved.

In comparison to different approaches that are much less accurate, such as MM, these methods normally end up taking up a higher amount of computer time, disk space, and memory; however, with the modern advancements that we see today in CS and technology, it is not becoming much of an issue when it comes to the consideration of these aspects.

3.3.1.3. Advantages

There are a couple of advantages that come with the use of this method. Firstly, it has proven to be very useful for a wide range of systems. Secondly, it does not depend on experimental data. Thirdly, it is also able to calculate both excited states and transitional states (Figure 3.5).

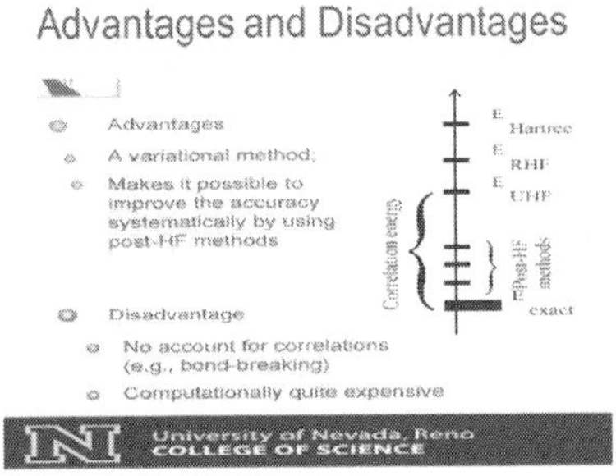

Figure 3.5. Some of the advantages and disadvantages of the restricted and unrestricted Hartree-Fock method. It shows that it is possible to improve on the accuracy of this method through the use of post-HF methods.

Source: *https://slideplayer.com/amp/9795208/ (accessed on 3 April 2020).*

3.3.1.4. Disadvantages

Despite the advantages, there are also some disadvantages that need to be considered. First of all, this method is quite computationally expensive. One needs to consider other methods and see if it is worth paying for the Ab-initio method instead. Secondly, this method is limited to systems that are small with 100 to 1000 atoms. Lastly, this method is also limited to short sampling times and/or short time dynamics.In general, this method is considered best for: small systems (tens of atoms); systems that require a high level of accuracy; systems that involve electronic transition; and molecules that do not have any available experimental data (Spellmeyer, 2005).

3.3.2. Semi-Empirical Techniques

Semi-empirical methods are simplified versions of the HF techniques, however, they make many approximations, and they also use some empirical data parameters. These techniques are considered very important when it comes to computational chemistry, especially when having to treat large molecules in a situation where the HF method is quite expensive without the ability to use approximations. Utilizing empirical parameters has proven to provide some allowance of including election correlation effects within this method.

Within the HF calculations framework, it is possible to approximate or completely omit some parts of the data, for example two-electron integrals. So as to provide a correction for this omission or approximation, there is parameterization of semi-empirical methods. This means that a set of parameters is used to fit the results, generally in a manner that is meant to ensure the production of results that are closest to experimental data, however, they could also agree with ab-initio results (Leszczynski, 2012).

There are some simplifications that are used in this method. Semi-empirical methods normally look up to empirical methods, where there is no explicit inclusion of the two-electron part of the Hamiltonian. Within π-electron systems, Erich Hückel proposed the Hückel method. When it comes to the valence electron systems, Roald Hoffmann proposed the extended Hückel method.

It is much faster to use semi-empirical calculations in comparison to the ab-initio methods. This is mainly due to the fact that they utilize the zero differential overlap approximation. This however, has a limitation especially if the results that are provided are very wrong, due to the fact that the computed molecule does not have an enough similarity to the molecules that are found in the database that is used for parameterizing the method (Leszczynski, 2012).

This method has proven to be very successful when it comes to describing organic chemistry, where there is only extensive use of few elements and also because the molecules have a size that is moderate. However, with different parameterization, semi-empirical methods were also used with nano-structures and solids.

3.3.2.1. Commonly Used Semi-Empirical Methods

1. *Hückel Method*: This is one of the simplest and earliest semi-empirical methods that were invented. The calculations that are found in this method work by modeling only the p valence electrons that are found within a planner conjugated hydrocarbon. The interaction that is found between atoms that have bonded is described by a parameter. In this method, second atom affects do not occur. The calculations in this method normally quantitatively make predictions of orbital coefficient and reject orbital symmetry. It is possible for these calculations to provide qualitative insight into compounds that are conjugated, or crude quantitative information as well; however, they are hardly used

today. The main use of these calculations as of today is in the classroom by students, due to the fact that it is a calculation that one can do by hand.

2. *Extended Hückel*: Valence orbital's that are based on ionization potentials as well as experimental electron affinities, and orbital overlaps can be modeled through this calculation. This is also called the tight binding calculation in some of the different physics literatures. A simplified single sub atomic orbital representation that is based on atomic radius can help in obtaining orbital overlap.

The main advantage of this method of calculation in comparison to the Hückel calculation is that it is able to ensure modeling of all valence orbitals. The main reason why these calculations are of high interest today is due to the fact that the method is quite general when it comes to using it for all the elements that are found on the periodic table. It may not be a method that is extremely accurate nor sophisticated; however, it is used many at times for inorganic modeling because there are not many methods that can involve the full periodic table and still have a reasonable CPU time requirement. In addition to inorganic modeling, it is also used for computing band structures which are calculations that are highly computationally intensive. Due to this factor, extended Hückel method is preferred for these calculations of band structure. The Hückel method has proven to also be very convenient when it comes to viewing orbital symmetry. Despite all these advantages, this method has been known to be fairly poor when it comes to the prediction of molecular geometries (Wilson, 2013).

3. *The Pariser-Parr-Pople (PPP):* This method is generally an extension of the Hückel method where other different heteroatom other than hydrogen is allowed. This method is not used much, but it is in situations where the electronic effects requires are minimal. For example, that has been in-cooperation of terms that are based on PPP in molecular mechanic calculations for the description of aromaticity. This method is also known for the development of parameterized simple analytic expressions for properties of molecules (Wilson, 2013).

4. *Complete Neglect of Differential Overlap (CNDO):* Of all the neglect of differential overlap methods, this is the simplest. This method works by modeling valance orbital's by only utilizing the lowest number of basis sets that can be utilized of Slater type

orbitals. This method has only been able to prove to be useful for some results in hydrocarbons; however, it has not been useful in much else. It is however, sometimes still utilized for the generation of the initial guessing on hydrocarbon ab-initio calculations. The improved parameterization of the CNDO/ 1, which is the CNDO/ 2 method, is what is used for performing all the CNDO calculations. There is also a CNDO/S method that has undergone parameterization for the reproduction of electronic spectra. This CNDO/S has helped in improving the yield when it comes to predicting excitation energy; however, it has done this at the expense of poorly predicting molecular geometry. The CNDO/2 method has also been extended for the inclusion of elements that have occupied d orbitals. Due to the limited accuracy when it comes to the results, these techniques have not yet been used all over (Wilson, 2013) (Figure 3.6).

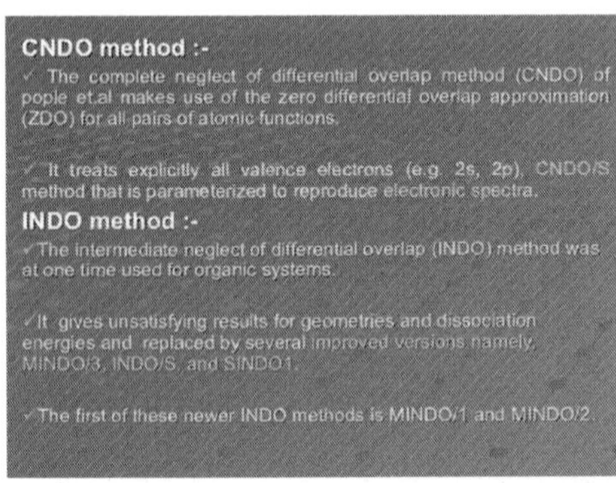

Figure 3.6. A comparison of the CNDO method and the INDO method. The two main INDO methods that are used are MINDO/1 and MINDO/2.

Source: *https://www.slideshare.net/dragnerkar/molecular-mechanics-and-dynamics (accessed on 3 April 2020).*

5. *Modified Intermediate Neglect of Differential Overlap (MINDO)*: Of these, there are three main methods: MINDO/1, MINDO/2, and MINDO/3. The most used and the most efficient and effective method of these three is MINDO/3. MINDO/3 has been able to use qualitative results for organic molecules. There has been a superseding of this method today due to the fact that there are methods that are much more accurate than this, such as the parameterization method 3 and Austin model 1. It is however,

sometimes still used for obtaining an initial guess for calculations using the ab initio method.

6. *Modified Neglect of Diatomic Overlap (MNDO):* This method has proven to provide qualitative results that are very reasonable for many different organic systems. There are several popular semi empirical programs that have been able to incorporate this method, in addition to the MNDO program. As of today, this method is still being utilized, however, the initially mentioned more accurate methods that are parameterization method 3 and Austin Method 1 are much more popular. This method, however, has shown to sometimes provide results that are quantitatively and qualitatively incorrect: There is underestimation of computed electronic excitation energies; There tends to be high activation barriers; It does not compute the conformer as the lowest energy; the computation of the barriers to bond rotation are normally too small; computation of the sterically crowded molecules as well as the hypervalent compounds are normally too unstable; the prediction of the four membered rings is too stable; the prediction of the oxygenated functional groups on the aromatic rings is normally too out of plane, etc. (Wilson, 2013).
7. *Austin Model 1 (AM1):* When it comes to organic compounds, this is the method that is most popularly used. The AM1 works by predicting the heats of formation much more accurately in comparison to MNDO, however, there has been some documentations of a few exceptions when it to comes to the Bromine atom. Depending on the information that is desired as well as the nature of the system, it is advisable to either use the Austin method 1 or parameterization method 3 which will both be able to provide the most accurate results that can be obtained when it comes to organic molecules, when using semi empirical methods.

The Austin method 1 has shown both strengths and limitations when it comes to providing results. It is possible to improve activation energies with the use MNDO. When it comes to aluminum, the Austin method 1 is able to make a better prediction when it comes to the results, in comparison to the parameterization method 3. The paramidalization of Nitrogen is poorly predicted by Austin method 1. The results it provides for Silicon dioxide are not bent enough. Limitations have been seen when it comes to the Austin method 1 energies, such as the prediction of five membered rings to be too stable, and the prediction of rotational to be 1/3 the actual barrier. The heat of formation that this method predicts tends to be inaccurate for molecules that have a charge localization that is high. This method also tends to poorly predict the geometries that involve phosphorus. They also predict extremely stable alkyl group energies, which are considered a systematic error. The Nitro groups that are obtained are of a much higher positive energy. When it comes to hydrogen bonds, the prediction is always correct in terms of its strength, but most of the times it's wrong when he comes to its orientation. In general, the Austin Method 1 is able to make better predictions than MNDO, however, not as well as the parameterization method 3 (Young, 2004).

8. *Parameterization Method 3 (PM3):* This method normally utilizes almost all the similar equations as the Austin method 1 while having a set of parameters that have been improved. When it comes to organic systems, this method is also currently very popular. It is actually known to be much more accurate in comparison to the Austin method 1 especially for hydrogen bond angles; however, the Austin method 1 has proven to be much more accurate when it comes to the hydrogen bond energies. Both the Austin method 1 and the parameterization method 3 are much more popular in comparison to other methods in the Semi empirical group, due to the fact that they have algorithms that are available for including solvation effects within the calculations.

The Parameterization method 3 also has both pros and cons. When it comes to the overall heats of formation, AM1 and MNDO provide the most accurate results. The level of accuracy is also much better in hypervalent molecules. The parameterization method 3 also makes a prediction that the barriers to rotation that is found on Carbon-nitrogen bond that are found in peptides are normally too low. When it comes to the bonds that are between the Silicon and the halide atoms, the prediction that is made is too short. The parameterization method 3 is also known for providing incorrect prediction of germanium compounds' electronic states. When it comes to the sp3 Nitrogen to always be pyramidal. There is also prediction of some spurious minima. The accuracy of proton affinities is not correct. It produces polycyclic rings that are not flat. The charge that is predicted on Nitrogen is incorrect. The distances that are non-bonded are too short. The bonds in Hydrogen are shorter. In general, when the comparison is made, the parameterization method 3 is much more accurate than Austin method 1 and MNDO (Young, 2004) (Figure 3.7).

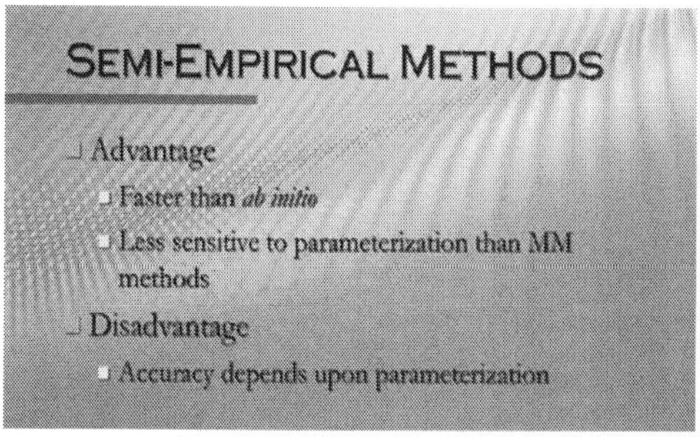

Figure 3.7. Some of the advantages and disadvantages of the semi-empirical methods. These methods are much faster than the ab initio methods.

Source: https://www.slideserve.com/dagan/molecular-modeling-semi-empirical-methods (accessed on 3 April 2020).

3.3.2.2. Advantages

This method has a couple of advantages including: it is able to calculate both excited states and transition states; and in comparison to the ab-initio method, it is less demanding computationally.

3.3.2.3. Disadvantages

Some of the disadvantages of the semi empirical method include: when it comes to rigor, it is less rigorous than ab-initio methods; and for parameters, it needs experimental data and sometimes it may also need data from ab-initio methods.In general, the semi-empirical methods are best used with: systems that are medium sized such as hundreds of atoms; and systems that involve electronic transition.

3.3.3. Molecular Mechanics

MM models molecular systems with the use of classical mechanics. It is assumed that the Born-Oppenheimer approximation is valid, and there is calculation of the potential energy of all systems, as a function of the nuclear co-ordinates with the use of force fields. The study of molecular systems can be done through MM, with systems that range in complexity and size from small to large material assemblies or biological systems that have thousands to millions of atoms. All the methods that are used in atomistic MM have to have certain properties. These include:

All-atomistic MM methods have the following properties:

- The simulation of each atom occurs as one particle.
- A radius is assigned to each particle. The main one that is used is the van der Waals radius. In addition, each particle is assigned a constant net charge (generally gotten from experiment and/or quantum calculations), and polarizability.
- The need to treat bonded interactions as springs that have an equilibrium distance that is equal to the bond length which is either calculated or experimental.

It is possible to have a couple of variations when it comes to this theme. For example, there are some simulations that have been able to utilize the representation of a united-atom, in which the intermediate Methylene unit or each terminal methyl group was considered as one particle, and also simulation of large protein systems with the use of the bead model that works by assigning two to four particles to each amino acid (Young, 2004).

The transferability of parameters is the main assumption when it comes to molecular mechanic method. When you describe this in a different way, the particular molecular motion that is associated with the energy penalty, for example, when the single bond of a carbon-carbon is stretched, will be similar between all the molecules, from one to the next. This helps in providing a simple calculation that can undergo application to molecular systems that are very large.

This method can only perform highly if four specific factors are available. These are:

- The energy expression's functional form.
- The data that is utilized for the parametrization of the constants.
- The methods that are used for the optimization of constants from the data.
- The user's ability to use these methods in a manner that is consistent with the weaknesses and strengths.

So as to ensure that the transferability of parameters is able to provide a molecular description that is good, there has be the use of atom types by force fields. In general, this refers to describing the sp3 carbon by different parameters when compared to a sp2 carbon, etc. Normally, it is important to understand that atoms that are found in aromatic rings are normally treated in a different manner in comparison to sp2 atoms. There are even some force fields that normally ensure parameterization of the atoms for functional groups that are different. For example, it is possible to describe the carbonyl oxygen through various parameters, in contrast to the carbonyl oxygen that is found in a ketone.

The greatest advantage of this method is that it makes it possible for one to model large molecules, such as segments of DNA and proteins. This is why this method is considered the main tool of computational biochemists. It is also able to properly model intermolecular forces (Young, 2004) (Figure 3.8).

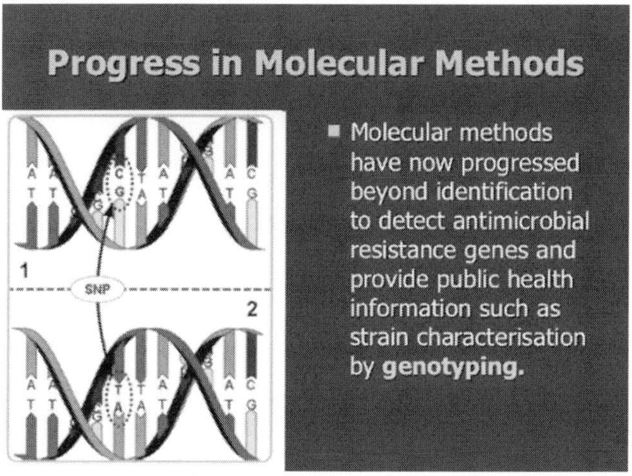

Figure 3.8. There has been a lot of progress in the development of molecular methods. We have been able to achieve strain characterization through genotyping for the diagnosis of infectious diseases.

Source: *https://www.slideshare.net/doctorrao/molecular-methods-in-diagnosis-of-infectious-diseases (accessed on 3 April 2020).*

The main disadvantages of this method are that, within the method, not many chemical properties that are not defined, for example, excited states in the electronic form. Due to the fact that terms that are found in chemical bonding are included in an explicit manner in the force field, without some form of mathematical manipulation, it is not possible to ensure examination of the reaction in which the bonds are either broken or formed. So as to be able to work with systems that are extremely large and complicated, software packages that are meant for MM normally have graphic interfaces that are powerful and easy to use. Due to this factor, most of the times MM is used, it is because it is easy to implement not that it is the best system that can be used for the description of a system. Due to the level of sensitivity that they have to parameterization, the most advisable method to follow when choosing a force field is by looking for studies that are similar in the literature, as well as validating the results of the test against those that are experimental (Young, 2004).

3.3.3.1. Uses of Molecular Mechanics

Over the past years, MM has mainly been used in the field of molecular dynamics. This field aims at utilizing the force field for the calculation of forces that act on each particle, and modeling particle dynamics as a suitable integrator, in addition to predicting trajectories. Molecular dynamics trajectories are able to be utilized for the estimation of probe kinetic properties, such as reaction mechanisms and rates, as well as for thermodynamic parameters of a system, only if provided with enough sampling and subject to the ergodic hypothesis.

MM can also be used in energy minimization, where they use the force field as an optimization criterion. In this technique, an algorithm that is appropriate, such as steepest descent, is used in finding a local energy minimum's molecular structure. There is then a corresponding factor of the minima to the molecules stable conformers and it is then possible to model the molecular motion as inter conversions between and vibrations around these stable conformers. Therefore, it is quite common to find methods of minimizing local energy in combination with methods of optimization of global energy, so as to equip the minimum global energy as well as other energy states that are low (Wilson, 2013).

At temperatures that are finite, we find that the molecules tend to spend much more time in these states that are low-lying, therefore dominating the molecular properties. It is possible to accomplish global optimization through the use of the Metropolis algorithm, simulated annealing, as well as other Monte Carlo methods. It is also possible to achieve this through the use of various deterministic methods of continuous or discrete optimization. While only the enthalpic component of free energy is represented by the force field, there is a possibility to achieve the inclusion of the entropic component by using additional methods, such as normal mode analysis. We have been able to calculate binding constant, active site coordinates, protonation equilibria, protein folding kinetics, and to design binding sites, through molecular mechanic potential energy functions (Wilson, 2013).

3.3.3.2. Advantages

Some of the advantages that are found in MM include: this technique normally relies on potential that require to be supplied in one way or another; and it may be inaccurate sometimes due to the fact that the potential that have been supplied are utilized way past the proven range of validity.

3.3.3.3. Disadvantages

Despite its advantages, it also has a few disadvantages such as: the force field that is used in particular is only applicable for a limited class of molecules; It needs experimental data and sometimes it may also need data from ab-initio calculations; and it is not able to calculate electronica properties.

In general, it is best for: processes and systems that have no forming or breaking bonds; and large systems of approximately 1000 atoms.

3.3.4. Other Methods Used

3.3.4.1. Density Functional Method

This is a method that is used in competition of quantum mechanics modeling in materials science, chemistry, and physics for the investigation of the electronic structure of many different systems in the body such as condensed phases, molecules, and atoms. With the use of this theory, it is possible to determine the properties of a many-electron system through the use of functional, that is, functions of another functions, whereby in this situation, is the especially dependent electron density. This means that the term DFT is derived from utilizing functional of the electron density.

The DFT is considered to be one of the most versatile and popular techniques that is found in computational chemistry, computational physics, and condensed matter physics. In the 1970s, this technique was found to be very popular when it came to calculating aspects in solid-state physics. However, up to the 1990s, it was not accepted as a fully accurate method for quantum chemistry calculations, which is the period in which approximations that were used in the theory had greatly been refined in a way they could model the exchange in a better manner as well as correlation interactions (Figure 3.9).

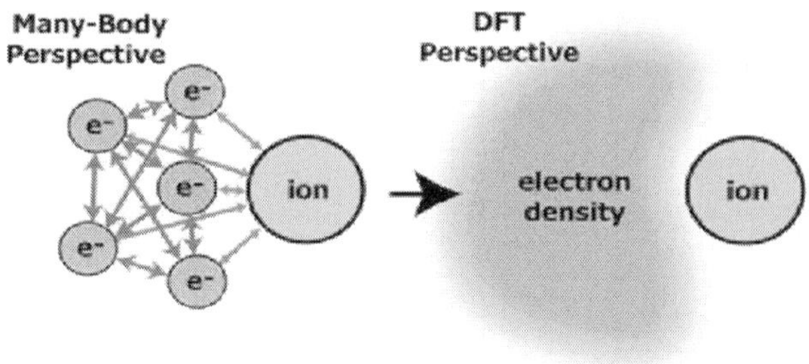

Figure 3.9. The visual representation of the density functional theory, with the many body perspective and the density functional theory perspective.

Source: *https://www.researchgate.net/figure/Density-functional-theory-DFT-abandons-the-manyparticle-electron-reality-in-favor-of_fig2_259406317 (accessed on 3 April 2020).*

In comparison to traditional methods such as the descendants of HF theory including electron correlation and even the exchange only HF theory itself, the computational costs in this method are relatively low. Due to the fact that the DFT has become a tool that is considered very important in nuclear spectroscopy methods such as perturbed angular correlation or Mössbauer spectroscopy, so as to come to an understanding as to the reason in which specific electric field gradients are found within crystals (Wilson, 2013).

No matter how much computational chemistry has advanced, there are still many issues when it comes to using the DFT for properly describing: calculations of the band gap and ferromagnetism in semiconductors; dopant interactions, global potential energy surfaces, transition states, and some strongly correlated systems; charge transfer excitation; Van der Waal's forces especially when it comes to depression; and intermolecular interactions that are critically important in understanding chemical reactions.

When dispersion is incompletely treated, it can lead to causing a great negative effect to the level of accuracy of the DFT, especially when it is used without corrections and alone, when it comes to treating systems that are fully dominated by dispersions, for example noble gas items that are interacting, or where there are many other effects, such as biomolecules, that are significantly competing with dispersion. There has been development of new methods within DFT that have been designed in a manner that is able to deal with this problem through being able to alter the functional or by including additional terms in a specific topic that has being researched on. A similar method referred to as the classical DFT normally utilizes a formalism that is quite similar when it comes to the calculation of properties of classical fluids that are non-uniform (Wilson, 2013).

3.3.4.2. Methods for Solids

The methods that are used for solid-state physics in computational chemistry normally follow a similar approach as that which is followed for molecules; however, they have two differences. The first difference is that the solid's translational symmetry must be used, and the second difference is that, there is a possibility for one to use basis functions that are completely delocalized, for example plane waves, instead of using molecular atom centered basis functions.

A band structure generally describes the electronic structure of a crystal, which helps in defining the electron orbital's' energies that are found at each point within the Brillouin zone. Semi empirical and ab-initio calculations normally work in achieving orbital energies, and this means it is possible to use these methods to perform band structure calculations.

Due to the fact that calculating the energy for a molecule is time consuming, it is evident that calculating the energies for all the molecules for the entire list of points in the Brillouin zone is even much more time consuming. It is possible for calculations to utilize some post HFmethods such as DFT, and Møller-Plesset perturbation theory to second order, or just use the HF method itself (Wilson, 2013).

3.3.4.3. Quantum Mechanics/Molecular Mechanics

This is a hybrid approach which involves molecular simulation methods that deal with a combination of the strengths of quantum mechanics, which is accuracy, and MM, which is speed, therefore providing the opportunity for the study of chemical processes in both proteins and solutions. This approach was introduced in 1976 by Levitt and Warshel. Together with Martin Karplus, they all won the Nobel Prize in 2013.

The greatest advantage of the quantum mechanics/MM methods is that they have a high level of efficiency. This involves being able to do simulations using classical MM in a very straightforward case scales as the big notion, where the number of the atoms in the system are represented by N. This can be due to the fact that in electrostatic interactions, each particle normally has an interaction with everything else.

- ***Interpretation of Molecular Wave Functions*:** The Richard Bader atoms in molecules model was created for being able to effectively link a molecule's quantum mechanical model as a wave function that is electronic, to concepts that are chemically useful such as valence bond model, the theory of Lewis pairs, bonding, functional groups, and atoms in molecules. Bader was able to demonstrate that these chemistry concepts that are empirically useful are easy to relate with the topology of the density distribution of the observable charge, regardless of whether it is calculated or measured from a quantum mechanical wave function. Atoms in molecules analysis of molecular wave functions normally undergoes implementation, for example, the AIMALL software package (Figure 3.10).

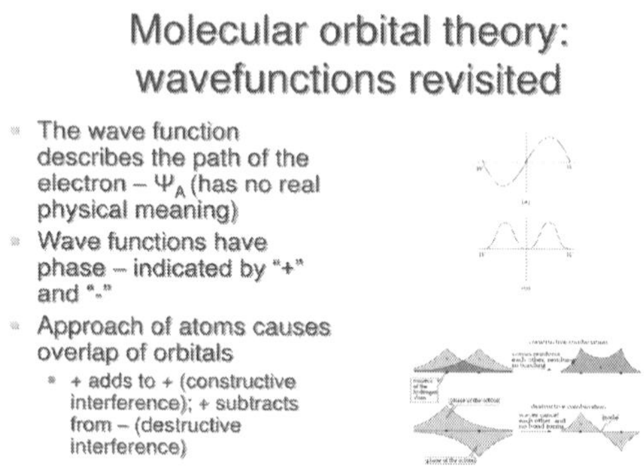

Figure 3.10. A revisitation of the wave functions. These help in describing the path that is taken by an electron.

Source: https://slideplayer.com/amp/6373567/ (accessed on 3 April 2020).

- ***Software Packages Available:*** There are many different available computational chemistry software packages that are self-sufficient. There are some that are inclusive of and only concentrate on a range that is very specific, well some are able to cover a wide range. There are even others that only have one specific method. Some of these include:

The molecular design software-this software is designed for the modeling of molecules. It helps in providing extensive support in the development of molecular models de novo. In comparison to the normally used programs for molecular modeling, for example those that are used for quantum chemistry and molecular dynamics, this software is able to support the construction of molecular models in a direct manner, including:

- Supporting the different aspects of the development of force fields;
- Optimizing geometry;
- Development of partial charges;
- Building solvated systems, crystals, and molecules;
- Conformational editing and interactive molecular drawing; and
- Molecular graphics.

Bio molecular modeling programs for nucleic acids-some of the commonly used programs for nucleic acid simulations include:

- MD for Molecular dynamics;
- Monte Carlo;
- Replica Exchange Method;
- Hardware accelerated;
- Implicit water; and
- Explicit water.

Quantum chemistry computer programs and solid-state physics software-these programs are utilized in computational chemistry for the implementation of quantum chemistry methods. Most of these are inclusive of some post-HF method and the Hartree-Fock method itself. It is also possible for this to be inclusive of semi empirical quantum chemistry methods, MM, or DFT. These programs could either be commercial software or open source software. Majority of these are normally large, most of the contain a couple of separate programs, and over the years, they have been greatly developed (Leszczynski, 2012).

Valence bond programs-these are used for modern valence bond calculations which are done through the application of the valence bond theory especially when it comes to computer programs that are highly competitive when it comes to the economy and accuracy with programs that are designed for the HF method, as well as other various molecular orbital based methods.Protein structure prediction software-these are software's that are mainly used in making predictions of protein structures, inclusive of transmembrane helix and signal peptide prediction, secondary structure prediction, ab initio methods, protein threading, and homology modeling. Some of these include:

- *Biskit*: This works by wrapping external programs into workflow that is automated.
- *RaptorX:* This works by detecting homology from remote areas, predicting binding sites, and 3D modeling.
- i*ntFOLD*: This is used for predicting protein-ligand binding residues, prediction of domains, Intrinsic disorder prediction, 3D model quality assessment, and 3D modeling as well as tertiary structure prediction.
- *ESyPred3D:* This is used for 3D modeling, alignment, and template detection.
- *FoldX*: This is used for protein design and energy calculations.
- *Molecular Operating Environment*: This is used for relaxation using MM force fields, rotamer libraries for side chain conformation, loop modeling, use of multiple templates and accounting for other environments such as ligand volumes that have been excluded, and also for identifying templates. These are just but a few of the software's that are available for use in computational chemistry.

Chapter 4

Computational Electromagnetics

CONTENTS

4.1. INTRODUCTION

The current society relies fully on the electromagnetic equipments and methods and some examples are radio, telephones, televisions, microwave, and satellite communication methods, medical imaging equipments, transforms, and electrical motors. Some of these examples are used in wide ranges of these circumstances; like radar is used for fire-control, weather forecasting, airport traffic management, tracking of missiles, guiding of the missile and safety in traffic (Figure 4.1).

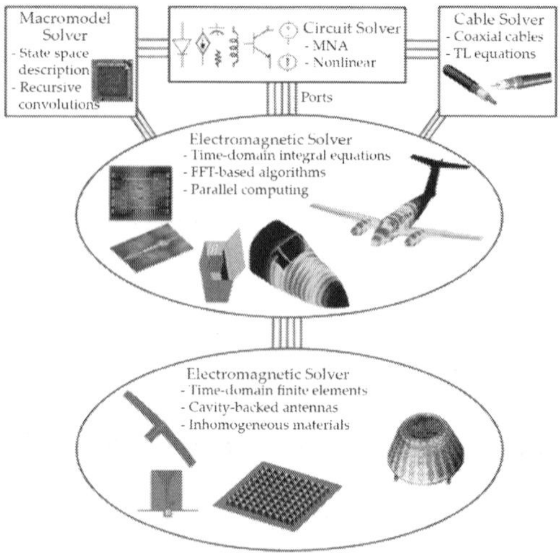

Figure 4.1. The computational electromagnetic is growing area slowly with the growing demand of software and study of electrical equipments.

Source: *http://users.ece. utexas.edu/~yilmaz/CEM_APPLICATIONS/ (accessed on 3 April 2020).*

In the electrical control engineering, the computational electromagnetic is well recognized for the study and design of generators,' shields, transforms, and also electrical equipments. In the implementation of microwave, the computational electromagnetic is the up to date equipment, which is being implanted for the creation of modern microwaves nets and aerials and also in the microwave ovens. The summarization and estimation for the RCS or the radar cross section for the stealth equipments has been the driving engine for the creation of many developments of new modern knowledge in the computational electromagnetic. With the growing command of electromagnetic compatibility also creates new computational dilemmas.

Computational electromagnetic or the CEM, electrodynamics computational or the modeling in computational is the procedure that is used to model the interface of the CEM areas with substantial matters within the surroundings. This usually is concerned with computationally competent approximations of the equations of Maxwell, which is normally used to estimate the aerial routine, electromagnetic consistency, radar cross fragments and the electromagnetic signal broadcasts when it is not in open spaces. This is a particular section of computational electromagnetic transactions with rays of electromagnetic that are spread out and later absorbed by minute particles.

4.2. BACKGROUND

A number of actual-world electromagnetic troubles such as electromagnetic spreading, electromagnetic emissions, or creations of waveguides and many others are not logically quantified, for the masses of uneven geometrics that are found in the real plans (Ladeveze, 2012).

Computational mathematical techniques are able to defeat the failures that are obtained from the closed shape solutions of the equations of Maxwell, which occur under a variety of constitutive associations of the media, and the boundary situations. Hence, making, and the computational electromagnetic or CEM vital towards the plan, and the modeling of the transmitters, radar, outpost, and additional systems of communication, nanophotonic strategy and elevated paced silicon electronics, therapeutic techniques, telephone transmitter plans and along with other applications. The computational electromagnetic usually tackles the troubles of computing electric E and the magnetic H areas transversely in the difficult areas for example to estimate the aerial emission patterns for any randomly fashioned aerial organization. As well as estimating the energy flow course and this is known as the poynting points, a transmission lines standard form, media-created signal distribution as well as the dispersion and the spreading can be calculated from the magnetic and electric areas.

The computational electromagnetic models can and cannot presume equilibrium, simplifying the actual world organization idealizing the spheres and the cylinders, as well as other ordinary geometrical stuffs. The computational electromagnetic models expansively make use of the equilibrium, and answer for reduction of dimensionality from three spatial sizes to 1D and even 2D. The Eigen value trouble formulation of the computational electromagnetic permits for the estimation of stable conditions for the usual modes in an organization. Transient reaction and the impulse area effects are precisely modeled by the computational electromagnetic in the time sphere by FDTD. Arched geometrical substances are considered more precisely as limited time basics finite element methods or the non-orthogonal bars. The ray broadcasting techniques can tackle the power course within the transmission lines. Computational electromagnetic is the request that is detailed, even when dissimilar techniques will come together to the exact area and energy distribution in the same modeled field (Ladeveze, 2012).

4.3. OUTLINE OF THE METHODS

One particular advance is discretizing the room into provisions of bars to include the Orthogonal and the non-orthogonal and tackle the puzzles of Maxwell on every position of the network. Discretization consumes the computer remembrance; hence tackling the problems will take considerable time. Big-scale computational electromagnetic troubles face remembrance and CPU restrictions. This computational electromagnetic crisis calls for supercomputers with very high presentation clusters processor vectors parallel. Usually these formulations entail moreover time-stepping via the problems which occur within the entire sphere instantaneously or via the lined mold inversion toward estimating the size of the foundation features, but as created by limited elements procedures, or else the medium yields by the means of the transmitting matrix procedures or even estimating the integrals by use of techniques of moments or even by using the swift Fourier and the occasion iterations when estimated via the split-step procedures or by the Beam Propagation Methods (Ladeveze, 2012).

4.3.1. Selection of Methods

By selecting the correct procedures to tackle different problems is very essential; as selecting the incorrect one lead to having wrong outcomes or even outcomes that take extremely long to calculate. Nevertheless, the name of the procedure at times does not explain how it is implemented, particularly for business tools, which mostly has several problems.

4.3.1.1. Essential Puzzle Solvers

1. *Disconnected Dipole Estimate*: This disconnected dipole estimate procedure is a simple method meant for computing spreading with assimilation via points of random shapes. The formulations are made on vital shapes of the equations of Maxwell. The discrete

dipole approximations are a rough estimation of the range goal via a limited display of polarizable facts. These particular facts to attain the opposite poles moments in reply of the confined electrical fields. Dipoles of itinerary cooperate with each other through their electric areas; hence, at times the discrete dipole approximation is at times known also as joined dipole estimation. The consequential relationships of the structure in the puzzle are normally tackled by means of conjugate gradient course. Discretization medium has symmetries which are essential shapes of equations of Maxwell and has difficult forms; which permit Fast Fourier change to numerous matrix periods vector throughout the conjugate incline courses.

2. *Methods of Moment's Element Methods*: The methods of moments also known as MoM or the boundary element method also known as the boundary element procedures is a mathematical procedure for tackling solutions of incomplete discrepancy puzzles which are been created like the basic. It can be implemented in various particular fields of engineering science and these are liquid mechanism, acoustics, electromagnetic, rupture mechanism, and flexibility. Ever since the 1980s, methods of moments have become widely accepted, since it needs only calculating the margin values, as opposed to values all over the gap. It should be considerably well-organized within the conditions of computation income for crises which have tiny exterior or capacity fractions. Theoretically, it operates via building networks above the created exterior. Nevertheless, for a number of crisis, border elements procedures are considerably computationally are fewer competent than size-Discretization procedures and this include finite element procedures, finite difference procedures, and finite volume procedures. The boundary factor formulation naturally gives an increase to completely populated matrix. In this way, the storage necessities and computational occasion will be likely to develop as per the cube size within the dilemma. By comparing, restricted aspect matrix should be normally lined which means the basics should be simply close by linked and the necessities used for systems matrix usually developed together by the dilemma size (Zingoni, 2010).

Density procedures such as several pole enlargements or to a coping traverse for rough estimations or matrix structure that are implemented to remodel for this crises, although by the expenses of extra difficulty and by a successful rate that relies' a wholly on the character and the size within the predicament. The boundary element method is appropriate for crises for which can be designed by the Green's function. These typically entail areas in linear harmonized media. This place significantly limits the variety and the overview of the crises appropriate for boundary elements. Non-linearity's can be incorporated in the formulations, even though they normally commenced capacity components involving the capacity that are discretize prior to resolutions, eliminating a necessary benefit of the boundary element methods.

3. *Fast Multipole Methods*: The FMM or the fast multipole methods is a substitute for the method of moments or even the Ewald summary. This is a precise imitation method that requires less reminiscence and a CPU power than the method of moments. The fast multipole method is centered on the multipole expansion techniques. The fast multipole methods can also be used to speed up the methods of moments.
4. *Plane Wave Time-Domain*: Despite the fact that the fast multipole procedures are helpful for the speeding up of the methods of moment's answers of essential puzzles which are fixed before occurrence-sphere of influence of the kernels of oscillatory, the PWTD or the plan wave time-domain algorithms uses related thoughts to speed up the methods of moments which are explanation of the time-area essential puzzles which connect the retarded possibility.
5. *Incomplete Factor Equal Circuit:* The incomplete factor equal circuit or the PECC this is 3D full-wave modeling technique that is appropriate for the collective circuit and electromagnetic study. Contrast to the method of moments, the partial element equivalent is a packed range method that is suitable beginning with the dc to the greatest occurrences resoluted by the network. Within the partial element equivalent circuit procedure, the important equation is explained as the law of Kirchhoff's voltage is useful to an essential partial element equivalent circuit compartment whose outcome is a total result for the 3D geometrics (Zingoni, 2010). The corresponding circuit formulations permit for the extra spice category of circuit elements so as toward the effortlessly incorporation. Study of the models significantly applies toward the occasion and the occurrence areas. By course, puzzles coming

originating partial element equivalent circuit are simply created by means of a customized sphere scrutiny before the customized nodal scrutiny creation. As well giving straight up to date answer, it has a number of other advantages over the methods of moments study for this set of crises because any kind of course factor is able to be incorporated within simple ways which are suitable stamps of the matrix. With partial element equivalent circuit, procedure has lately been prolonged to comprise non-orthogonal geometries. The copy expansion, which is steady by the usual orthogonal solutions which consists of the puzzle illustrations the sizes together with a common hexahedral and four-sided figure basics. This helps in maintaining the figures of the unknowns at the smallest amount and hence reducing the computational occasion for the non-orthogonal geometries (Zingoni, 2010).

4.3.1.2. Discrepancy Puzzle Solvers

1. *Limited-Divergence Occasion-Area*: The limited-divergence time-area is an accepted computational electromagnetic procedure, which is very easy to comprehend. Having remarkably simple achievements for a full signal solver. This is the smallest amount of an arrangement of magnitude that needs very little work to execute an essential limited divergence time-area solver than the technique of time or the finite element procedures. The limited-divergence time-areas are the only procedure where an individual can practically execute themselves in a rational time outline, but will rather be for a precise problem. Because it is a occasion-field technique, the answers should cover up an extensively occurrence variety by means of a single imitation, giving a occasion pace be tiny enough to go with sampling the puzzle theorem for the preferred maximum occurrence. By limited-divergence time-areas is under the broad category of the grid-based discrepancy of the time-domain mathematical modeling procedures. Equations of Maxwell which are incomplete differential appearance are usually customized to central-dissimilar equations discretize and applied in the software (Zingoni, 2010).

The cyclic method is normally used to solved these equations; the electric scope is tackled at immediately at the particular time, then later the magnetic area is tackled later a given time, and this procedure is repeated continuously. The present finite-difference time-domain vary from close by

DC, the ultralow-occurrence geophysics that link the whole earth-ionosphere waveguides via the microwaves, this are the radar mark knowledge, aerials, wireless connections equipments, modern interconnects, biomedical management, and imaging to the detectable light. The finite-difference time-domain has its strengths like it has very simple modeling of difficult material patterns; there is no matrix attack concerned; very simple to adjust to similar processing and very simple to create broadband information, and the ability to execute both transient and the stable state study. The finite-difference time-domain has its weakness to the net thickness is resoluted by well arithmetical particulars within the dilemma; there is stairway mistake for arc's arrangement; required by the net the whole imitation area; and the ABC (PML) to shorten the unbounded problem area (Zingoni, 2010).

2. *Discontinuous Occasion-Area Procedures:* The irregular Galerkin occasion area methods is among several other methods that have turned out to be very popular lately because it has integrated both the advantages of limited quantity occasion areas the procedure and the limited factor occasion area procedures. Similar to the limited volume occasion area, the mathematical change that is used to replace the information among neighboring essentials, hence all operations of the irregular Galerkin occasion areas are limited and simple parallelizable. Like the finite element time domain, the discontinuous Galerkin time domain that employs the shapeless net and be able for the high-order correctness if the elevated-order hierarchical foundation purpose is adopted. The discontinuous Galerkin time domain procedures are extensively implemented for the multiscale crises that are concerned with masses of unknowns.
3. *Multiresolution Time-Domain*: The MRTD also known as the time multiresolution area this is a copying alternative toward the limited divergence of the occasion of the area procedures that depend on the signal study.
4. *Limited Factor Procedures*: The limited factor technique is normally implemented to discover the estimated answers of the partial equations differential or the PDE and the essential equations. The approach to the answers are both based on eradicating the occasion derivatives totally this is the steady condition problems, or representing the partial differential equations (PDEs) into a corresponding ordinary equation differential, which are then tackled by the use of the standard

procedure like the finite dissimilarity any many others. In tackling the incomplete disparity puzzles, the main problem be how in the direction of building a solution estimates that are equations to be investigated, except the one which are mathematically steady; this means to facilitate the mistakes that happen in the input information and the intermediate estimations do not build up and demolish the wipe out the importance of production results. The various methods of tackling with them; this has a number of disadvantages and advantages. The finite element procedure is the best way of tackling the incomplete discrepancy solutions over the difficult areas or as the preferred precisions that differ above the whole area (Zingoni, 2010).

5. *Finite Integration Techniques*: The finite integration technique is a Discretization spatial system which is used to mathematically tackle the electromagnetic area crises in time and concurrency spheres. It conserves the basic topological features of the uninterrupted equations like the management of energy and charge. This particular procedure covers the whole collection of electromagnetic from the fixed up to the high occupancy, while then optic applications are the bases for the simulations of tools in a business. The crucial strategy of this approach is to implement the equations of Maxwell in the basic form to a place of staggered grids. This method is extremely unique due to its high elasticity in the geometric modeling and the boundary managing as well as the absorption the arbitrary substance distribution and the material properties for example anisotropy, dispersion, and non-linearity. The use of a steady double orthogonal network for example the Cartesian net, combined with the precise time integration plan like the leap-frog-plan, leading to the calculating and recollecting-efficient algorithms, which are usually modified or the temporary field study in the frequency of radio also the RF implementations.

6. *Simulated-Spectral Occasion Area*: This particular category of marching-in-time computational procedures for the equation of Maxwell also uses the separate Fourier or the discrete Chebyshev changes to estimating the spatial derivatives of the magnetic and electric area vector mechanism that are set in the 3-D lattice of the component cell or the 2-D network. The pseudo-spectral time domain causes insignificant arithmetical phase rate anisotropy

mistakes that are virtual to the finite-difference time-domain and hence permitting crises of much superior electrical dimension to be constructed.

7. *Pseudo-Spectral Spatial Domain*: The PSSD tackles the equation of Maxwell by moving them forward in a selected spatial course. The areas are consequently held as a purpose of time and perhaps any transverse spatial magnitudes. The procedure of pseudo-spectral because of time derivatives estimated in the occurrence domain of with the help of FFTs. This is because the areas are apprehended as features of time, this supports the arbitrary dispersal in the broadcast medium to be quickly and precisely modeled with the least effort. The options to broadcast ahead in space as opposed to time, subtleties usually come with it, mostly if the reflections are significant.
8. *Broadcast Line Medium*: The broadcast line medium can be created in numerous ways as a straight set of basics that are lumped with solvable straightforward by a course solver as a traditional network of essentials or through a disperse matrix technique. Transmission line matrix is very flexible investigation strategy that is very similar to the finite-difference time-domain in all capabilities, although more codes are more likely to be accessible with the finite-difference time-domain.
9. *Locally One-Dimension*: This is an implied technique, that occur in two-dimensional folders, the equation of Maxwell that are divided into two, while in the three-aspects case equations of Maxwell have been divided into three organized spatial commands. Constancy and dispersal investigations of FDTD-LOD three-dimensional procedures in details.

Other methods include:

- The EME also known as the Eigen mode expansion is a thorough bidirectional procedure that is used to replicate electromagnetic broadcast which only relies on the decay of the electromagnetic areas into a base set of Eigen modes locally. By solving the equations of Maxwell that are found in every restricted cross-sector the Eigen modes are created. The development of Eigen mode can be used to tackle the equation of Maxwell in 3D and

2D and can give a complete vectorial explanation given that the mode solvers are vectorial. It provides very tough advantages as opposed to the finite-distance time-domain procedures for the modeling of visual waveguides, making it widely accepted as a device of the modeling of silicon photonics and fiber visuals tools.

- The PO or the physical optics is a term used for the high concurrency approximation or the short wave-lengths rough calculations that are usually used in visual, engineering electrical and practical physics. This is a transitional technique that is between geometric visual, that totally ignores the wave properties and the complete wave electromagnetism; which is the exact theory. The term physical means that its more substantial than optics of geometric and it is not that it is precise a substantial hypothesis. The estimates consist of using the beam optics to approximate the area on the exterior and later integrate that area over the exterior to give a rough estimation of the transmitted or dispersed area. This represents the born estimation, as in the facts for the dilemma is considered as perturbation.
- The UTD also known as the consistent hypothesis of diffraction is the highest occurrence intended for tackling the electromagnetic dispersion of crises from electrically tiny discontinuities or discontinuities in various dimensions that happen at the same position. The UTD estimates close to the field electromagnetic area as quasi visual and uses beams diffraction coefficients foe every diffracting object-source mixture. These particular coefficients are then used to estimate the field power and the stage for ever route away from the diffracting position. These areas are then added to the occurrence areas and reflected areas are acquired for a total resolution.

4.4. CORROBORATION

Corroboration is the major problems confronting the stimulation clients of electromagnetic. The consumer has to recognize and master the power sphere of its replication; gauge is how distant is the outcome from the reality. Moreover, to better answer this matter involves three steps which include;

comparison involving simulation results and analytical formulation, cross-comparison among codes, and comparison of simulation outcome with capacity (Kaveh, 2013).Cross-comparison among codes-the best example is the cross comparison of the outcome from the method of moments and the asymptotic procedures in their power domains.

- Comparison of the stimulation results with measurements-the last validation procedure is made up by the comparison among simulations and measurements. For instance, the RCS estimation and the dimension of the compound metallic item at 35 gigahertzes. The computation equipments PTD, PO, and GO for the boundaries.

Validation procedures can evidently reveal that a number of differences can be explained by the differences among the investigational setup and its reproduction in the simulation surroundings.

4.5. LIGHT SCATTERING CODES

There are several competent codes for tackling the electromagnetic distribution dilemmas. Below are some of them:

- Electromagnetic disperse by cylinders' codes;
- Codes for electromagnetic disperse by spheres codes;
- Disconnected dipole approximation codes.

Solutions which are logical, like the solution of Mie for diffusion by cylinders or spheres, can be used to legalize more concerned with techniques.

4.6. COMPUTATIONAL ELECTROMAGNETIC IN PLASMONICS

In the field of electromagnetic, mathematical procedures have been vital in the growth of advanced knowledge in the last years. The fast growths of computer capability and estimation speeds make precise decisions of the very difficult problems possible.

This has been visible in the creation of microwaves millimeter signal mechanisms and aerials. Several years back, the blueprint of a transmitter was totally based on the straightforward systematic models or by the use of the strategies in experiment and mistakes; at the moment, simulations appear to be very vital to the plan as the actual capacity. The circumstances are rather different with the plasmonics (Figure 4.2).

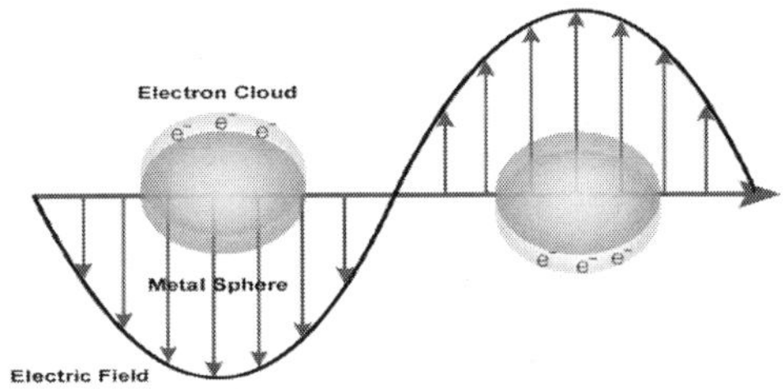

Figure 4.2. Plasmonics is rather a novel investigated area and the request of computational electromagnetic in the plasmonics can be specified as very current.

Source: https://nanocomposix.eu/pages/the-science-of-plasmonics (accessed on 3 April 2020).

There are still several problems that still need to be tackled and the missing connections that still need to be tackled. These plasmonic organizations that are considered are the structures that are arranged according to their extent of the wavelength which are at their frequency. Even though this occurrence variety is totally dissimilar from the long-established occurrence where computational equipments have been created for example the microwave occurrence, in majority of the cases no particular special methods of techniques have been implemented. BY now most plasmonic topologies have been reported in writing and have been analyzed or planned with the best-known mathematical procedures that have been establishes within the commercial software packages or developed in the in-house (Kaveh, 2013).

4.6.1. Basic Physical Modeling Differences

Below is the difference involving the classical topologies that are handled with the electromagnetic computational and topologies in plasmonic. The term classical is described as organizations at a much lesser occurrence such as the microwave occurrence, whereby computational electromagnetic is developed in a mature area.

1. *Frequency*: Foremost, it is vital to rule out that the interaction among the plasmonic organization and light in the occurrence bands are careful summarized with a very high level of correctness by means of the classical electromagnetic hypothesis. Even though the occurrences are instructions of scale that are advances in the plasmonics compared to these microwaves, the laws of

Maxwell are similar. Therefore, both scalable and linear. Even if the quantum effects are not considered, which still applies to the plasmonic implementation that is thought of, and because the organizations are not tiny, there is no basic dilemma. The original formulation o the equation of Maxwell can stay unaltered. The truth that this particular tiny level, no quantum factors have been considered as being really vital to the study. This means that the idea of a disperse, a tool that is able to be triggered by the electromagnetic signals rather than particles, still operate. Essentially, the combination connecting an electromagnetic light signal and the disperse plasmonic is therefore the same as the occurrence in the microwave and can also be investigated in the same particular way (Kaveh, 2013).

2. *Volumetric Currents*: The significance of the concurrency that is high is the tiny level of the basic building blocks of the topologies that are measured at the nanoscale. Therefore, there are two major issues that are connected. The first, intervention knowledge nowadays is only simply used to create the 3D form of structure for example the volumes. The thin sheets of 2D, the thickness of the metal instructions of the degree that are much minute than the transversal scope of the prototype, are normally used as the occurrence in the microwave such as the conducting area or strip are very impossible. The second one is the nanostructures that work at the plasmonic occurrence the skin intensity may be similar with the structural size, so that the currents should flow above the whole volume and the tool has to be described with the volumetric currents. The surface current explanation is not even enough.

3. *Material Characteristics*: The microwave occurrence, mostly the substance properties are very steady above the occurrence bands that are measured. Despite, the losses, majority of the metals act in the same manner this are high-quality conductors. The conductivities and the permittivity's may differ with instructions of the degree over this occurrence bands.

4. *Modeling Techniques*: In the modeling, field techniques are introduced and divided on the foundation of their result technique for example the finite elements or the FE, finite integration techniques (FIT), finite-difference in time-domain, integral equations (IE) are all tackled by the MoM method or the method of moments. Based on their hypothetical specificities, the

purpose of each technique in the plasmonics case is discussed. The structure of computational electromagnetic is seen well in the microwave investigative society. This society deals with the organization in the arrangement of the wavelengths.

5. *Limited Factor Procedure*: The limited factor technique is used to tackle discrepancy equations. The areas within this factor are articulated in conditions of several essential functions such as the polynomials. Its subdivided gap is essential such as the tetrahedra. These languages are fixed into the practical of this equations and the difference of the purpose made to zero. The product is an Eigen value matrix equation whose explanation produces the areas at the nodes. Finite element method gives life to a very sparse equation matrix, which can only be tackled using the devoted matrix, numerical technology that leads to a very fast explanation at times, bearing in mind the mass figures of the unknown. Finite element method is usually formulated in the occurrence area. This means that the methods of moments, the explanation are estimated for every occurrence of interest.

4.6.2. Software Tools

Some viable solvers and other intellectual tackles are being thought-out:

1. ***Material Characteristics***: Strong unreliable objects uniqueness might appear unimportant toward applying in the essential equation system, in various cases more severe consequences arise. Such as the Green's purpose estimate schemes are based on the details that the substance properties do not alter over the occurrence band of attention. Any specific implementation o the method of moments-integral equation needs this vital repose into its formalism, which probably wants to be modified. The main benefit of the method of moments-integral equation as compared to a time field technique such as the finite-difference time-domain this is because the ellipsometric measurement information can be implemented straight into the device, with no additional fit. The finite-difference time-domain methods evolved for the visual range fit in the dielectrical response of the metal.
2. ***Occurrence of Layers:*** The integral equation procedure solvers are created by the function use of Green. Green procedures are created for the multi-layered organizations like the surroundings

standard of the arrangement may feature any random figure of horizontal, infinitely extended, dielectric, and metallic structures, which are taken into consideration systematically. These surroundings are mainly appealing for plasmonic organizations; this is because they are usually deposited on an even covered dielectric substrate such as the glass. The volumetric essential equation mechanisms are replaced by the equal volume currents, which look as the main unknowns in the consequential IE. The substrates used in regular situations are enormous as compared to the wavelengths; the edge effects are particularly tiny and can be ignored. It can be analyzed that the plasmonic organization has very particular contents which create the integral equation-methods of moment's solution quite appealing (Zingoni, 2010).

4.6.3. Commercial Software Tools

1. ***High Frequency Structural Simulator: Finite Element Method*****:** Due to it being the very first equipment in the market and with its simplification and elasticity, the high frequency structural simulator is one of the equipments widely used in the manufacturing microwave and the millimeter wave plan surroundings. The main aim of the high frequency structural simulator is to remove the parasitic boundaries which are S, Y, and Z, the envision of the electromagnetic areas 3D the near-and-far areas, and to produce the SPICE replicas are all supported on the 3D finite element methods, result to the electromagnetic topology which is under deliberation. This particular software is widely accepted and is implemented for all types of purposes. Various results for the plasmonic topologies can effortlessly be found by Google search of the words plasmonics and high frequency structural simulator. The major step with a new model project is to describe the geometry of the organization. This process is repeated until one of the depart criteria is content. It is essential to note that the high frequency structural simulator offers no arched elements for a better rough calculation of curved objects. This means that the web along the curved surface has to be selected very well. This can be acquired with the surface estimation limits. In conclusion the resolution for example the electric and magnetic areas, currents, and S-parameters can be visualized in 3D, 2D and 1D. All results can be exported as

records. The Optimetrics toolbox is obtainable for optimizations, limitation, understanding, and numerical study (Ladeveze, 2012).

2. ***Comsol Multiphysics: Finite Element Method*:** Comsol Multiphysics implements the restricted element technique to tackle the fractional differential equations in the 3D and the 2D. This is a multiphysics system, which states that not only can it handle the electromagnetic, also it can handle procedures, acoustics, liquid dynamics, and heat transmitted. The geometry, substance parameters and the boundary circumstances have to be put up in the graphical user interface commonly known as the GUI. After defining the limitations and the domains the web is created. This consists, the range of the basic functions and the curved web elements, they are implemented for the rough estimation of the curved limits. The meshing is driven by particular figures of the nodes and their allocation on each perimeter of the particular model. The Comsol multiphysics give a very broad range of matrix solvers that are used to tackle the methods of equations. The straightforward solvers are more suitable for the tiny problems and the iterative solvers are appropriate for bigger problems. The Comsol Multiphysics can be created from the 2D and the 3D plots. The Quantities resulting from the electromagnetic areas such as the power, power loss, and poynting vector are accessible as the predefined variables. The Comsol Multiphysics does not permit the boundary sweeps or the optimization. The model put up with the graphic user interface can be saved by the Matlab draft, which can be effortlessly be customized. The Matlab draft tools can also be implemented to a topology to optimize it (Ladeveze, 2012).

3. ***JCM Suite: Finite Element Method*:** The JCM suite is parcel software that is based on the finite element method. It made up of devoted equipments for certain imitation dilemmas that appear in the nano-visual and plasmonics. It is made up of disperse equipments, broadcasting mode equipments and the character mode of tools. The harmonic time of the crises can be created in the 3D, 2D and the 1D. The topologies can be separated or may happen in the periodic patterns or a combination of both. The electromagnetic areas are discretizing with the highest arrangement edge essentials. JCM suite consists of the repeated mesh creation.

4. ***CST; Finite Integration Technique***: The microwave studio is founded on the finite integration technique. This permits they selection of the time area as well as the occurrence domain methods. In spite of, the occurrence of the transient, Eigen modes, and the occurrence domain solvers within the CST MWS, the time area solver estimates the broadband manner of the electromagnetic tools in one imitation that operates with the random fine concurrency resolution. The creation of the curved organization by the use of the perfect boundary estimation methods and the modeling of the perfect thin electric conducting sheets by the use of the thin sheet method, tries to deal with the usual difficulties that are inbuilt to the finite-difference time-domain procedures for the organizations that are classical, a number of mesh types can be selected. The usual mesh creator detects the major points inside the organization and later the mesh nodes are located. The consumer can physically add extra fix points on the arrangement, and fully manage the figures of the mesh ranks, with them coordinating with modification to the particular wavelengths. Power based variations of the web permits to develop it in a predefined figure that passes that provides a mesh modification of the complicated plan features for the cost of longer general simulation periods. Even if the finite integration technique that manage the substance parameters that alter over the dielectric volume definite.

The CST is a common purpose software parcel being the actual contestant for the high frequency structural stimulator that was used before in the microwave areas, has drastically become popular with time. Also used in the study and plan of the plasmonic organizations, better outcome results are acquired with the CST which is found in literature. The dilemma that occurs at times with CST in the occurrence response if the equipments settings are not suitable (Ladeveze, 2012).

4.6.4. Non-Commercial Software Tools

1. ***Lumerical; Finite-Differences Time-Domain***: Since measuring the topology, occurrences group desirable, and the nature the excitation, it estimates the system, disperses manner and the emission of the organizations under deliberation, and is founded on the mixed full-signal. The possible explanation of the Electric area essential explanations, initially it was implemented on

the surface currents of the 2D. The new hypothetical methods were created and used within the structure. This is vital in the analysis of its purpose in the field. This in turn leading the very initial established replicated outcomes within the field. That is widely used in the plasmonics. The MAGMAS is founded on the incorporation of the triangular and rectangular net cells. The whole mesh management is obtained from the physical meshing form. The graphical interface user is accessible.

2. ***Extra Non-Viable Gears that are Establish Within Text*:** At this instance plasmonics is generally experimentally motivated investigation field. Such as in the area traditional aerial study, several papers can be found on modeling as such. Majority of this papers are mostly concerned with the report of the physical phenomena happening and the irregularly just stated the mathematical device being used. Majority of the researchers in the plasmonics area implement the commercial device accessible. Even the use of the magnetic flow formalism to explain the holes, typical at the microwave occurrence, already have been implemented in the plasmonics. Nevertheless, these devoted developments cannot be divided under the headings, investigation, and structure in the sense that they have restricted the handling a broad range of various topologies.

3. ***Benchmarking*:** At the moment, physicists, and engineers rely a lot on the highly dedicated full signal electromagnetic areas solvers to examine, expand, and optimize their blueprints. Computer-aided investigation and optimize have replaced the plan processes of the of iterative investigation modifications of the original design. It obvious that the essential answer technique for a software device may considerably influence the competence and correctness by which particular arrangements types are summarized. However, the business focus gradually raises switches from such key theoretical considerations to improve in the field of layout devices and system-level design devices. For this reason, users tend to get the bad impression that particular solver is mechanically suitable to tackle any type of difficulty with the arbitrary accuracy. This investigation is specific on the restrictions and the capabilities of the useful electromagnetic modeling methods that are usually concealed from the consumer.

4. ***Benchmarking in Literature*:** In the literature field, fewer comparisons amid the solvers in the area of plasmonics are seen. The finite element method solver that is accessible in the studio is implemented and not the finite-distance time-domain solver. The output limitations considered is the electric area power that links both fields. All the solvers experimented are based on the finite element methods in the occurrence domain, it can be predicted that the major issues with the solvers for this particular topology are similar.
5. ***Comparison between Differential and Integral Equation Techniques*:** When determining the degree of difference and the IE methods are compared. This is achieved by selecting representative solver from each class and by using it to investigate the essential plasmonic topology. In this particular class various types of techniques are used, but the Lumerical is selected, because it is extensively used in the business solver in the plasmonic society. The basic topology chosen is the plasmonic dipole, and this is a organization that can operate as a disperser, but it can also operate as the actual nano-aerial. The major outcome of this segment is that it comes up with a ending on various computational aspects that are concerned with the modeling of the nano-structures with both of the solvers.
6. ***Modeling of the Feed*:** The very first limitation deliberated is the impedance that is seen when the nano-device functions as a broadcaster or the receiving aerial. MAGMAS uses a physical modern filament w width. While the Lumerical does not have a built-in actual feasible modern energy model. It uses a more less sensible pure electrical dipole power. It is observed that there is an outstanding agreement in the development of the curves for example the input impedance with the occurrence of the different widths of the power current filament in the MAGMAS. A similar contract was also seen in both silver and gold dipolar.
7. ***Plasmonic Dipole*:** This is an arrangement that is made up of two nanorods which have opening in between. When the opening is short-circuited it functions as a single bar, and when the opening is open, it acts as a tool that creates an improved electric area. When it is linked to other nanocircuits, it may operate as a nano-aerial in cooperated in the broadcast and is received. The two rods may be made up from metals such as AI, Au, Cr, Ag, and Cu.

8. ***Quality of the Input***: The computational electromagnetic solvers in general create the right outcomes without failure for a large number of different organizations only if the two situations are met.

The consumer has enough common background in the area, with a more precise knowledge about the answer method which has been used in the solver that is being used. Moreover, if not being used in the proper way there is a big danger that the solver is not used well.

9. ***Modeling of Loses:*** The significance of taking into account losses is clear. The metals at the plasmonic occurrence may be neglecting the outcome would be total mistakes outcomes. The difference among the time domain and the frequency domain solvers, because the finite-difference time-domain based device which works in the time domain. The material information has to be altered from the functions of occurrence into functions of time. This is a very hard process, involving a difficult and is a topic to a variety of constraints.
10. ***Meshing***: The mesh value and declaration are the major factors in the correctness of the solver. The electromagnetic pairing between the segments that are nearby may be dissimilar significantly due to the particular meshing implemented, particularly in parts of the organization where fast topological changes happen. This particular issue was studied by the performing convergence work in conditions of the decisions of the meshes.

4.7. ELECTROMAGNETIC FIELD SOLVERS

The electromagnetic field solvers also known as the field solvers are detailed programs that are used to solve the equation of Maxwell straightforward. They create a fraction of the field of the electronic plan mechanization, and they are usually used in the plans of the incorporated circuits and printed circuit boards.

They are used when a resolution from first values is wanted, or the highest correctness is necessary. The removal of parasitic course models is very important for various aspects of physical proof like the timing, signal integrity, substrate pairing, and control grid investigation. As the circuit speeds and densities increase, the necessitate has grown to account precisely for the parasitic effects for bigger and more complex intersect structures. The electromagnetic complexity has developed from the capacitance and resistance, to inductance and even the full electromagnetic signal broadcast. The increase in density has developed for the study of the passive tools like the integrated inductors. The electromagnetic manner is controlled by the equations of Maxwell and all parasitic removal that create the equation of Maxwell (Zingoni, 2010).

That shape can easily be logical similar plate capacitance solutions, may even entail a whole arithmetical answer in a complex mains arithmetical signal broadcast. In the design removal, logical procedures for straightforward or easy arithmetical are able to be implemented anywhere correctness are not important the pace, except when the numerical pattern is hard and when the accuracy weight do not permit overview, geometric explanation of the suitable shaping the equations of should be engaged. Suitable shapes of equations are normally tackled by various sets of procedures. First it implements the differential shape within the central equations and requires the Discretization or meshing of the whole domain in which the electromagnetic areas reside. The two widespread methods in this primary position are the finite distinction and finite factor procedure. The resulting linear method arithmetical structure that must be tackled in wide but thin that contains very few non-zero entries. Sparse linear explanation procedures, like the sparse factorization, conjugate-gradient, or multigrid procedures can be used to tackle these methods, the most excellent of which need CPU occasion and recollection of occasion, anywhere the figure in the essentials in Discretization. Nevertheless, most crises in plans of electronic mechanization are the exposed difficulties, also known as the external crises, also because the areas reduce gradually to perpetuity; procedures can involve very large problems.

Secondly, sets procedures are essential solution procedures that involve the Discretization sources of the areas of the electromagnetic. These sources can either be substantial amounts, like the exterior indict thickness within the capacitance difficulty, arithmetical equations consequential within the request of the theorem. Once the sources are implemented on two-dimensional outside for three-dimensional dilemmas, the procedure usually known as the border factor technique. The exposed crises, the origin of the area are seen in a lesser area than particular areas within, and hence the dimension of linear processes created via the essential solutions procedures are smaller the finite element method. Vital solutions procedures, nonetheless they can create dense when the entries are not zero procedures creates these procedures likely be the finite element method particularly for the tiny crises. These procedures need recollection toward accumulating plus the tackling through the straight removal or the greatest in tackling the problem. The rising route paces and thickness require the answer of gradually more complex intersected, building thick integral equation approaches inappropriate owing to rising development computational rates which increase crises dimensions. In previous decades, a lot of efforts have been done into raising the essential also the differential solution procedures, also the random walk procedures (Zingoni, 2010).A procedure of Discretization by truncating is necessary by the finite element method uses have significantly eliminated figures of basics necessary. The essential equation become mainly popular for intersect removal of sparsification methods, at times known as density of matrix, hastening, or the free matrix methods, which has brought about the development storage plus explanation moments to essential solving the equations (Zingoni, 2010).

In integrated circuit field, sparsified necessary solution methods are normally used for tackling of inductance and capacitance removal crises. The casual-walk procedures have evolved to maturity of the capacitance removal. Crises that requiring the result of whole equations together the discrepancy and essential problem solutions are very frequent.

4.8. SHOOTING AND BOUNCING RAYS

The shooting and bouncing rays or the SBR procedure in computational electromagnetic was created for computation of the radar cross section. Ever since, the procedure has been widespread to be used also for installed aerial presentations (Figure 4.3).

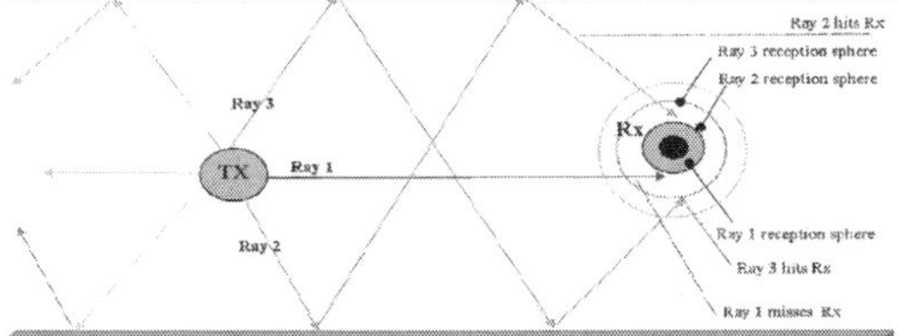

Figure 4.3. The shooting and bouncing rays procedure is an estimation method applied to high occurrence. This particular method can be used in the GPU computing makes the computation very efficient.

Source: https://www.researchgate.net/figure/Graphical-view-of-shooting-bouncing-ray-tracing-SBRT-method-in-an-indoor-scenario_fig1_331528582 (accessed on 3 April 2020).

4.8.1. Extending SBR for Edge Diffraction

Ever since the estimation described assumes that the radius of curvature is big compared to the wavelength, the diffraction from edges required to be handled individually. The shooting and bouncing ray's method can be extended with physical theory of diffraction (PTD) so as to include edge diffraction in the replica.

- Recent progress of computational electromagnetic;
- Advanced-arrangement vector essentials;
- Edge essential hybridization techniques;
- Asymptotic with hybridization techniques;
- Occurrence-area limited factor technique;
- Quick multipole technique;
- Multilevel quick techniques; and
- Quick high arrangement technique.

The needs of electromagnetic simulation include:

1. ***Electromagnetic Requirement***: In assurance or the smallest amount of interruption to the surroundings also towards giving assurance for an accurate effort in the surroundings.
2. ***Electromagnetic Interruption***: To create healthy plan in the regular surroundings. The electromagnetic becomes dangerous and becomes in the logic speed enhancement (increase in frequency, time decrease in transition) high occurrence release amplified.

Methods development (dimension reduce, lump capacitors reduce, digital stage reduction incorporation enhancement), margin noise reduction and other responsive to high frequency conflict power electronic growth (controlling of digit, frequency switching and increase in power) making it hard for normal electromagnetic release fulfillment and planning of robustness.

4.8.2. Problems and How to Tackle Them in the Field of Electromagnetic Investigation

In earlier days, these electromagnetic field simulators paid a closer attention to the solution of very simple aerials or even the microwave mechanisms. This limitation was mainly because of the limited computational resources. In the early year of 2000, two major changes took place in the computational electromagnetic fields and this include various computational electromagnetic procedures were incorporated thus using their diverse intrinsic power, and other competent solvers of the matrix were created utilizing the process of patterns element meant for the quick computations (Zingoni, 2010). With these developments, they permitted more complex and large aerials, and even enabling the combination of the operating surroundings. With quick solvers, the optimization of the difficult problems has become sensible. With the diverse improvement in the antenna plan and requirements on the computational electromagnetic equipments are now determined by the subsequent;

- The efficiency, wide-band, despairing among various aerial, latest equipment, incorporation of the transmitters inside the devices for example telephone tools also stages such as vehicle problems, self-driving cars, anti-impact detecting instruments, intra-vehicle message and may others.
- Fast production of message processes: The propagation of processes manages the necessitate to restrict the unnecessary interference connecting. Compatibility of the electromagnetic study which frequently related to difficult processes and difficult surroundings, such intervention can be caused by a number of rays, defensive, with pairing systems. Such examples include, electronic waves created unnecessary emission above a broad choice and these areas can stimulate waves within the wire connect, generating interfering different processes.

It has usually been foremost perimeter of diverse tackles for over 15 years or so. The following are usual examples:

- Traveler in vehicle: the finite element method is implemented to the human body to many various parts be in attendance, while methods of moments before the multilevel fast multipole method are implemented in the cars.
- Transmitter reflector by means of difficult supply: Multilevel fast multilevel fast multipole methods which are implemented to the difficult nourish, while physical optics is implemented to the wide reflector.
- Ships on the radar: multilevel quick multipole technique is applied within the transmitter, while uniform theory of diffraction is useful to the floor above the vessel.
- Wire connects in vehicle: Multi-performer broadcast line solver is practical to the wire package, at the same time as methods of moments are applied to the automobile body.

Chapter

5 Computational Fluid Dynamics

CONTENTS

5.1. INTRODUCTION

Though the computational fluid dynamics is studied under computer science (CS), it is a branch of fluid mechanics. It entails the use of numerical analysis as well as algorithms in solving problems dealing with fluid flow. In the current systems dealing with gases and liquids, computers are extensively used in carrying out calculations that are later on used in the simulation of the interactions involving gases, liquids, and various surfaces that are defined using conditions. It is therefore a key resource useful in understanding the natural elements around mankind such as water, wind, air, and earth. For instance, in water, it is useful in carrying out analysis on phenomenon that includes storms, floods, and sea waves. A good computational fluid dynamic in high computers can be useful in the predictions of such phenomenon.

The computational fluid dynamics involves fluid flow analysis. In order for us to understand what fluid flow analysis is, we need to have knowledge on fluid flow. Fluid flow is under the fluid dynamics principle in physics. It entails the study of liquids and gases in motion while subjected to certain conditions such as unbalanced forces. There are different types of fluid flows which include the uniform and non-uniform fluid flows, steady, and unsteady flows, laminar, and turbulent fluid flows, comprehensive, and incompressible fluid flow, rotational, and irrational fluid flows and one, two, three dimensional fluid flows (Mittra, 2012).

There are different properties of fluid flows that are useful in fluid flow analysis. They include viscosity, temperature, density, pressure, and specific weight, volume, and gravity. Therefore, fluid flow analysis is the testing and prediction of the behavior of systems that entail fluid flow. It is useful in designing and increasing the performance of the fluid flow systems. The computational fluid dynamics is one among the fluid flow analysis used. It involves the application of Newton's second law in fluid motion. There also some assumptions that are made in computational fluid dynamics for instance, "

The stress in a fluid is equal to the sum of a given diffusing viscous term and a pressure term." It also sought to verify the correlation between density, pressure, velocity, and temperature of the fluid in motion.

For the computational fluid dynamics to work, it was required that some computer software to be used in the process. This software is equipped with algorithms and formula that can be used in carrying out various calculations dealing with fluid flow (Mittra, 2012).

5.2. COMPUTATIONAL FLUID DYNAMICS AS AN INTERDISCIPLINARY TOPIC

It contains fluid mechanics, numerical analysis, as well as CS. As stated above the CFD contains principles of fluid mechanics involving the study of aspects of fluid flows and the relevant equations that are used in calculations. It also looks into the fluid properties that may be affect fluid flow such as density, temperature, pressure, and velocity among others. As a physics-based topic, it makes use of the Navier-Strokes equations in showing the relationship between all the fluid properties of a moving fluid (Figure 5.1).

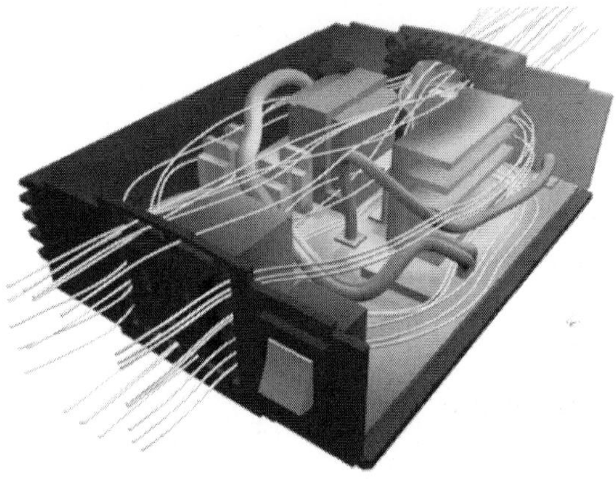

Figure 5.1. The computational fluid dynamics is an interdisciplinary topic as it entails combinations of different disciplines from different topics.

Source: https://www.npd-solutions.com/cfd.html (accessed on 3 April 2020).

Numerical analysis as its name indicates deals more with numbers. Therefore, the numerical analysis principles are incorporated into the CDF to assist in calculations which may later on be used in showing the behavior of the fluid in study. It may also be used in making future predictions on the tendencies of fluid for instance in sea waves.

CS is also part of the CDF hence the name computational as computers are involved in the CDF analysis. Computers play a significant role as most of the analysis in done using them. The other disciplines are integrated into the computational part. There are software that are used in facilitating the CDF. CS is critical in the CDF as practices such as simulation will require one to have knowledge on CS. Principles of CS such as programming are used in the creation of the software and programs used in the CDF. Algorithm principles are also used with the numerical analysis to create suitable algorithm that will be useful in the conduction of calculations (Mittra, 2012).

All the three disciplines are interdependent in the CDF. They all play a crucial role in ensuring that the analysis is able to yield proper and accurate results as some of these results are used globally for planning purposes. Therefore, based on the understanding of all the disciplines used in CDF, we can conclude that CDF is the use of physics, applied mathematics as well as computational software in the visualization of gas and liquid flows and its effects on objects it flows past (Mittra, 2012).

5.3. HISTORY OF COMPUTATIONAL FLUID DYNAMICS

This method of analysis has been used since the early 20th century though it was not greatly applied in several fields. For instance, the CDF was initially known as a tool used in the analysis of airflow around objects such as cars and airplanes. It was therefore limited to specific areas that were seen to generally involve the use of water and air. This was until recent days that researchers identified that the CDF can be extensively used in other fields other than those that directly deal with liquids and gases. This has also led to several adjustments being made to the CDF to provide a larger platform for its use in the given areas and hence wider application areas (Sheng and Song, 2012).

One of the needs that led to the expansion of the use of the CDF in other areas included the increased complexity of the cooling infrastructure used in server rooms. It was solved by incorporating the CDF as a data center. Its major role is to analyze thermal properties. It is also used in the designing and modeling of a good airflow. It is therefore equipped with data and information on the content and layout of the data center allowing the CDF make use of this information to generate a three-dimension mathematical model on a given grid that can allow viewing of the model at different angles (Sheng and Song, 2012).

This system of analysis is mostly used by control system analysts as it will enable them use their generated computer programs to control different variables in air or liquid flows. It is resourceful in identification; more so in industries, of areas where cold air is wastes or where air is mixing and enabling proper control and management. It is useful in easy handling and management of IT equipment by allowing management of the cooling infrastructure allowing efficient working of such infrastructure saving costs on the maintenance and repairing of damaged computers.

5.4. SOFTWARE USED IN COMPUTATIONAL FLUID DYNAMICS

There is a variety of software used in CDF analysis. The user decides on the type of software to be used based on what the software has to offer. Some of the software used in CDF includes SimScale, Open FOAM, ANSYS, Autodesk, COSMOL multi-physics, SU2 code, Exa-Corporation, and the Finite element method software.

5.4.1. Autodesk CDF

This is the most common software used in CDF. It is commonly used as simulation software. This software is a product of the Cadac group. It is a software that when used gives off accurate, fast, and flexible fluid flow results. It also provides tools used in thermal simulation. These tools are used in predicting the performance of the product for instance a cooling infrastructure. It is also used in optimizing designs and validating the future prediction on the performance of the product. This is all done before the product is manufactured allowing individuals to easily market some of the products that they have invented using the software.

This software is commonly used as it is easily available for users who can readily access it at the comfort of their homes through online purchases. This software has a variety features that are used in ensuring that it works effectively.

The following are some of the features of the Autodesk CDF:

1. ***Flow Control Applications***: This feature allows optimization of the product design. It allows the changing of various variables to facilitating the improvement in the flow distribution as well as the pressure distribution. Therefore, the user is able to make a prediction the performance of a device when a certain pressure is used and can therefore decide on the pressure ranges and other factors that will affect the flow in the product.
2. ***Thermal Prototyping***: This prototyping is carried out on the computer removing the need of having physical prototypes. The CDF have tools that can be used in creating the thermal prototypes.

Different models can be produced that will show the different modes of heat transmissions either solid to solid or solid to liquid. The manufacturer is therefore able to know which airflow model is more suitable to be used in the product to facilitate cooling among other things.

3. ***Free Surface Modeling*:** This feature is useful in understanding how liquids and gases will interact when placed in a given surface. It therefore enables simulation of the interfaces that occur between gases and liquids. It is mostly useful in carrying out analysis such as model flows in waves.

5.4.2. AutoCAD

The Autodesk software under it has the AutoCAD which has been used for product designing, civil infrastructure, construction, and product designing. It is a major part of the Autodesk software and has been greatly used due to its human friendly program that even a beginner can use. It has been useful in creating 3D models that have been useful in computational dynamics. It offers great modeling and visualization features useful in creating the objects in a 3D format. Therefore, some of the features it contains include the 3D modeling visualization, photorealistic rendering, section planes, visual styles, photo studio data linking, data extraction, tables, layout, and layout view ports, import 3D models and user interaction features among others. This branch to some extent has been used in computational fluid dynamics.

1. ***Advantages of Using Autodesk Software*:** It consumes less time. This software makes it easy for an individual to develop the 3D images of the project in question. For instance, if it is to develop an image of the airflow or liquid flow of the architecture to be developed. The user interface has been made such that it is suitable to get the concepts applied in making the 3D designs of the structure.

It offers a variety of features. This features apply in terms of the designs to be made. One of the processes in the computational fluid dynamics is knowing the design of the infrastructure to be made. By knowing the design one is able to gauge variables such as the rate of airflow and liquid flow. This feature allows one to come up with different designs of the software and is able to identify the modifications to be made for the air/liquid flow structure to work.

It has well established drafting tools. These tools have been generated based on geometrical dimensions which are a huge part of the CDF. This feature allows an individual to come up with accurate designs of the object that has either been created in 3D or 2D. It also has the auto check feature which allows the reuse of the designs that had already been generated. This will allow the saving of time as well as resources. It has a feature that allows the reproduction of documents as well as the visualization feature. This software has many other advantages that include the easy application of new ideas among others. As everything has a good side, it also has a negative to it.

2. ***Disadvantages of Autodesk Software***: Some of the disadvantages include the fact that it requires a relatively large memory space for it to run. This is attributed to the fact that several 3D designs will be made in it therefore, plenty of space will be required. For computers that may not be able to offer such type of storage space then it will be required that they purchase hard drives to supplement the storage space. It may require that an individual has problems solving abilities as well as critical thinking. This is useful in the handling of the software program that may be at times be complex for the user.

It may at times require individuals to be trained on how to use the software and the installation of the program may be quite costly as the individual will have to purchase the software. It may require the user to have a computer with a relatively strong CPU. This is due to the fact that the software at times draws relatively large amounts of the computer processing power. It may be quite costly for the individual to purchase such hard drives.

5.4.3. Simscale Software

This also part of the software that is used in the CDF. This is a software product that is based on cloud computing. It is a product of the SimScaleGmbh. It is used in a variety of analysis apart from CDF. They include the Finite element analysis as well as thermal simulations. This software makes use of open source codes that include the open FOAM for the CDF and the code Aster and Calculix for the FEA. This software creates a platform where users are able to run various simulations and therefore are able to facilitate design changes. Some of its features include the following:

For the CDF, it has the computational fluid dynamics module. This module as stated above makes use of the Open Foam open source. This source is used for fluid flow simulations. With the use of the SimScale software, there are two types of CDF analysis that can be conducted. One is the steady state while the other is the transient analysis. These two facilitate the following:

1. ***Thermal Module***: This module makes good use of the Open Foam for various thermal interaction problems. These interaction problems include the solid-solid thermal interaction and the solid-liquid interaction. It also makes use of other open sources such as the Code Aster and Caclulix for the thermo-structural analysis. This allows it to facilitate the uncoupled thermo-mechanical simulations that deal with either the conjugate heat transfer or the convective heat transfer analysis. With such, a platform is created so that both the steady-state and the transient simulation can be carried out.

The fluid simulations incorporate the use of turbulence models to achieve its goal. As the CDF deals mostly with liquids and gases, we focus more on the conjugate heat transfer. This type of analysis deals more on the thermal energy transfer involves in a solid-liquid scenario. Only recently, it was included into the portfolio for SimScale physics.

2. ***File Format***: For the file format, SimScale makes use and creates a platform for the importing of geometrical formats to be used by it. Some of the file formats include the IGES, BREP, STEP, Autodesk Inventor, Parasolid, SolidWorks, and ACIS among others. In a mesh type format, the following are examples of the formats used: Open Foam, MED, CGNS, EGC, and UNV among others. The geometry features are used in the calculating of the rates of gas or liquid flow and therefore play a crucial role. Other geometrical formats include the On-shape format. This feature can be directly obtained/imported from the CAD platform which is part of the Autodesk software.

Some of the industrial applications of the SimScale software in CDF include aerodynamic wheel profiling. This software is used in most auto motive companies such as the Tokyo Wheel use this software to carry out wheel profiling for the carbon fiber racing wheels. Some of the technologies used in aerodynamic wheel profiling such as the QRC use the SimScale software to make use of the thermal simulations to carry out tests on multiple variations of the RF tester that they use (Davidson, 2010).

The SimScale software as mentioned above can also be used in the FEA module and makes use of the Solvers Code Aster as well as Caclulix. The use of such codes facilitate both linear and nonlinear dynamic or static structure analysis. Each code has its own given function for instance Code Aster is involved in simulations dealing with multi-physics coupling, porous media, fatigue, damage, fracture, and geo-materials among others. The Caclulix on the other hand is used in creating a platform where users can build, calculate, and also post-process some of the finite element models. Though this may not be relatable to CDF, it is just but a clear demonstration of the extensive uses of the SimScale software (Davidson, 2010).

3. ***Advantages of the Simscale Software:*** It is fast. The SimScale software has components such as the LBM solver which may commonly be present as Pace-Fish. This was created by the numeric system. This element has its own Cartesian mesh engine which makes the work of the user to be defining the flow domains or the physics in study. The solver run time in the LBM solver generates the grid that will be used during the analysis. The use of the Cartesian grid makes the process to be much faster. Another advantage is that it is also less prone to error and is more tolerant towards other types of geometry.

The LBM solver is usually programmed to work at higher speeds. This has led to the implementation of other features such as the Lattice-Boltzmann method to allow for a parallel architecture of the system to run. This will facilitate the running of multiple GPUs while created in parallel and thereby producing results that are far much quicker compared to other types of typical NS transient simulation (Davidson, 2010).

Another advantage is that it allows a much more accurate analysis thereby producing results that can be termed to be realistic. This will mean that users of this software will not be required to forfeit the speed of the software in order for them get accurate results. This makes the software to be more preferred compared to the rest.

5.4.4. Ansys software

This is a product of the Ansys Inc. a company that is based in Pennsylvania. This company is known to manufacture multi-physics simulation software that is used in various ways that include product designing, operation as well as testing. This company's previous membership was sold to another company there by allowing it to acquire other design samples as well as technology that is useful on fluid dynamics. It also facilitated other physical analysis and electronics design. This software is useful in developing and marketing of engineering simulation software used in various analysis programs. Like in the SimScale software, the Ansys software is also useful in the finite element analysis software.

This software is also useful in the simulation of computer model of structure useful in the mechanical and electronically analysis of temperature distribution, electromagnetism, elasticity, toughness, and fluid flow among others. It is more like the concepts that are used in architecture. For instance, the software us useful in establishing how a certain product will function under certain specifications. This therefore removes the need of one having to conduct crash tests or building test products so that an overall product is produced (Sheng and Song, 2012).

This is beneficial as it saves time and resources allowing them to be incorporated into other parts of the manufacturing process. This software is very useful in making predictions of the running of various products. For instance, through simulation it is able to determine how long a bridge can run even when subjected to heavy traffic. Therefore, allowing different strategies can be put in place in order to save resources while ensuring good quality of the product to be manufactured.As most of the CDF software makes use of simulation, in the Ansys the simulations are conducted using the Ansys workbench system which is part of the products of the software. It works by allowing the user to break down the larger structures in the modeling process into smaller components. These components are modeled and tested each on its own. The following procedure may be followed. The user begins by establishing the dimensions of the Object in question. Then the user adds the properties of the object such as the weight, pressure, temperature among other physical quantities. After that, the software takes on the duty of creating a simulation and makes an analysis of the movement, temperature distribution, fractures, electromagnetic efficiency, as well as the fluid flow among others.The software is also useful in developing other software. For instance, it is used in generating data management software which is used in data management and backup, teaching, and academic research. This software is easily available to the user and is usually sold on a subscription basis (Sheng and Song, 2012).

Feature of the Ansys Software

- *Unequalled Depth Feature*: This provides users with unequalled technical depth in the given simulation domain. The domains usually vary. It may be fluid analysis, structural, thermal, meaning, electromagnetics analysis among others. The feature offers variable functionality levels depending on the user or domain requirements. This software also offers rich domain acquisition and a variety of technical solutions depending on the experience of the analyst.

- *Unparalleled Breadth*: This software offers a richness in terms of functionality in the broad range of disciplines in CDF be it structural, explicit, thermal, electromagnetics or fluids. The software provides a variety of analysis types as well as mashing tools that supports the different domains that are to be simulated.
- The domains form the pillars of the Ansys software constituting to the unparalleled breadth in the simulation industry.
- *Comprehensive Multi-Physics Features*: Multi-physics is a huge part of simulation in CDF as most of the designs will involve disciplines in physics. The Multi-physics features in the Ansys software is unique from other simulation software. This is made possible through the technical depth and breadth offered by it. Also the scalability of the products is coupled up with Multi-physics in simulation. The unique capability of Multi-physics in Ansys software is flexible, well architecture and robust in the software system making it easy to solve very complex coupled physics analysis in a given environment.
- *Engineered Scalability*: This is made possible through the scalability features. For most users, scalability us a very crucial aspect that is considered when they want to purchase any software either for short term or long term use. The Ansys software engineered scalability ensures that the user acquires flexibility required in the designing process. It gives on an ability to use a technology that is equal to the level of the problem encountered. It offers a wide range of computing resources offering it on the basis of availability and the extent of appropriateness of the technology. According to the technology the user will employ, the technology is able to scale up to suit it.
- *Adaptive Architecture*: This is availed by a variety of architectural features provided by the software. The architectural features are of great essence as it is used in the designing process. It is also used in the development of in house codes as well as solution designs. It also provides an avenue to carry out customization

of the design to be generated. The Ansys has a simulation architecture that is flexible and can fit into different organizational requirements. Ansys workbench is therefore referred to as the simulation strategy backbone. These are but some of the features present in the Ansys software.

- *Advantages of ANSYS Software*: It is flexible. This means that it can be used in a variety of technologies and can be used to carry out a variety of analysis. It is also readily available ad the users can purchase the software online or physically from the manufactures. It also avails a variety of tools that can be used in the process of simulation of the CDF designs.
- *Disadvantages of ANSYS Software*: It is costly when used for long term. This is because the software is sold to user in a subscription basis and they will therefore require to pay on a given frequency making it costly.

5.5. SIMULATION

Simulation is the major methodology used in the CDF. Simulation refers to the visualization of an object showing how it would work it were to be actualized.

It is com only used among developers as it removes the need to carry out operations such as crash testing or building of test subjects thereby saving time and resources that could be used in further developing of the software. It therefore employs the making of objects in a 3D manner thereby allowing the object to be viewed in any angle that the user requires (Figure 5.2).w

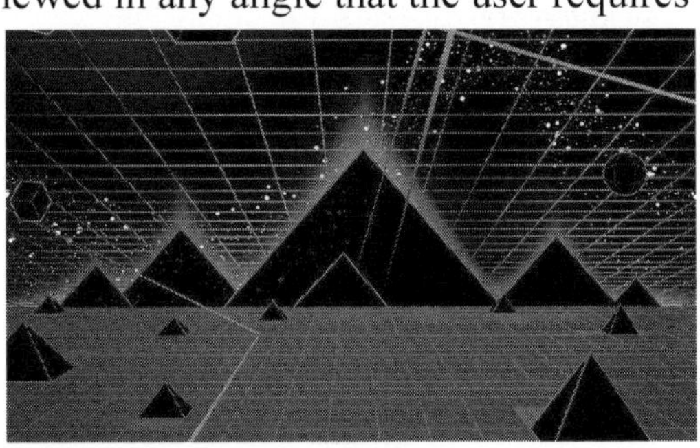

Figure 5.2. Computer simulation.

Source: https://medium.com/@gokulmohanty/do-we-exist-inside-of-a-computer-simulation-67299e535c6d (accessed on 3 April 2020).

Simulation is usually done alongside a program that fits in the variables that are to be measured in the project. By so doing after making a simulation of the product to be designed, one is able to conduct comprehensive analysis on the model that is to be produced. In the case of the CDF, simulation allows the creation of fluid flow designs and its used in different manufacturing plants to determine the type of products that should be developed. For instance, in aerodynamics simulation is used in the construction of the airplanes knowing how the airflow in the airplane will occur. It therefore allows one to come up with an airplane that is efficient in its working (Sheng and Song, 2012).

There are different types of languages that are used in simulation but are grouped into two. That is the continuous simulation language and the discrete simulation language. There also different types of simulation. They include the live simulation. This involves the use of living beings operating the system. It therefore requires the presence of individuals to facilitate the simulation. There is the constructive simulation which involves the simulated individuals running simulated systems. There is also the virtual simulation that involves real individuals running the simulated systems. In the case of the CDF, it makes use of the virtual simulation as an individual will be required to run the system by changing some of the variables among other things.

5.5.1. Advantages of Simulation

Some of the main advantages of using g dilation include:

- It allows the study of the future behavior of a system even before it is built. With simulation, one is able to come up with a design and vary the variables and is able to. Make use of the simulation analysis results to make some predictions on the behavior of the system.
- It gives off accurate results. Compared to the analytical model approach, simulation offers higher levels of accuracy in the obtained results. This is because some of the simulation software used allows the use of up-to-date technology that will be useful in ensuring that the generated results are of high levels of accuracy.
- It enables one to identify possible problems in a system. For instance, one is able to identify a possible glitch in the system through the use of simulation. It also enables users to carry out the what is analysis.

5.5.2. Disadvantages of Simulation

It is quite expensive for one to build a simulation model. It may also be quite costly to conduct a simulation. For some individuals, they find it quite hard to interpret the results from the simulation.

5.6. NUMERICAL METHODS USED IN COMPUTATIONAL FLUID DYNAMICS

A fluid in motion follows the Navier-Stokes equation. This equation was formed as a result of a combination of laws that have been derived from the law of conservation therefore elements such as mass, energy, and momentum are involved in some numerical methods used in CDF. The equation deals mostly with the establishment of variables such as flow velocity, the temperature, pressure, and density.

The use of these equations favors the use of simulation to conduct this form of calculation as it is nearly impossible to conduct this analysis with the use of analytical methods. The computational fluid dynamics as a discipline involves it being used alongside other theoretical and experimental methods to get quality results.

The machines used during CDF are required to be modified and fitted with numerical methods that are required in the process of simulation as well as analysis. Some of the numerical methods used in CDF include the: finite difference method, finite volume method, finite element method and the spectral methods among others.

- ***Finite Difference Method*:** There are some equations that are used in the finite difference method. This method works by removing the infinitesimal limiting process and replacing it with another in a derivative based calculation. The infinitesimal gives an indication of the degree of the error as a function of mesh spacing. By replacing the infinitesimal limiting process, the error is divided by two when the grid spacing is, x also divided by two. This is referred to as the first order method.

The different methods applied on a FDM are usually at a minimal of second order in terms of accuracy though this may not be the case in some given scenarios. Even with such, the FDM is still a common and preferred numerical method for obtaining solutions. This is attributed to the fact that it is simple, efficient, and has a relatively low computationally cost (Sheng and Song, 2012).

The major disadvantage of this method is that it tends to have a geometrical inflexibility which results to the applications being even more complex domains. This challenge can be elevated by using some techniques that will suitable fit the computationally mesh to computationally domain.

- ***Finite Element Methods***: This method was developed as a solution to the geometrical inflexibility challenge in the FDM. It therefore deals with problems related to complex computationally regions. It works by having the PDE being recast into a form that is variational. This causes the mean errors everywhere to be of small values. Discreet ionization is then done by dividing computational domains into elements of either triangular or rectangular shape. The solutions in this case are interpolates by a polynomial of usually low order. In this method, the unknown variables are known as collocation points. This method was used in CDF to deal with advection dominated problems.
- ***Spectoral Method***: This method is a high level method different from the finite difference and finite element methods that are of the 2nd and 4th order. The low orders also have a local approximation property meaning that a given collocation point is affected by a given number of points around it. The spectral method as a high order method has a global approximation property. This means that its features are of global approximation property. The functions in this case include the interpolation, polynomial as well as trigonometric functions. By using the high end method, it ensures that there is a good rate of convergence. The rate of convergence is usually dependent on the smoothness of the solution in question. Therefore, for infinitely smooth solutions, the error will decrease exponentially (Sheng and Song, 2012).

The spectral method in used in carrying out computations related to homogeneous turbulence and is effective as is requires simple geometries to do the computations. It is also used in atmospheric models in its convergence elements and a regular spherical shape of the computationally domains.

- ***Finite Volume Method***: For this method, it carries out simple computations as simple geometry is used. It involves the solving the integral form of the main equations. This facilitates the local continuity property to be in a continuous manner. This method is usually used in aerodynamics applications. They are applied in areas where strong shocks as well as discontinuing of solutions occur (Sheng and Song, 2012).

5.6.1. Factor Considered When Selecting a Numerical Method

- ***Computational Cost*:** The time taken by the CPU to solve a system of equations varies substantially from one method to another. Compared to all other methods, the finite difference method is usually the cheapest numerical methods. This is based on the grid point. It is then followed by the finite element method and finally the spectral method.
- ***Accuracy*:** On the basis of accuracy then the spectral method is the best to be used. It delivers a higher accuracy per grid point basis in comparison to the FDM and FEM. It therefore gives of a much less error value compared to the other numerical methods.
- ***Backward Difference*:** It is an illustration of an implicit method. This is because the unknown is used in evaluating the slope of the solution. This is done on the right hand side. Usually, finding the value of the unknown is easy when using a scalar or linear case scenario. In other further complex equations such as the case of a nonlinear right hand side or combination of several equations, a nonlinear system of equations may require it to be inverted.

Based on the above criteria, the user while looking at the numerical method to be used, is able to choose the most appropriate method to employ. The numerical method employed may also be dependent on the type of software that is being used to facilitate CDF. Though some software have capabilities of incorporating all the available numerical methods.

- ***Equations Used in CDF:*** There are a variety of equations that are used in the various processes such as simulation in the CDF. It brings about the essence of CDF being referred to as a group of computational methodologies. It therefore employs the use of various equations on solving problems on fluid flow. Though there are some assumptions made which are physics based. The equations are used to solve the problems at hand. There are various systems of equations used in CDF.

5.7. HIERARCHY OF EQUATIONS USED IN CDF

The following are some of the laws and equations used in CDF are discussed below:

1. ***Conservation Laws*:** The conservation laws constitute the most crucial equations that are used with CDF. This is in the view that some equations can be deduced from them. In the case of studies

involving single-phase, compressible flow and single species some of the laws considered include the conservation of linear momentum, energy, and mass are considered.

2. ***Continuum Conservation Laws***: Equations deduced are as a result of mass, momentum, and energy being locally conserved. They can therefore move by means of continuous flow. This when the C, L starts. The other point of view is when the CL starts but in this case a continuum medium is assumed. In this case, the system of equations is referred to as unclosed since one will be required to develop further equations or relationships. For instance, an equation showing the relationship between temperature and quantities such as internal energy or enthalpy. It involves the use of equations of state that consists of ideal gas laws and also developing constitutive relationships for viscous stress tensor as well as that of diffusive heat flux.
3. ***Compressible Navier-Stokes Equations***: The CCL laws are first considered. There are assumptions that are made in the Newtonian Viscous stress tensor as well as the Fourier heat flux. These equations are required to be argumented with an EOS and caloric EOS. This is done in order to obtain a closed system of equations.
4. ***Incompressible Navier-Stokes Equations***: This is a deviation from the compressible Navier-Stokes (CNS) equation but it is dependent on it. These are based on the assumption that density is always constant. These equations can also be serviced by making an assumption that the March number is relatively small. The same assumption is made on the temperature difference in the fluid. This results to the conservation of mass as well as momentum equations being decoupled from the energy conservation equation.
5. ***Compressible Euler Equations***: These equations are derived based on the equations in compressible Navier-Stokes equations (CNS). It is serviced based on the assumption that there is a friction less flow experience no diffuse heat flux.
6. ***Weakly Compressible Navier-Stokes Equations***: They are also made from the CNS. It is made based on the assumption that density difference is dependent on temperature only. This means that pressure will not cause a deviation in the density. The equations are mostly used in ideal gas equations. In some cases,

these equations are referred to as the CNS equations having a low March-number approximation.

7. ***Boussinesq Equations*: These equations follow the principle that density variations are negligible in every environment in exception of the gravity term in the momentum-conservation equations. This means that the density will multiply the gravitational acceleration. This is based on the assumption that fluid properties such as heat capacity, viscosity, and thermal conductivity are kept constant. These are mostly used in micro scale meteorology.

8. ***Ideal or Potential Flow Equations*:** in these equations, it is assumed that there is zero fluid-particle rotation and the zero divergence. By so doing, the resultant flow field is solely determined by the given geometrical boundaries. The ideal flows equations are used in CDF to facilitate the initialization of simulation.

9. ***Linearized Compressible Euler Equations*:** In the use of these equations it is assumed fluid properties such as density, pressure, and velocity can be represented using given equations. These equations are generally used in computational aeroacoustics.

10. ***Sound or Acoustic Waves Equations*:** While using this way it is assumed that the Mach number at the base state is relatively small. Therefore, the resultant equations for variables such as density, energy, and momentum can be distorted and manipulated to for a pressure equation which is better off referred to as sound wave equations.

11. ***Shallow Water Equations*:** It these equations it assumed that density though in different environments is always. The velocity component is neglected. The velocity component in this case refers to the one perpendicular to the wall. The velocity component that is parallel to the wall is considered and is referred to as spatially constant. These equations are used in a case scenario where a flow near a wall. In this case wall-parallel length-scale of interest is set to be much larger than the wall-normal length in question.

12. ***Boundary Layer Equations*:** For these equations the equations for the incompressible CNS are considered for the boundary layers. It is assumed that there is the presence of thin regions located close to the walls where the spatial gradients are perpendicular to the wall in question are fairly larger compared to those parallel to the wall.

13. ***Bernoulli Equation*:** In these equations it is assumed that the varying values of density are dependent on the pressure variations.
14. ***Steady Bernoulli Equation*:** It starts from the Bernoulli's equation. It works from the assumption that there is a steady flow. When one starts seducing the equations from the EE equation then they have to make an assumption that the flow will be steady. The derived equation is integrated along a streamline.
15. ***Stokes or Creeping Flow Equations*:** If these equations are derived by using the CNS or the one for incompressible the inertia flow is neglected. The assumption can be proven when the Reynolds number is considerably low. The resultant equations are linear in nature making it quite simple to solve the equations.
16. ***Two Dimensional Channel Flow Equations*:** In the case where there is a flow between two infinite parallel plated, the equations are derived by using the CNS equations. It is therefore assumed that the flow is steady, well developed and two-dimensional. The assumptions made do not work for all situations. Such situations include the micro channel flows and compressible flows.

5.8. APPLICATIONS OF CDF

Some of the applications of CDF include:

1. ***FD Simulation*:** It is also referred to as CDF modeling. This type of simulation has its engineering based on given scientific process modules that run on the basis of CDF theory. It us used in the resolving of various fluid flow problems such as those involving flow velocity, temperature, chemical concentrations and density in areas containing flows. It is also among the numerical methods used in calculation of nonlinear differential equations that have a relation to fluid flow.

This type of CDF simulation is used in various industries with an aim of achieving perfect product designs by making use of both COMPUTATIONAL tools as well as theories related to fluid dynamics.

2. ***Industries That Use CDF Modeling*:** The CDF solution is applied in industries for the purpose of carrying out analytical tasks. The most common industries that make use of the CDF simulation include: turbo machinery, Oil, and gas industry, product design and optimization,

energy generation, processing engineering, building HVAC, aerospace/aeronautics as well as petrochemicals among others.

The industry known to commonly use CDF modeling is the building HVAC. It is used in generation of highly accurate options that will be used in the designing process. This ensures a high level of efficiency by the HVAC system.

5.9. ADVANTAGES OF CDF

This can also be viewed as reasons why CDF consulting, which is one of the uses of CDF, is being commonly used:

- For one, the use of CDF allows the user to get an overlook of the performance of a system even before it is executed. They are therefore able to make any amends if necessary.
- It allows one to identify the changes required in a given design layout even before the system us installed. With such changes, the performance of the system will be further improved.
- CDF models enables the user to acquire accurate and detailed information cowering properties such ad heating, ventilation as well as air conditioning.
- CDF provides methodologies that suit the latest technologies used in HVAC allowing both theoretical and experiments to be done.
- CDF modeling produces results that are reliable. More to that it allows saving of costs. This leads to the reason why the analysis reports from such relied upon.

5.10. LIMITATIONS OF CDF

1. ***Physical Models***: Among the challenges of the CDF in terms of physical models is Thai it is dependent on physical models used in real world processes. This means that the accuracy of the results is dependent on the accuracy of the physical models.
2. ***Numerical Errors***: As the CDF calculations are carried out using machines, it presents the chances of having numerical errors. Some of the errors are brought about by rounding off as well as truncation errors.
3. ***Boundary Conditions***: The accuracy of the CDF model is dependent on the initial boundary conditions provided by the numerical model.

Chapter 6 Computational Ocean Modeling

CONTENTS

6.1. INTRODUCTION

Computational Ocean modeling involves using computers for education to get the insight of systems that are complex and complicated. An individual can understand these complex systems by using computers in the process of using mathematical calculations, knowledge in physics and having knowledge in computer science (CS).

Computational ocean modeling is a model that has many variables that show the character of the system that is being studied. Simulations which is the ratio of output to input is carried out by making all the variables to be able to fit and that are combined and then they are tested to check how what was changed has affected the system. What is obtained from the model simulations is used to assist the people carrying out research to foresee what is going to be the outcome of the real and actual system that is being studied as a response to the alternating conditions?

Modeling is useful since it helps the people carrying out research to carry out a lot of experiments using their personal computers (PCs) to know the main experiments that the researcher needs to use know the solutions that they need to use in case of a problem arising or solving a problem that is being faced.

One important feature that the computational models that are present in today's world enables researchers to research many biological systems at many different levels. These levels range from; molecular processes, cell to cell interactions and many other biological levels, for instance, organ level research. Multiscale modeling is therefore applied and which is studying multiple levels together.

6.2. COMPUTATIONAL MODELING ACCELERATING DISCOVERY

For one to understand and gain deeper know-how of how computer modeling works one has to keep in mind the process when one is baking a cake that is involving more than twenty ingredients. This will enable them to understand more about the computational modeling because when an individual wants to bake a cake they have to know how each ingredient adds up to the flavor of the cake and how each ingredient contributes to the taste of the cake once it is finally ready. One way to know this is an individual can bake many different cakes each using one of the ingredients each try of the cake. By doing this a lot of time will be spent and therefore will be ineffective. To save on time and avoid any inconveniences, an individual can easily input all the twenty or more ingredients into a computer model and then she/he writes and explains to the computer the function of each of the ingredient and the flavor each add to the cake and once is done the computer will now have the idea of the function of the flavors and it will be able to interact with the ingredients. In case of any additional ingredient, they can always be added at any one time and therefore the computer can explain how different cakes will come out when different ingredients are used at a faster rate than the one used before (Mittra, 2012).

In the case where you have no idea of the effect of the ingredients and how it will change the flavor of the cake, by using computational ocean modeling there is a possibility of altering the number of ingredients as many times as desired until one comes up with a cake that he/she desires. This will be way easier and way faster than having to bake on the cake after another each inputting a different amount of the ingredients bake and this will be time-consuming and it will waste a lot of ingredients in the process.

The major advantage of computational ocean modeling is that it gives scientists and researchers and also engineers the ability to come up with variations easier and faster by saving cash that could be used and materials that could go to waste by using their PCs (Mittra, 2012).

6.3. EXAMPLES OF COMPUTATIONAL OCEAN MODELING AND ITS USE IN THE STUDY OF COMPLEX AND COMPLICATED SYSTEMS

As seen earlier, computational ocean modeling is used for studying those systems that are complex and complicated. Examples of computational ocean modeling include the following:

1. ***The Weather Forecasting***: Weather forecasting is the study of the weather and how the weather patterns are likely to be to predict and plan for future occurrences. Studying the patterns of the weather is done by using models of the computer ocean that help in carrying out analysis and foreseeing the future of the weather basing their facts on the many factors of the atmosphere that are present. The importance of doing this is to carry out proper prior planning of the future so as to predict the future and what would be expected. For instance, if there is a possibility of tsunami one can be aware and evacuate people who may be affected before

that time and therefore they can prevent many deaths that might occur if they fail to do this. Carry out proper prior planning of the future so that they may predict the future and what they expect it to be for instance if there (Figure 6.1).

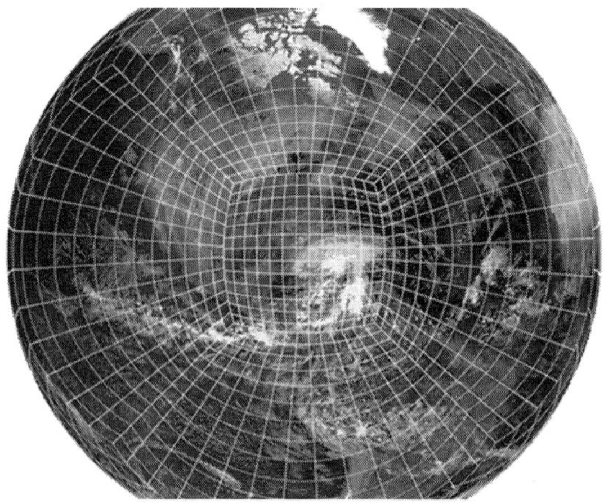

Figure 6.1. Computational ocean modeling used for studying weather systems.

Source: *https://portermedium.com/2019/06/the-next-generation-weather-model-is-here-what-it-means-for-your-forecasts/ (accessed on 3 April 2020).*

2. ***Building Better Aero Planes***: Better aeroplanes are required to have the ability to fight for their countries. Better flight aircraft are invented by using complex equations that help to determine how the aircraft will react in different environments and how different external environments affect the planes. For instance, using computational wave modeling to create the aircraft by using the complex equations, in case of turbulence one can determine how the aircraft is going to react when it faces turbulence before they create the aero plane. Also, air density can be determined before the aeroplane is built and how it will affect the planes. So by using the computational ocean modeling, we can determine how different external conditions affect the aero plane and when you invent the aircraft you can invent one that is not affected by these external conditions (Sheng and Song, 2012).
3. ***Studying Earthquakes:*** Computational wave modeling is also used for studying earthquakes. Earthquakes are very dangerous and they may cause a lot of harm if they are not dealt with

before they occur as they can cause a lot of deaths of people and therefore computer wave modeling is used for this study. It also helps in discovering how the structures should be built to avoid being affected by earthquakes.

6.4. IMPROVING MEDICAL CARE AND BIOMEDICAL RESEARCH USING COMPUTATIONAL OCEAN MODELING

Researchers use the idea and knowledge of computational ocean modeling to develop and invent models of blood vessels, blood flow and heart valves. When an individual is injured such that they cannot use their vessel, they are normally implanted with these models that assist them to live longer. In inventing these models, the use of computational ocean modeling because there is a need to know if at all the creations will work and coming up with the models. Computational ocean modeling is also used in the creation of tools that health workers use for doctors. These tools that the doctors invent they use to make decisions on the kind of treatment that the patient needs at any one-time and, therefore, it is of great benefit to the doctors and health workers for providing treatment (Mittra, 2012) (Figure 6.2).

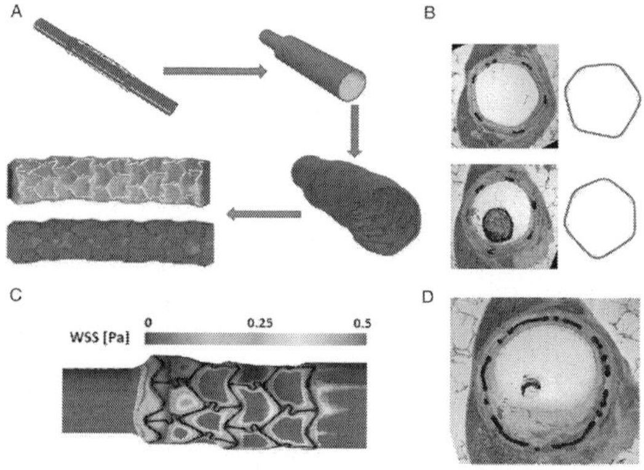

Figure 6.2. Computational ocean modeling is also being used in the medical field for medical research and to come up with biomedical research.

Source: https://heart.bmj.com/content/102/1/18 (accessed on 3 April 2020).

Computational ocean models are also used in the surgery of the eye because it is used in the coming up with the technologies that are used in the surgery of the eye. An example is the human cornea model that was invented with the knowledge of computational ocean technology that is used to come up and in the technology and surgery of the eye.

Computation ocean modeling is also used in the modeling and inventing of drugs and medicine that are used to cure diseases in the early stages. For instance, if there is an outbreak of an illness the researchers will use the knowledge and computational ocean modeling to invent the drugs that will cure the illness. These drugs that are invented using computational ocean modeling are assured to be safe for patients' consumption. The use of the computational ocean training helps to determine and ensure that the drugs, once they are consumed with the patient, will heal the illness and will not cause any side effects that may harm the patients extremely but will be effective and will work (Mittra, 2012).

6.5. NIBIB-FUNDED RESEARCHES DEVELOPING IN THE AREA OF COMPUTATIONAL MODELING

1. ***Speeding up the Healing Process of a Cut or Injury:*** In some countries like the United States and other third world countries and basically in the whole world, individuals who are suffering from illnesses like diabetes and other conditions like obesity normally face a major problem because when they get injured their wounds take a very long time to heal. In this process, they can develop major conditions and these wounds can get infected and they will have to take a lot of time to cure them. These individuals can only be cured by adding a new skin fibroblast in the wound region and with these, it enables the platelets to be more agile and to heal the wound way faster than before. The use of the computational ocean modeling assists in the coming up with the model of the fibrin pallets that are installed into the wound of the patients that enable them to perform more than they could and their healing process is speeded. This will enable individuals with this condition to be assured of getting healed (Mittra, 2012).
2. ***Reducing Osteoarthritis Following Knee Surgery*:** Anterior cruciate ligament tears are a knee injury that occurs very often to people. Many surgeries are normally conducted to help reduce these cases and to ensure that every joint regains its stability. It is, however, dangerous as the people with this condition are in more likely danger of contraction osteoarthritis in the early consent. Since it is a condition scientist are forced to carry out research

on this condition known as OA and gain an understanding of why it affects the patients. With the use of computational ocean modeling, the scientists are can look into the making of the muscle-bone, soft tissues and others and they, therefore, can study and understand more about this condition. This model is also used t carry out tests to find out what is needed in a surgery that will cause an effect and to study and understand more about this illness. This model is therefore of great use and it is used by many scientists to come up with the cure for OA and therefore the more it is being introduced in the research, the more advantageous it is proving to be.

3. **Mu*ltiscale Modeling of Microbial Biofilms for Improved Treatment of Antibiotic-Resistant Infections:*** Antibiotic-resistant infections are dangerous infections because when they are cured using an antibiotic they become resistant to it and they fail to be cured. Most infections are used to be cured using an antibiotic which cures faster and when an infection decides to be antibiotic-resistant it means that it resists treatment by antibiotics. Some common infections like the common cold can be cured using an antibiotic at first but with time they develop resistance to the antibiotic in case the individual with the infection does not take the drugs as prescribed or they do not follow the drug prescription and therefore when the infection gets resistant, it cannot be cured with the antibiotic anymore unless stronger means are used to cure the illness. The researchers, therefore, use the computational ocean modeling to come up with ways that they can use to cure the illness in the easiest way possible without having effect of cause and effect and harm to the individual who is resistant to antibiotics. IT is therefore advantageous when the use of computational ocean modeling is inputted in this (Mittra, 2012).

6.6. COMPUTATIONAL MODELER

Basing our argument on the fact that if an individual want to understand how they can get rid of ocean wastes and the papers and plastics that are normally there they have to first understand and gain knowledge on the behavior and the properties of these plastics and papers. In the same way, does an individual gain understanding of the computational ocean modeling. An individual can acquire the amount of know-how by carrying out advanced data analyses at several levels. Therefore, when they aim the knowledge on these they can easily understand the computational modeler.

6.6.1. Qualifications of an Individual Carrying out Computational Ocean Modeling

An individual who is undertaking computational ocean modeling has the following qualifications that enable them to carry out their duties.

1. ***Creativity*:** An individual who is carrying out computational ocean modeling is creative. Creativity is the coming up of new ideas and discovering better means of performing a duty. Creativity is required in the process of computational ocean modeling to discover new models and therefore to understand the computational ocean models that are in existence. Creativity ocean modeling is a complex system that is used to understand the systems that are there is the requirement of a creative mind.
2. ***Problem Solver*:** Problem-solving is the ability to deal with a situation and to come up with the most suitable solution to solve the problem and situation at hand. Problem-solving involves a lot of creativity where the individuals who are solving a problem have to creatively think of ways to solve an issue. Individuals who are undertaking computational ocean modeling are problem solvers because they are faced with various problems that may arise at the time of their work and they need to have the skill on problem-solving so that they can come up with the most appropriate solutions for them.
3. ***Willingness to Travel*:** An individual who is undertaking computational ocean modeling must be ready to travel often to different countries and continents since his/her work cannot be limited to one place . Accompanying the willingness to travel is the ability to fit in and adapt to new conditions. Individuals who have the willingness to travel should also have the ability to adapt to new areas such that they do not need to take a lot of time to adjust to this. The advantage of adjusting to the new environment is not only that they can avoid a lot of time but they can also have the ability to fit into the new conditions without having to waste a lot of money solving problems that they may face.

Good communicator: An individual who is a computational ocean modeler is one who is a good communicator. Communication is the sending of information from one person to another. A good communicator is one who can send information from one person to another in a way that will ensure that is effective and that the information that is received is the one that was intended to be received when it was sent. Computational ocean modelers require the individuals modeling to be good communicators so that they can send the information and share their ideas in ways that will be understood and in ways that will not be misinterpreted or taken wrongly. The advantage of communication that is effective is that also ensures and enables the individuals carrying out computational ocean modeling to know and understand each other even more. They can relate effectively with one another and this can help them to work together without any undesirable issues arising in the organization.

4. ***Teamwork*:** It is the ability of individuals in an organization to work together without having any complications and misunderstandings among them. Computational ocean modelers are individuals who understand the systems and they are therefore individuals who work together with many other colleagues since working on their own may be tiresome and extremely boring. The computational ocean modelers, therefore, have the skills of teamwork such that they can work with other individuals easier than working alone and they can achieve more. Another advantage of teamwork is it helps work to be done efficiently and to the best. When the computational ocean modelers have teamwork they can work together as a team to get things done without any quarrels or wars and therefore they can work things out fully such that the outcome of their work is perfect and one that was desired before. When the work is done perfectly, the organization grows better and peace is maintained in the organization at all times therefore the organization will always have a peaceful environment to work in at any time.

Self-driven individuals are individuals who can work in any environment at any one time without being supervised, that is, they can work in any environment unsupervised. It is a qualification for individuals who are undertaking computational ocean modeling to be self-driven because self-driven individuals often know what they want in life and they work hard and strive to achieve it. They are not lazy and their employers are assured that they are safe with the work being in the hands of these individuals. Being self-driven therefore rises a lot of opportunities for the computational ocean modelers that enables them to get promotions and a lot of praise.

Another qualification for computational ocean modelers is that they are very curious. Curiosity is the ability to want to know more and not being satisfied with the little knowledge that one has. Individuals who are undertaking computational ocean modeling are required to be curious such that they want to know more about the systems so that they can do and perform more research that will enable them to acquire more and more information that they may require and it may be of help to them. The advantage of being curious is that one gets to understand more and more.

Another responsibility and quality that a computational ocean modeler has are that they should be solution-oriented and by this, it means that they are always thinking about the solutions to problems. Everything that a computational ocean modeler thinks or does should be to come up with solutions and solutions to problems that may arise. When the computational ocean modelers are solution-oriented, they can perform their work way more diligently than before and they can show a more positive outcome in their work. They should, therefore, be at all-time solution-oriented in all they do.

Intrinsic motivation is the ability of an individual to motivate themselves no matter the situation they are going through. It is when one can give themselves a word of encouragement to encourage them even though many individuals will be against them and will demotivate them. Intrinsic motivation is an important tool and qualification of a computational ocean modeler because many individuals who are in the computational ocean modeling face a lot of challenges. They also need the motivation so that they can work for long hours without giving up. The computational ocean modeling is a complicated process that the individuals face a lot of pressure when they are working and the modelers can get tired and feel like giving up and not going on but with the intrinsic motivation it enables the individuals to keep up with the work and not give up very easily. Though intrinsic motivation is important, there is also motivation from other people which may also be of great importance.

Another qualification for a computational ocean modeling is that they should be goal-oriented and by goal-oriented is that they use and they set goals which they plan to achieve and they work towards the achieving of these goals. Setting goals is an important part of not only the computational ocean sector but of also all other sectors that the individuals or different people may be working in. By setting goals, it enables people to remain self-driven and to remain on their track and want to achieve what they want at the end of the entire process. It is important because it ensures that individuals achieve what they aim for at all times.

Lastly is having the motivation to work such that the individuals have the drive and the aim to perform certain work and they are motivated to do it. My motivation in work, the individuals are more likely to be more excited about performing the work and they do not feel objected or forced to perform their work. They are self-driven and they have a goal. They get excited when they know that they are going to perform their work and by this, they can show greater output and results at the end of the day when compared to individuals who may fail to have the motivation to work.

6.6.2. A New Computational Framework for Multi-Scale Ocean Modeling Based on Adapting Unstructured Meshes

This model is specifically designed in a way that it shows a better representation of the solution structures that are coming up as it shows them in a three-dimensional view which is more desired than the one before it came about. The algorithm that is used is one that ensures there is the use of levels that are anisotropic that can solve situations that are complex and complicated. These algorithms are also able and they can load parallel mesh optimization that enables the resolutions to be different at different times.

This new computational framework that is used that enables the multi-scale ocean modeling is opposite and different from the computational ocean models that usually present in the current world today.

In the current world, the computational ocean models are designed with a laid basis on static structured grids but the new computational framework is used that enables the multi-scale ocean modeling has unstructured static grids and they are being preferred by more individuals in the current world of today. They are especially preferred by the oceanographic community which is the community that deals with the oceans and the environs of the ocean itself.

The new computational framework is used that enables the multi-scale ocean modeling involves using unstructured static measures that are more preferred by many other individuals and they have the anisotropic adaptability in three dimensions (Sheng and Song, 2012).

6.7. HOW DOES COMPUTATIONAL OCEAN MODELS GIVE THEIR RESPONSE TO HURRICANES

As stated by G. R Halliwell computational ocean models respond to hurricanes. The main place that the hybrid computational ocean model is found is in the Mexican gulf and it has been used for the past years since its existence to study computational ocean modeling response to hurricanes in an area where there are complicated and complex features of the ocean, for example, the loop currents and the eddies. This process is a key process that carries with it a lot of importance that include improving ocean model performance and by these we mean it improves how the ocean performs and how the performance has effects. It also leads to the study improvement of forecasting of the hurricanes by individuals who forecast the hurricanes and therefore it has proven advantageous (Sheng and Song, 2012).

The ability to differentiate between the temperatures of the surface of the sea initially and later on after hurricane Ivan is also enabled and the simulations and infrared satellite measurements readings. Therefore, it has caused and led to better and more improved options of the new computational framework is used that enables the multi-scale ocean modeling and has positive advantages that are attached to it.

6.8. COASTAL OCEAN MODELING PROJECTS

Coastal ocean modeling projects are projects that are done by scientists and coastal ocean modelers. The coastal ocean modeling works like a channel between the governmental operational and investigation associations that gives permission for and allows splitting of statistical models, views, and software devices. They are many projects that are taken in the field of computational ocean modeling and they are studied and explained further by other scientists to get the main idea that was being looked for initially in the study of computational ocean modeling.

A problem that computational ocean modelers face when they are carrying out their projects is that they lack enough time to perform their duties. This is disadvantageous because they have a lot of work to perform in a small amount of time and failure to perform their duties may cause them getting fired and therefore they are always competing with time and they always are busy trying to reach deadlines that are set for them (Blazek, 2005).Another problem that is faced by computational ocean modelers when performing their functions is demotivation because in their work progress they face a lot of problems when it comes to working. These problems that they face can easily make them tired and demotivated. Many individuals may fail to understand what they are going through and this may easily make the computational ocean modelers to feel demotivated and to solve this they are advised to take some time off where they can spend time with their families and they can use this time to regain the energy that they may have lost and when they go back to work they will tend to perform better than they did before (Blazek, 2005).

6.9. GETTING TO UNDERSTAND WHAT PART DOES THE PHYSICAL ENVIRONMENT PLAY WHEN IT COMES TO MARINE ORGANISMS IN TROPICAL ECOSYSTEM

This, on the other hand, was invented by L. M. Cherubin and it states that is an interesting discovery. Marine organisms are the living organisms that live in the water especially in the oceans and marine. The marine organisms include the fish, the sharks, the dolphins, the snails, the seashells and many others including the octopus. These living organisms cannot survive in any other condition or environment if it is not the ocean. There are many marine technologies are present nowadays. They carry out their research concerning the ocean as a feature to empty life, they see it as just a place empty of water and by this, they can look deep into the things that are contained in the ocean while they become keen to avoid effects that come about due to the presence of currents and waves that may affect the whole study. The meaning of this is that the paths of the concerns that may be causing stress or distraction cross at very minimal times and it can be taken into consideration since both fields are faced with challenges that are complex and complicated and therefore it will be pointless to consider the complexities without having the understanding that is required. Researchers, however, bring together their efforts and money to work together as collaboration in their studies and research by doing things together like communicating to each other on what they have found so that they can give us information of what will happen that may cause an impact in our lives. By giving out and carrying out a research on the physical environment and how it affects and the effect on marine ecosystems enables the interaction between the researcher and the living organisms in the marine areas especially if the research is an open one. In the areas where there is facing and time of biodiversity collapse and changes in climate, not only on land but also in aquatic environs having a close interaction with the living organisms that live in the water is an important and significant face. These interactions should involve internalizing and contemplating the interactions of these living things in the marine with where they live and the environs of the ocean. Biodiversity is having different organisms interact in the different environment to survive while climate change is the changing of the patterns of the weather from time to time.

Some endangered species are also present in any environment that is normally protected and if they are not given the protection they deserve they may end up dying and becoming extinct. The marine endangered species that exist include the Elkhorn coral and the Nassau grouper which are some species of fish. Scientists normally study how the process of transporting eggs and larvae through the motions of the oceanic waters.

They also have to use what they know and what they have learnt in ocean physics about how the transportation of organisms that live in a large sum of water takes place.

A scientist called Claire Paris who was not only a scientist or a researcher but was also a computational ocean modeler in the University of Miami took to read about how the marine organisms behave like how they move around, what they are capable of and their development through different stages of their short or long life span. She also studies how these marine organisms react and behave to changes in the environment. She was in partnership with other individuals and their research was mostly about the species that are tropical and are found in the Caribbean Sea.

In the Caribbean Sea, there is danger and threats since the ecosystems are slowly becoming worse due to the upcoming and growing threats that are present there. Claire Paris and er team, therefore, took to gain knowledge and understanding about the living organisms in the marine and their reaction to the surroundings that bear with them a lot of risks, for example, carbon dioxide, temperatures that are warm, polluted surroundings and many others.

It is harmful and disadvantageous if the transport changes a lot from what they were initially used to more complicated patterns due to the changes in the climate.

There is the use of computational ocean modeling that is used to stimulate the circulation of the ocean such as the MICOM and ROMS in computational demanding configurations.

6.10. GRID OCEAN MODELING THAT IS UNSTRUCTURED

Unstructured Grid Ocean Modeling was invented by a scientist called Mohamed Iskandarani. He spent most time of his work experience performing development of unstructured grid ocean models. These rid have the function of making complex coastline in different models of the computer and they ensure there are multi-scale simulations. Grid ocean modeling has seen the growth of computational ocean modeling as it uses a lot of concepts that are derived and got from computational ocean modeling. It, therefore, is a major scientist discovered that more research is being carried on concerning it.

6.11. PROBLEMS THAT COMPUTATIONAL OCEAN MODELERS FACE

Just like all other careers, computational ocean modelers also face a lot of problems during their working process and as they carry on with their daily duties. The problems that they are most likely to experience include the following common problems; a lot of workloads, lack of enough time, demotivation, quarrels with their colleagues, getting tired and exhausted and having the urge to give up. These problems are discussed further and possible solutions to them stated to come up with a better understanding on what one should be ready to face in case they want to undertake computational ocean modeling as a career in his or her life and as they are planning for their future lives (Wendt, 2008).Computational Ocean modelers face a problem when it comes to performing their work and duties because they are expected to perform a lot of duties. In computational ocean, modeling the individual must understand the complex and complicated systems and it is not an easy process to understand and have knowledge of this and therefore the individuals spend a lot of time trying to understand them and in the process, they may get tired and exhausted more.

Lack of enough time. computational ocean modelers face a problem when it comes to lacking enough time to carry out their duties as they have a lot of things to do. Most of the computational ocean modelers lack family time and they do not have a lot of time to spend with their families. This makes most of them prefer not having a family at all so that they can have enough time to carry out their duties. These workloads can be minimized by the individuals being more organized and carrying out their work in an organized manner so that they can prevent having to redo a certain job (Wendt, 2008).

Demotivation is another problem that is faced by computational ocean modelers because in their work progress they face a lot of problems when it comes to working. It will also give them the opportunity and time to bond with their families and get rid of any stress that may be eating them up. If the situation is very complicated, then the computational ocean modelers are advised to visit a health facility where they may get tested. They can also see a counselor who can help them to avoid and get rid of stress (Wendt, 2008).

Another problem that they may face is the problem with quarrelling with their colleagues. It is logical that when people are facing and working together they are most likely to quarrel from time to time and minor disagreements occurring. The solution to these problems is that the individuals working together with the computational ocean modelers to each perform their duties without interfering with the work of the other individual and with these; they will each avoid having quarrels. Since having a lot of work to do can also cause stress, the individuals can also be given some time off like once per week where they can go and relax their minds. Team buildings should also be held where the workers go out and play and do several activities which will enable them to build a bond within each other. When this bond has created the workers and colleagues can perform their duties easier without having to interfere with each other. Another way to solve the issue of quarrels from workers and between workers is by making strict rules that may be set to prevent workers from having disagreements. These rules are properly defined and explained to each worker (Magoules, 2011).

Another problem that computational ocean modelers face is that they lack enough time to perform their duties. This is disadvantageous because they have a lot of work to perform in a small amount of time and failure to perform their duties may cause them getting fired and therefore they are always competent with time and they always are busy trying to reach deadlines that are set for them.

Chapter

7 Computational Structural Mechanics

CONTENTS

7.1. INTRODUCTION

Computational mechanics of structures also known as structural mechanics refers to the use of computers in carrying out calculations of the deformations, stress equivalents and the deflections within already existing structures or structures to be created (Figure 7.1).

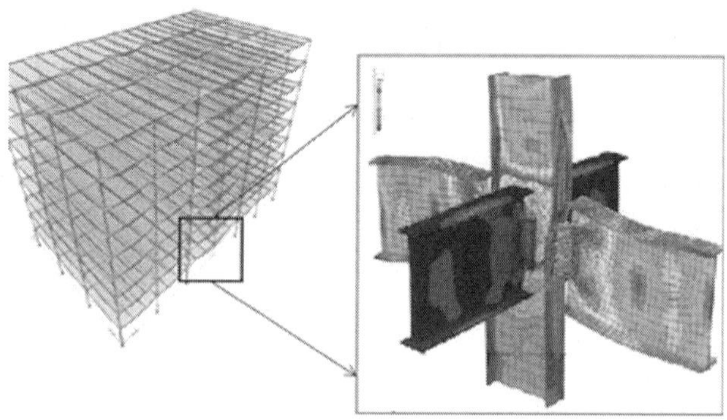

Figure 7.1. The computational structural mechanics is used in facilitating performance evaluation on already existing structures. It is also used in creating designs for structures to be created or even existing structures.

Source: *https://aeroengineering.us/services/computational-structural-mechanics-2/ (accessed on 3 April 2020).*

For an evaluation to be made, an analysis is first carried out on the structure. Therefore, CSM can be said to be a subject of structural analysis. As a subject to analysis, it requires one to obtain data that will be used in analysis process. Such data includes the structure's geometric representation, structural loads data, material properties, as well as the support conditions. Such data is added to the computer and is referred to as input data. Once input data is entered in the computer, it under goes analysis to produce output which is released to the user. Variables used in computational structural mechanics include deformation, deflection forces, and stress.

Deformation refers to a change in shape or size of an object. Therefore, some objects are subjected to displacement as a mode of deformation. In CSM, deflection refers to the relative in displacement mostly the external deformations. For internal deformations, the change in displacement is referred to as strain. Deformation is subject to the deflection forces. When these forces act on a body or an object, it causes an alteration in the shape and size of the object. This is due to the strain that is experienced by the body. Therefore, deformation, and deflecting force are inter-related. Strain also has a linear relationship with the stress on the object while deformation has an elastic relationship with stress.

There are different types of deformation dependent on the type of material, size as well as geometry of the object. It also depends on the forces that are inflicted on the object. They include the permanent deformation also known as plastic deformation. This type of deformation is irreversible meaning that the state of the object after being subjected to a series of forces is maintained. There is also the temporary deformation. This type of deformation is different from the permanent deformation in that after the object is subjected to a force, it has the ability to regain or recover it initial shape and size. It is also referred to as the elastic deformation (Blossey, 2006).

The elastic deformation is inflicted in mechanical and structural engineering. While being used it follows the infinitesimal strain theory that may be referenced to as small strain theory. This theory in exclusive for materials such as elastomers. Under elastic deformation, there is the linear elastic deformation. This type of deformation is usually governed by Hooke's law. In this case, the stress inflicted is also referred to as the elastic modulus which when applied produces a resulting strain. This type of strain is limited to certain types of materials. Other form of deformation includes the metal fatigue and fracture. The metal fatigue applies for metals known to be ductile. This type of deformation is experienced in the flight industry where this deformation caused the failure of aircrafts.

The fracture deformation is almost similar to the physical deformation in that it is also irreversible. In this type of deformation, once the object has exceeded the elastic limit a breakage is encountered. Stress is a quantity that is used in expressing the internal forces experienced by an object. It is common for people to confuse between stress and strain as some individuals may insist that it is the same thing. However, stress refers to the forces experienced by the object while strain refers to the measure of strain is the measure of the level of deformation in the object. Stress has an SI unit called Pascal (Blossey, 2006).

There are different types of stress which include the mechanical stress. Linear approximation is used in establishing the relationship between the mechanical stress and deformation. There is also the normal and shear stress. Simple stress which is presented in three forms uniaxial normal stress, simple shear stress and isotropic normal stress. There is also the cylinder stress commonly experienced in materials such as wheel, pipes, and pillars among others. In the computational structural mechanics may involve the study of the effects of stability on structures.

It also entails the study of non-linear behaviors of structures. This type of study is mostly under the applied mechanics. Therefore, being under applied mechanics, it involves the study of the behavior of structures when they are subjected to mechanical loads including the buckling in column, deflection of a thin shell, vibration of a beam and bending of a beam. Some of these aspects are considered when designing of structures so that they are efficient in the long run. As stated, computational structural mechanics is the use of computers in conducting analysis. However, there are different methods used in analysis. They include the energy method, direct stiffness method and the flexibility method. The stated analysis methods have been modified and integrated to the finite element methods. This therefore leads to two methods used in carrying out analysis and that consists of the plastic analysis method and the finite element method (Blossey, 2006).

7.2. PLASTIC ANALYSIS METHOD

7.2.1. Energy Method

This involves the use of energy principles in analysis. The energy principles used are related to structural mechanics. The principles are used in expressing or defining the relationship existing between stresses, deformations, material properties, displacement, and the external effects that are represented by the work done or energy in the object. Based on the fact that energy is a scalar quantity, the relationships established are convenient and effective. They also provide a different approach when it comes to generating equations of bodies that have an ability to be deformed in solid mechanics. The generated equations have extensive applications such as being used to obtain approximate solutions for relatively complex solutions as well as being used in partial differential equations (PDEs) (Ladeveze, 2012).

Some of the general principles used include the virtual work principle. This states that, "in equilibrium the virtual work forces applied in a system is equal to zero." Under this principle there are the principle of virtual displacement as well as principle of virtual forces. The term virtual refers to something that is not real. Virtual work refers to the use if the principle of least action in conducting a study on forces and movement in mechanical systems. The virtual work principle is taken in the case where a body is considered to be in a free diagram. The body in this case is assumed to consist of infinite number of differential cubicles. There are various states considered when using the virtual work principle. This principle is applied in real life whereby it will require one to come up with an equilibrium that is based on real stresses and forces. The virtual displacements used in this case have to maintain consistency. To achieve this, equilibrated virtual forces and stresses are used calculations by making use of the virtual work equation. The virtual work principles obtained from the two different states that are usually independent of the material behavior.

There is also the principle of virtual displacements. These principles are generated as a result of the modification of the virtual work equations. This involves the use of varying notations that are user in the case of supported bodies. In the process of generating these principles, variables such as the virtual displacement and strains are varied by using the variation notation and are later on specified. The virtual displacement is verified to be zero relative to the surface in question. This means that the work done by the forces will equate to zero. The virtual displacement will be subject to the external forces. By so doing the equation used in virtual work will be defined as the principle of displacement. This principle is applicable in scenarios where the displacement is quite large and is also real though it will require complex values of strains and stresses. Virtual displacement refers to the observing of an equilibrium configuration in a mechanical system noting how it react to small kinematic perturbation.

In the principle of virtual forces, there is a specification made such that the virtual stresses and forces are a deviation from the real stresses and forces. Like in the principle of virtual displacement, the virtual forces are assumed to be zero making the equations for the virtual work to be the basis of its principle. This brings about its other name which is the principle of complementary virtual work. In making the equations for this principle, variables such as the displacement boundary have to be considered (Ladeveze, 2012).

The virtual work principles are used in structural mechanics in solving problems in structural mechanics. All the principles under it such as the one for displacement as well as virtual forces are included in solving the problems depending on the variables provided. The equation in this principle are effective and correct.

7.2.2. Flexibility Method

It is also referred to as the method of consistent deformation. This may be attributed to the fact that this method has been in use for a long period of time in carrying out calculations dealing with structural systems. It is therefore referred to as a traditional method. This method is used in carrying out computations on displacement as well as forces in structural systems (Ladeveze, 2012). Though it is referred to as a traditional method, there are some modifications made to it so that it is somewhat modernized and it makes use of equations being currently used. The modern use makes use of matrices in its calculation allowing it to be referred to as the matrix force method. The term force is used because this method deals with calculations involving member forces being the major unknowns.

Under the flexibility method, the term member flexibility also arises. This is applied in the case where the material used is not stiff. In the equation used, there is the value of the spring stiffness which also has to be obtained. In the case where the material used is stiff, the equation becomes modified so that the matrix stiffness method is employed. The two methods have each their own variations such that in the case of the material beings stiff, the member stiffness relations can be integrated. This is only made possible through the use of the nodal equilibrium and the compatibility conditions that are in the flexibility equation. The nodal equilibrium equations are used to remove the need of the system being statically determinate. In order to do so, these equations are modified by minimizing the number of independent unknown number of forces. These equations make use of principles used in vectors. For most of these equations to be efficient, it is required that the system should be stable in nature (Ladeveze, 2012).

Under the flexibility, method there is the primary system. The system in this case in the statically indeterminate systems. It involves the identification of the value of a vector X which is also known as the vector of redundant forces.

1. ***Advantages of the Flexibility Method*:** This method allows the use of the Gauss-Jordan elimination process in lessening the number of redundant forces. The process is known to be effective as it allows the use and selection of redundant forces. By so doing it facilitates numerical stability. This method more so the one of matrix is a much easier method to use if it is to be implemented and used in carrying out automatic computation. It is also advantageous in that it allows for extension so that it

can be used in advanced applications. Some of the extensive application methods include the non-linear analysis, vibrations, and stability among others. This makes this method suitable for use in the general purpose structural analysis software packages. Most users prefer this method because it is less intensive in the aspect of computation. It is also good tool in learning as it will allow learners to gain more knowledge on equilibrium.

2. ***Disadvantages***: Some of the disadvantages of using this method is the fact that it does not have much knowledge on structural behaviors and as CSM revolves around structures, it increases risks levels.

7.2.3. Stiffness Method

It houses the direct stiffness method which is also called the matrix stiffness method. This method is more digitalized in the sense that it is used in computer-based analysis, due to the fact that it is computer based, it has the ability to carry out analysis involving complex structures such as the case of statically in determined structures. It borrows some of the concepts use in flexibility method. The concept borrowed is the use of matrices in carrying out the calculations. As mentioned earlier the method is composed of stiffness relations their relations are used in carrying out calculations on the member forces as well as the displacement in structures. For the implementation of the finite element method, the direct stiffness method has been a major contributor.

The finite element method borrows concepts from the direct stiffness method. It champions for the use of simpler idealized elements being interconnected at the nodes. it entails the use of one general equation which can be used in other elements being considered in the calculation. In making the equation, variables such as the material stiffness of the elements are compiled to form one matrix equation. The process entails the use of matrix mathematics. The equation is then used in determining the behavior of the structure being idealized. This method allows the establishment of unknown forces and displacements (Ladeveze, 2012).

There is a process followed when using the direct stiffness method. For one it involves breakdown. This involves one identifying the individual parts that make up the structure. The elements are then disconnected at the nodes. The identified elements are the analyzed individually and are then used in generating member stiffness equations. The next stage is the assembly.

This involves the relations developed from the individual element being recombined. The elements are recombined to form the original structure. The obtained stiffness relations are converted into a global system for the whole structure. The structures are then combined to form the matrix. While combining there are two major rules that are followed. They include the compatibility of displacements as well as the force equilibrium at each node. The last stage is the solution stage which involves the system being expressed as a single matrix equation.

The advantages and disadvantages of the matrix system are the same as those for the flexibility method. Some of the applications of the direct stiffness method include it being implemented into computer software for the sole purpose of evaluating complex structures that have a huge number of elements. It is greatly used in the field of structural analysis. In this field, this method has been greatly used in structural modeling thereby allowing users create a structure model and define the structure properties. The program then takes the role of creating the elements as well as develop global stiffness relationships (Ladeveze, 2012).

7.2.4. Approach of Plastic Method

This method is applied on objects that tend to have a nonlinear behavior more so those that have ductile properties. They are therefore able to attain greater bending extents and strengths which can be illustrated using the linear elastic bending analysis. There are some assumptions made when using this method. In the case of a n elastic bending analysis in a straight beam, the assumption is that the strain distribution is linear and the plane sections maintain its state. The assumptions cause a linear stress distribution within the object within a plastic analysis and the results stress distribution is termed to be nonlinear and is dependent on the nature of the bean's material. For one to limit the plastic bending strength also referred to as a plastic moment can be made in the case of the consideration of the upper limit on the bean's lad carrying capacity capability of the entire beam. There are certain factors that can be considered to be a major factor contributing to the failure of a beam. They include the global or local instability of the formula used. This is before the elastic limit is attained at any given length (Zingoni, 2010).

For this to be removed, one is required that the beams should be checked for quantities such as the local crippling, local buckling as well as the global lateral-torsional backing modes contributing to the failure. It is important for one to know that there are some reflections required for the development of stress that to be used in the plastic analysis. These reflections are to be excessive and consistent to the point of in compatibility. This creates the need for one to have separate analysis carried out. This will ensure that the design deflection limits to not exceed what is expected. In special cases, the load limit is made in such a way that detrimental permanent deformation does not occur. To meet this qualification, several separate analyses are conducted and more analysis is done exceeding the required standard. Stress is known to affect the internal surface of the object therefore large quantities of stress will affect the internal load distribution more so in statically indeterminate beams. This quantity is greatly affected by large deflections. The internal load distribution is also incorporated in the calculations during the evaluation process (Zingoni, 2010).

In the above discussion, there is a term that comes up and that is plastic bending. This refers to an action that occurs when an applied moment on a material causes the external fibers to surpass the material's yield strength. The bending on the external surface of the material occurs when the loaded moment is at the peak. This means that the stress will be applied at the surface of the material. The outer surface will experience the stress and later on will distribute the stress to other parts of the material. By so doing, it reduces the chances of a failure occurring. At extreme ends, it ends up delaying the failure that would have been predicted using the elastic analytical methods. When the stress is distributed from a neutral axis, it becomes similar to the shape of a strain curve. This is based on the assumption that it takes the shape of a non-composite cross section. The cross section then under goes a relatively high condition of plastic bending and therefore behaves as a plastic hinge.

There are various theories used in understanding the behavior of stress and bonding. One of the theories includes the elementary elastic bending theory. This theory places emphasis that the bending stress will vary proportionally with the distance from the neutral axis. However, the plastic bending illustrates high levels of accuracy and a higher level of stress distribution. The resultant areas of the cross section tend to vary between the yield and the greatest strength of the demonstrated by the material. Within the elastic region of the cross section, it is said that the distribution of stress varies linearly with the distance.

The distance in this case is from the neutral axis to the onset of the yielded area. This means that the expected failure will take place when the stress distribution estimates the material's stress-strain curve. The largest value being that of the ultimate strength. Not every area of the cross-section will have exceeded the yield strength (Zingoni, 2010).

For student learning computational structural mechanics, some of the topics they learn include the beam theory. It houses the Euler-Bernoulli beam theory which is also referred to as the engineer's beam theory or classical beam theory.

This theory is a simplified version of the linear elastic theory. It provides a method of calculating the load capacity of the material as well as the deflection characteristics of the given beams. It mostly deals with cases of small deflections. Some refer to it as a special case scenario of the Timoshenko beam theory.

This is used in mathematical models and have been useful in developing the plate theory and is a useful resource in structural and mechanical engineering. This theory has been used in developing various equations that can be used in structural and mechanical analysis. They include the static beam equation and dynamic beam equation. In this theory there is an axis referred to as the neutral axis. It is used to refer to a state where the beam under study is not under any axial loading axis. Some case examples of this theory is the three-point bending which is known to be a classical experiment in the world of mechanics. This is the case scenario of a beam at rest on roller supports. The beam is then subjected to concentrated load that is placed at the center of the beam. The cantilever beams are also discussed under this theory. They are used in assisting individuals to have a better understanding on beams and are therefore fit to solve any problems concerning structural mechanics. Lastly is the statistically indeterminate beams. This beams are known to be complex in nature (Zingoni, 2010).

Some other topics in the CSM include buckling, plates, and shells, earthquake engineering, torsion, trusses, stiffening, structural dynamics as well as structural instability.

7.3. FINITE ELEMENT METHOD IN STRUCTURAL MECHANICS

This method was developed to be used in the solving of complex problems in the line of structural mechanics. It is a wee established that is preferred by, most users in the event of complex systems. It consists of infinite elements being conned at certain points known as nodes. The connection involves them being connected to one another hence it becomes an inter connection. Finite elements possess properties such as thickness, Poisson's ratio, density, coefficient of thermal expansion and the shear modulus among others. This computation method was generated from the matrix analysis structures. This was when the stiffness and displacement matrix approach was created and introduced. They were developed on the basis of engineering models that were currently existing (Zingoni, 2010).

During the development of this method, there were some practical considerations made. The included the conditions of the symmetry that were exploited in an aim of having minimal sizes of the model. At the nodes, the displacement compatibility had to be ensured. The same case applies for the element edges. They are imposed through the use of constraint relations. It is also a requirement that the behavior of the element should capture and entail the suppressive actions of the real system. This should be the case globally and internationally. The support constraints used should be good conditioned and will great care be imposed to the nodes on the symmetry axes. To produce acceptable accuracy, the element mesh used should be relatively fine to suit the system. These mesh are generated through the use of facilities provided for by the commercial software packages.

Compared to the virtual work principal, the finite element method is said to use a traditional approach during its development. This is well elaborated in the theoretical overview of the finite element method displacement formulation. This theoretical approach given an illustration of the process taken when converting the elements to a stage where they produce solutions. It also gives an outline on some of the equations used while generating this method. Mathematical matrix is also involved in the process. The systems generated and used are also indicated in the theoretical formulation. The theoretical approach is also use in showing the relationship existing between the virtual work method and the finite element method. Equations are used in developing the relationship and similarities in both equations (Zingoni, 2010).

As it also discusses on the virtual work principal, we get to learn of the internal virtual work in a typical element. The element matrices under the principal refer to the system of matrices used that undergo a process that will lead to a typical element being defined. The matrices used undergo numerical evaluation through the use of the Gaussian quadrature for them to be numerically integrated and be used as a method in carrying out analysis. The finite element method being a high leveled technique is advantageous as it will enable the easy solving of complex equations in structural mechanics.

7.4. SOFTWARE USED IN COMPUTATIONAL STRUCTURAL MECHANICS

Some of the software used in computational structural analysis includes the open source structural analysis software, finite element analysis software and the nonlinear analysis software among others.

7.4.1. Finite Element Software

This software is the most common software used in CSM. It presents features that can be well used in the calculation, analysis, and evaluation of a given structure (Figure 7.2).

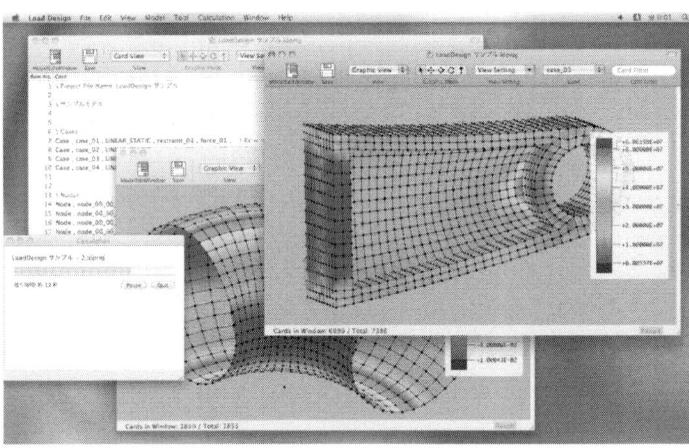

Figure 7.2. Finite element software presents a variety of features that can be adequately used in carrying out analysis.

Source: https://galusaustralis.com/2019/10/13513/finite-element-software-market-2019-strategic-assessments-ansys-dassault-systemes-msc-software-corp/ (accessed on 3 April 2020).

There are a variety of software packages under the finite element software. They are all used to carry out a variety of processes. They are referred to as finite element software packages as the make use of the finite element method in solving differential equations that are partial in nature. For instance, the Agros2D software has a variety of features that include a multiplatform open source application. This application is used in solving of physical problems. This is mostly used by users who have the Linux or Windows operating system (OP) as they have an operating speed that accommodate this kind of package. There is also the ANSA Pre-processor which has an advanced CAE pre-processing software features. This software package is used in the Linux, Max OSX, and windows OP. It makes use of the proprietary commercial software to facilitate its running (Kaveh, 2013).

The Calculi X software. This software was generated as an open source FEA project. It is composed of features such as the solver and a compatible ABAQUS file formatting tools. It also has the pre-post processing features which are used in the generation of input data used in the FEA and CDF applications. It uses the GNU GPL license for its running and it is used in the Linux and the windows OP. The DIANA FEA is a software package that makes of finite methodology features. This software is extensively used by the geotechnological, civil, and structural engineers. It makes use of proprietary commercial software licenses to facilitate its running and is also used in the Windows and Linux OPs.

The dell which makes use of the element codes and scaling to be used in comprehensive analysis. It makes use of the C++ languages in making and using of the element codes. It uses the LGPL license and they make use of the Linux, UNIX, Mac OS X and windows OP. DUNE software has the distributed and unified numeric features. This makes use of the GPL Version 2 license for its running and makes use of the Linux, UNIX, and Mac OS X OP. There are many other software packages that are under the finite element software packages. As demonstrated by the above samples, these software packages make use of a variety of features each different from the other though some software incorporates all the various features within it. Such software is commonly used by users as it is more beneficial. The features of the software can be distinguished using a variety of criteria. These criteria allow the comparison of the features. These criteria can include the license, graphical user interface, documentation, and mesh. In terms of the mesh, it is divided into the elements, mapping order, generation, adaptive refinement, input, and output, check, and the operation. It is also classified according to the parallel possibilities, solver, linear algebra, matrix-free, language used in the software. The more the features the better the functioning and the running of the software. These software packages should be made to be able to run properly and efficiently ensuring the efficient running of the software (Kaveh, 2013).

1. *Advantages of the Finite Element Software*: Some of the advantages include the adaptability capability. The finite element software in created in a manner such that it can be used and supported in a variety of application software and OPs. It also allows the adjustments of the specifications in order to meet the expected levels of accuracy. By so doing, it reduces the need for the generation of physical prototypes and thereby reducing development costs of such prototypes.

It is also used in maintaining high levels of accuracy. The software allows various modifications to be made to the equations used to minimize the levels of accuracy. This makes the FEM method to be practically used in solving problems related to the structural mechanics. This allows the maintenance of high levels of accuracy within the structures. In terms of modeling, the software allows the easier modeling of the complex geometrical and irregular shapes of the material. It therefore allows the modeling of both exterior and interior parts of the material. The user is therefore required that the user to identify the critical factor used in modeling (Kaveh, 2013).

It also a time dependent simulation. In structural mechanics, simulations are required in order for one to get an idealization of the structure to be evaluated. Some of the simulations used include the crash simulations. Such type of simulations tends to be time dependent. This software allows the simulations to be time dependent in that it is able to be done within a short period of time so that one is able to make the analysis in a period of time. It also comes in handy when one is required to come up with a virtual representation of the structure.

The software is advantageous in that it allows the easy establishment of boundaries. The software has features that allows the establishment of boundaries through the use if conditions that are used in the definition of the conditions of the models of structural mechanics. This therefore means that the boundaries are expressed as conditions. Such conditions include the point forces, thermal effects i.e., Changes in temperature and the distributed forces. It also allows for visualization. The visualization is made possible through the use of simulations. They are able to achieve detailed visualization of the designs (Kaveh, 2013).

2. ***Disadvantages*:** Some of the disadvantages of the finite element software is that they are quite difficult to produce. This is because

in terms of programming, it is quite difficult to program the finite element software. This is attributed to the fact that this software to a greater extent deals more with the integration of numbers and following rules on quadrant. The use of such type of variables may require individuals to have critical thinking skills and it may be quite hectic to program the software. It is also quite difficult to ensure that the software generated will be effective. Another disadvantage may be that for each of the software packages under the FEMs, they each offer their own set of challenges.

Under the FEMs software, apart from the packaging software there is also the simulation software under it. Simulation refers to the creation of objects allowing them to be used in creating a visual representation of the structure to be developed. By creating the simulation, one gets a vivid idea of what the structure looks like. The images created using this type of software are usually in three dimension images though they can also be presented using two dimension formats. Some of the simulation software used includes the open foam software, simscale, and the ANYSYS software among others. All these software have their own unique features that contribute to the creation of a good simulation which will allow for the use of well-developed systems in the process of evaluation and analysis (Ladeveze, 2012).

For most of these software the analysis is conducted in them such that they are able to combine both the simulation and analysis processes. The software is equipped with calculation systems and are fitted with formula that are used in calculation thereby making the process to be less hands on. All that is required is for the user to key in the data, come up with various designs of the structure and the computer does the rest. In the case of the finite element analysis, these computations can be automated so that they can be conducted by the computer without the need of the presence of a human being.There are merits and demerits of using simulation as a method of conducting analysis. Some of the demerits include the fact that it is quite expensive to come up and actualize some of the software used in simulation. In some extreme cases it is quite difficult to come up with the simulations as some of them tent to be quite costly more so for those dealing with the designing of complex structures. In the case of complex simulation, it is quite difficult for one to interpret the information on the results of the analysis. Some of the advantages include the fact that one is able a future prediction on the behavior of the structure. It is a much better approach compared to the analytical method of conducting analysis. This is based on the aspect of accuracy of the obtained results. Simulation tends to give higher levels of accuracy compared to the analytical approach as it gives off a wider area and techniques that can be used in conducting analysis (Ladeveze, 2012).

It also gives off a method that's facilitates the easy identification of problems encountered in the system. It scans for possible glitches within the simulation software. Let's take the case of the ANSYS software. The simscale software is also part of the software that is used in the CSM. This is a software product that is based on cloud computing. It is a well-known product of the SimscaleGmbh. It is used in a given number of analysis apart from CSM. They include the Finite element analysis as well as thermal simulations. This software makes use of open source codes that include the open FOAM for the CSM and the code Aster along with the Calculi for the FEA. This software creates a platform where users are able to run a variety of simulations. In addition to that, are able to facilitate design changes.

The most common software when dealing with simulation is the ANSYS software. It is common among users as its benefit them by providing your problem in an approach that it ensures proper services to the user. It is a product of the Ansys Inc. Which a company that is based in Pennsylvania. It is a company knows to manufacture multi-physics simulation software that are used in different ways that include product designing, operation as well as testing. The company's previous membership was sold and given to another company there by allowing it to acquire other design samples as well as technology that is useful on fluid dynamics. This also facilitated other physical analysis and electronics design. This software is very useful in developing and marketing of engineering simulation software that is used in various analysis programs. Like in the Simscale software, the Ansys software is greatly used in the finite element analysis software (Zingoni, 2010).

The software is to some extent useful in the simulation of different computer models of structure that useful in the mechanical and electronically analysis of variables such as temperature distribution, electromagnetism, elasticity, toughness, and fluid flow among others. It is common that these concepts that are used in architecture and therefore in a great way useful for computational structural mechanics. For instance, the software is useful in defining how a certain product will function under given specifications. This removes the need of one having to conduct crash tests or building test products/subjects so that an overall product is produced. This allows the saving of time as well as resources that would have been used. The company is able to use those funds to improve the features of the software.

The software is very useful in making predictions on the running and performance of various products. A case example is that through simulation one is able to determine the period that a bridge can run even when subjected to heavy traffic. This allows various strategies can be put in place in order to save resources but ensuring good quality of the product to be manufactured (Zingoni, 2010).Advantages of the SimScale software and the Ansys software include: they are fast. The SimScale and Ansys software have components such as the LBM solver which is commonly present as Pace-Fish. This was created by use of the numeric system. This element usually has its own Cartesian mesh engine that makes the work of the user to mainly be defining the flow domains or the physics in study. The solver run time in the LBM solver assumes the role of generating the grid is used during analysis. By making use of the Cartesian grid the process becomes much faster. Added advantage is that the solver is also less prone to error and more tolerant towards other types of geometry.

The LBM solver is often programmed to work at relatively high speeds. This has contributed to the implementation of other new and existing features such as the Lattice-Boltzmann method to cater for a parallel architecture of the system to run. This will allow the running of several GPUs while created in parallel and thereby producing results that are relatively quicker in comparison to other types of typical NS transient simulation (Zingoni, 2010).The other advantage is that they allow a higher level of accurate analysis thereby producing results that can be said to be realistic. This will in turn mean that users of this software will not be required to forgo the speed of the software in an aim them get accurate results. This makes the software to be more preferred compared to the rest.They are flexible. Flexibility mostly is applicable for the Ansys software. Flexibility means that the software can be used in a variety of technologies and has the ability to be used to carry out a variety of analysis. The added advantage is that this software are usually readily available and the users can purchase the software on the internet or physically from the manufactures. It also provides a wide range of a variety of tools that can be used in the process of simulation of the CMS designs. Some of the disadvantages include that they are costly when used for long term duration. This is because most of the time software is sold to user in a subscription package basis and they will be required to pay for the services of the software on a given frequency making it costly.

7.4.2. Open Foam Software

This is also among the software that is used in both computational structural mechanics and computational fluid dynamics. Though most at times it is used in computational fluid dynamics, to some extent it is used in conducting structural analysis. It contains a variety of features that allows it to be used in both cases of analysis. Its structure includes a layout that is made of various directories the most common are two. The first one is the Open FOAM version which has the software library having the directory layout within the side figure used. There is also the Third party which is made up of the software's third party libraries. This software is also used in simulation where by the simulation has a structure with a specified edit. In basic terms, it means that this software simulations are configured using multiple plain text input file whose location is across three directories. They include the system, constant and initial time directories. All the listed directories have their own components which are used in making the directories function properly. For instance, for the system directory, the files used include controlDict, fvSolution, fvSchemes, and the fvOption. The fvOption is an optional file that is freely available at the user's disposal. Other available files can also be grouped under system directory. For the constant directory the major file is the polymesh. There dictionaries can also be classified under this. The initial time directory includes the field files.

In this software, there is room so that other directories can be developed depending on the user requirements. Some of them are the result time directories such as the girl predictions which are a subject of iteration time or count. There is also the post processing that consists of data created by function objects such as data conversion (Zingoni, 2010).

1. ***Advantages of the Open FOAM*:** Some of the advantages of the Open FOAM software is that it is made up of a friendly syntax. This syntax allows easy solving of PDEs. It works by modifying the equation to a form that can be easily solved. It is also made up of wholly documented source codes allowing the user to make some modification to available source codes to achieve different results the advantage being that it can be restored to the original format. The software entails unstructured polyhedral grid capabilities useful during simulation facilitating the production of a variety of models. Along with this it has the automatic parallelization of applications. This is written in the software by use of the software's high level syntax. This software is cheap to

use because there are no incurred licensing costs. It can also be used for commercial purposes as it offers a variety of applications as well as models at the comfort of the user.

2. ***Disadvantages***: Some of the disadvantages include the fact it tends to cause problems to developing communities. This is because of the fragmentation that occurs. The fragmentation contributes to the rise of the number of forked projects. It also suffers from a deficiency of a graphical user interface. This means the interface offered are the open source and proprietary interfaces. Another challenge is with the programmers' guides which are known to be short of details that are crucial for the running of the software. It results to a slow process when one tries to add information into new applications or modify the functionality. This causes frustration to the user who may opt to use a different type of software.

7.5. EMERGING TRENDS IN COMPUTATIONAL STRUCTURAL MECHANICS

There are various trends that have been innovated in the world of computational structural mechanics. These trends have been introduced to make the process of calculations in CSM to be much easier and can be extensively applied to other fields. Emerging trends have included one being able to make new formulas to be used during the calculations. It has also involved new principles being invented that are in line with structural mechanics either the linear aspect or the nonlinear aspect of structural mechanics. Some of the advances in computational structural mechanics include the incorporation of the use of computers in computational structural mechanics.

It has involved technology being modernized to fit the use of CSM and allowing large scale computation of such structures. The use of technology has involved applications being made that facilitate the use of software used in carrying out computations around structural mechanics. The relationship between CSM and technology is not a recently developed channel. CSM is actually a discipline that has been formed as a result of the combination of other disciplines such as computer science (CS) and structural mechanics. Structural mechanics also houses other disciplines such as fluid dynamics and mechanics (Kaveh, 2013).

The combinations of these technologies with CS is the major form that brings out the relationship between the disciplines and technology. The use of knowledge in CS allows one to use their knowledge on CS to come up with codes that can be used in carrying out computations dealing with structural analysis. By so doing these codes have been useful in developing programs that are used to run software used in structural analysis. Technology being integrated into CSM has led to some of the methodologies used in structural analysis such as a finite element method being incorporated to computers so that the calculations are done automatically by the computers. The user is only required to key in data into the computer and to make changes to some of the variables in the computer and the computer automatically conducts an analysis and gives the user output which is the result of the analysis.

The integration of computers follows the aspect of it being used in carrying out simulations. Simulation is the representation of an object in a three-dimension format. Simulated object is not real but is said to be virtual. It is very useful in structural analysis more so for the diagrams that are to be used in structural mechanics. The user is able to identify the elements in the diagram, break them down, conduct an analysis, obtain results, and afterwards reunite the elements of the structure. This allows for a comprehensive analysis to be done. The simulations can only be done through the use of software. It is therefore required that the manufacture has knowledge on CS so that they can be able to create the software. Software avails the necessary tools that can be used in creation of the software.

Also among the latest trends in the use of the latest OPs. The use of such systems provides the user with a good environment that facilitating the efficient running of the software programs or packages. The use of the latest OPs ensures that the programs run at a higher speed. This ensures that once the programs are keyed in they are solved automatically and are solved within a short period of time. The user is then able to get feedback and the required changes are made to the formula or the models that have been generated as a result of comprehensive analysis (Kaveh, 2013).

Among the latest trends include companies using the CSM software to carry out evaluation of already existing structures or structures that are to be developed. Therefore, most of the building companies have their computers fitted with such software. With the help of this software they are able to make a prediction on the future behavior of the structure. This more so applies to structures such as bridges like those that are suspended from an object. If it is noted that there are many vibrations within the structure and it is unfit for the structure to be in use, the building companies are able to make some adjustments. They are able to identify the areas of weakness within the structure.

Engineers have also been among the group of individuals that have been greatly known to use the advanced computerized CSM. For them these systems allow them to easily conduct calculations on the structures. It has also involved the integration of certain programs for use in the analysis process. They are able to come up with modernized systems of conducting the numerical methods the most common being the modernized calculations of the finite element method. It has contributed to them being able to conduct analysis within a short period of time. It also allows them to conduct extensive analysis and evaluation of structures. With the use of technology, the individuals are able to conduct extensive research that allows them to make upgrades on currently existing software used for simulation. Also they are able to identify some of the demerits of the methods of analysis use. They are able to make some corrections to those methods. To some extremes when the computations to be done are extremely complex, they are able to use the internet to conduct research and innovate some methodologies to be used in the calculations (Kaveh, 2013).

The advantage of these is that they are able to improve the accuracy of some of the methodologies available. They also work on the flexibility of this method modifying them to work and be supported in a variety of the computer systems used. The emerging trends in computational structural mechanics are among the advances being made to technology to improve structural analysis. These trends are quickly being adopted by most individuals as well as companies to assist them in the fields of mechanics that they deal with. Most of the trends have also been integrated in to the existing systems.

7.6. JOB OPPORTUNITIES IN COMPUTATIONAL STRUCTURAL MECHANICS

Some of the job opportunities in CSM include one being a researcher. The job description will involve one conducting a variety of research in CSM mechanics and system modeling. They would be required to have experience in both linear and nonlinear mechanics that will be applied in conducting structural and thermal analysis. They will also be required to have knowledge on the various software that are used in structural analysis. Another job opportunity is one being an application engineer. This may be a physics based job opportunity that is based on computational simulations. They will be required to have knowledge on computational fluid dynamics, structural mechanics, fluid-structure interaction, structural acoustics, as well as electromagnetics with knowledge in radio-frequency. They also are required to have knowledge on software used in conducting simulation processes. Another job opportunity is working as a computational structural mechanics scientist. This means that they are involved in all manner of scientific research conducted in CSM. They come up with new formulas to be used during the calculations. Also they check for existing errors within the currently in the methods being used to conducts structural analysis. Currently there are few numbers of such researchers. This makes this job opportunity to be more marketable for many individuals and the salary is also good. One can also work as a code developer for computational solid mechanics. This deals more with programming as it will be required that they will be required to have knowledge on programming languages. Knowledge on programming is used in creating certain codes and also conducting the manipulations on the codes. One can get employment as an advanced material modeling and processing analytical engineer. This job opportunity is quite complex and the individuals will be required to have knowledge on a variety of disciplines. For instance, it will involve one having knowledge on quantum chemistry, statistical mechanics, plasma physics as well as proven mechanics. It will involve the applications of all the disciplines and using their interrelationship to make an analysis. There is also a job opportunity as a computational scientist. The individual is required to have knowledge on computational methodologies including the structural mechanics or computational fluid dynamics. Their major work is to develop the equations used during the calculations. Also they come up with principals used in conducting the calculation process. One can also work as a simulation and analysis personnel. They will be required to have knowledge on fundamental mechanics. They also need to have knowledge on structural mechanics. They will also need to have knowledge on finite element analysis as well as thermal analysis. There is also a computational physicist. Their work is to formulate and calibrate computation models. They also work with other experts in the fluid of fluid dynamics. Also, there is the structural dynamics that deal mostly in elasticity, plasticity, composite, and fracture mechanics. They deal mostly with permanent structures. They work in the development of structural hardening technologies.

Chapter

8

Computational Biology

CONTENTS

8.1. INTRODUCTION

Computational biology is a branch that involves the use of computers and the knowledge on computer science (CS) to get the understanding of structures and the processes of life. Biology is the study of the structures of the human being and the processes that a human body undergoes (Figure 8.1).

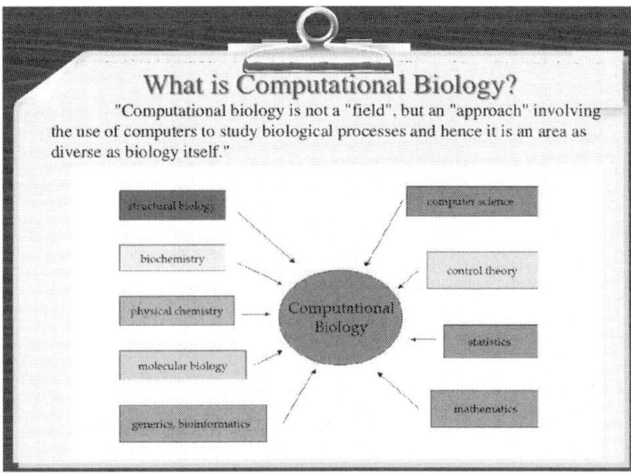

Figure 8.1. Computational biology involves the using of computational methods example algorithms to show how biological system operates and then the results are interpreted in a large scale.

Source: *https://www.slideshare.net/sajjanvsl/algorithmic-approach-to-computational-biology-using-graphs (accessed on 4 April 2020).*

By using computational biology, it helps the understandings of structures and functioning of a body such that one can form models from this.

The main audience and population that these topic targets are the population of people who have a very strong background when it comes to biology such that they have an inner understanding on what is biology and what biology involves. Computational biology just as the name states and from its definition it needs individual who knows what biology is and how systems of a body operate so that they can use this knowledge to apply the computers to get the knowledge of the systems. This, therefore, means that computational biologists most definitely undertook biology as a unit in their course too. Most universities will not accept a student to read computational biology and graduate from it if they lack the knowledge of biology or if they failed biology in high school. Also one has to pass in biology unit so that they can graduate with a degree or diploma in computational biology. Computational biology also needs individuals who have the skill in quantitative approaches. Quantitative approaches as a skill is a skill where an individual has the knowledge of approaching an issue based on amount or quantity and it is a skill that is very necessary for computational biology as it will be explained more in the course of this writing.

There are goals that computational biology study targets to attain which include the following goals. One by the study of computational biology it aims to enable students to gain the understanding of foundational methods in computational biology. By enabling students to gain the understanding of foundational methods in computational biology it means enabling students to know what computational biology from its basis is and to get to know everything about it and how they can apply computational biology. They are also made to understand the origin of computational biology (Blossey, 2006).

Another goal of computational biology study is that it gives students the exposure that they need so that they can carry out more research or they can begin their research. Computational biology involves the use of computers and therefore it can be improved with time into better models and therefore research has to be carried out to know how to achieve this. Since most students may fail to find information about a topic that they have no idea on, it is necessary and the goal of computational biology to equip students with the skills that they need so that they can work on improving on their research.

Computational biology mainly deals with systems biology. Systems biology is the part of biology that deals with the systems of the human body. It should, however, be understood that computational biology class is not a system biology class but it is the study of computational biology it may involve the study of some systems that are involved in the system biology class. It is therefore understood that despite computational biology involving the study of biology with the computers it is mainly tied toward the system biology more than the general biology (Blossey, 2006).

Computational biology also involves and deals in synthetic biology. Synthetic biology is the field of biology that deals with redesigning an organism or reshaping an organism for useful purposes by engineering them to have new abilities.

The act or redesigning organisms into different organisms such that they acquire new abilities that they did not have. For example, if a human eye is not able to see it can be redesigned in such a way that it will acquire the ability to see once more. Just as we stated in system biology, computational biology class is not a class on synthetic biology but it may involve some parts that will deal with the synthetic biology. It should also be understood that synthetic biology may at most times depend on computational biology but this will be discussed further.

Lastly, computational biology deals in the algorithm but like before a computational biology class is not necessarily an algorithmic class but some algorithm may be involved. By applying algorithms, it gives the ability to apply a bioinformatics algorithm as part of the homework. By applying algorithm, it makes the study of computational biology more applicable and therefore computational biologist must know the algorithm.

Computational biology as a field falls into major fields and is taken as a part of biology. it falls in the field of synthetic biology which we have discussed earlier. It also falls in the field of development of methods for the analysis of biological data which involves how you analyze and develop data that involves the functioning of the human body and how it operates. It also falls in the sector of informatics and bioinformatics.

It falls under the field of computational biology, biology, and systems biology. Systems biology is the study of the systems which fall as molecular and cellular systems. Molecular systems are the systems that deal with the molecules while cellular is the systems that deal with the cells in a human body.

Molecular and systematic data and systems are therefore explained and modeled easily with the knowledge in computational biology.

In biology field, computational biology is applied as a way to study the synthetic biology which as seen earlier is the biology that deals in designing organisms to gain new abilities that they did not acquire before by engineering them and therefore computational biology must be applied in the study and applied in the coming up of the systems (Blossey, 2006) (Figure 8.2).

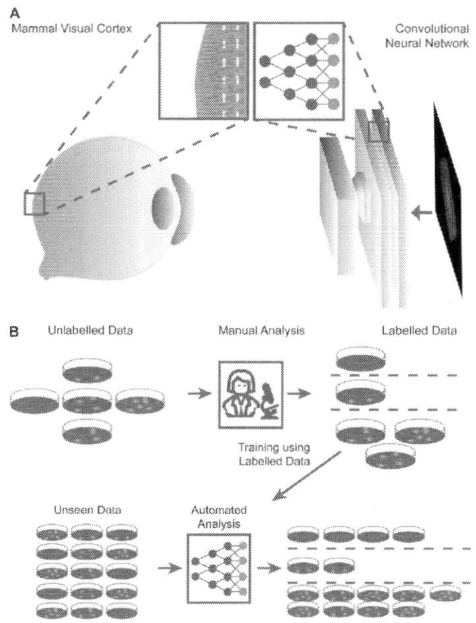

Figure 8.2. Computational biology using algorithms.

Source: https://www.researchgate.net/figure/Simplistic-illustration-of-an-artificial-intelligence-algorithm-and-its-applications-in_fig1_334042736 (accessed on 3 April 2020).

For us to understand computational biology we need to know the origin and generation of what was happening earlier on. In the years 1970s genome proteins did not exist. That is the genome sequences were not there. Genome proteins are system qualities that are used to identify the type of protein that is present. The plural genome is the gene and it is studied in biology. In these years, there were also no large sequences of data that could explain about the protein. Although the data was not present, the beginning of knowledge about proteins had started. The early scientists mainly performed the function of getting to know what the proteins are and how they are formed. They mainly dealt with getting the knowledge and the basic understanding of the proteins. They also did their research and they, therefore, began comparing different proteins together so that they could understand the different types of proteins from their differences. The scientists who were mostly behind this were two great scientists who were the Carl Weose and Margret Dayhoff who mainly behind discovering the proteins and the structures and the differences in the structures of the different types of proteins (Blossey, 2006).

The year 1980s mainly involved the sequence alignment search. In these years the database that was there on proteins began to increase. The use of system alignment and search started becoming more important and a lot of people came up with better algorithms that were better in times of speed as they faster algorithms. The main aim of coming up with a faster algorithm is that the scientists were able to align the protein structures and to understand more about the protein structures. The algorithm is understood as a set of rules that are set up to come up with a deeper understanding on how to solve a calculation and to be able to find a solution for a calculation most especially by the use of PCs. FASTA programme was majorly used and applied in the year of 1980 and it became fastly popular. BLAST system was also widely used and the individuals behind the writing of the BLAST included the following individuals. Ruth Nussinov, Michael Zucker, Bill Pearson, Webb Miller and many other writers. these individuals were mainly scientists and they were of great importance in the field of sequence alignment search. Algorithms will be discussed more in the course of this study to get a better understanding (Blossey, 2006).

In the year of 1990s, computational biology was noticed to increase and become more popular. The main factor and reason behind the development and increment of computational biology in the year one thousand nine hundred and ninety is that there was the development of microarrays. A microarray is a tool that is used in the laboratories that have the ability and the capability to detect how very many genes show their expressions at a single time. Computational biology also started becoming popular because there was the coming up of the first genome questions and sequences. The questions that were coming up about the genome is the questions that were involving how an individual can identify the genes that are present in the genome and many other questions that arose. There was a family of engineers who had the function and work of sequence labeling problems. The individuals that were behind this included David Baker, Pat brown, David Eisenberg and many other individuals that were present. This was the years when the computational biology begun and rose to seek popularity and the genes in the genomes understood more deeply than it was before.

In the year two thousand, there was the sequencing, assembling, and annotating f the genome. It enabled the sequencing of the genome in such a way that it made them more fashionable and now it was not only the genomes of the small organisms that were being sequenced but the sequencing of bigger organisms was enabled. The bigger organism that was there included the human such that the genomes of the humans were now being sequenced. These were the starting of the huge host of computational problems that included the challenge that is formed when assembling the genome annotating them and many other processes that were involved in the genome (Wünschiers, 2012).

Aside from this, in the year two thousand, there was also another phase that was also involved in the computational biology introduction which involved the computational biology become more biological such that it mainly dealt with the biological processes that were there. First of all, there was massively parallel data collection which involved the collecting of data in large amounts. Under it, there was the transcriptomics, proteomics, interactomics, and metagenomics. The next martin making computational biology more biological in the year two thousand is using sequences and array or the collected data to address the important questions that may arise. Many questions arose which was essential that answers to them are provided and computational biology also led to the rise of many unanswered questions. Some of the questions that arose were, for instance, the structure of the proteins where people wanted to get the understanding of how the structure of the proteins looked like and how this structures of this proteins are used to solve problems and to perform various functions in the human body. Other questions included the development and evolution of the proteins and how they grow.

Another way in which computational biology became more biological is that they used experiments that are they performed experiments and approached them experimentally. With is there was a rise in bioimage informatics which is a division of bioinformatics and computational biology. This is the using of computational techniques to study the bioimages. These bio images are the images of the molecules and the cells in an organism and therefore they can be studied by the use of bioimage to gain a deeper understanding of these images and to be able to find suitable solutions to problems that may arise or to problems that may be present (Wünschiers, 2012).

8.2. THE FOUNDATION OF COMPUTATIONAL BIOLOGY

Initially, computational biology began at almost the same time with the begging of CS. The scientists who were behind the coming up of computational biology was a person from Britain and he was both a mathematician and a logician and he went by the name of Alan Turing. Many people liked to refer to him as the father of computing. Alan Turing took the computers that were present in the start and used them to put up a model of biological morphogenesis.

The model of morphogenesis was a model that could show how the pattern and the form in organisms that are alive. He carried out this research in the early years of 1950 just before he passed away.

In this year, there was the development of the first computer that was known as the MANIAC computer that was developed in a large laboratory that was found and situated in New Mexico that was called the Los Alamos national laboratory. This laboratory was one that was mainly used to deal with the research of weapons.

The coming up of the new computers was then discovered in this laboratory. The computers have been in function as early as the year one thousand and fifty and they were used to perform functions that were around calculations that dealt with calculations in the genetics of the people living in an area that is populations genetics.

The situations that required individuals to carry out the original computational modeling in biology, it was the duty and responsibility of Turing and performed by a certain group of people in the city of Los Alamos (Singh, 2014).

In the coming years up to the years the 1960s, these computers have been used for applications that are more complex and complicated and therefore they have been used in the examining of the structure of the protein and how it looks like. With these movements and use of the computers to come up with the development of the protein structure using the computers, it led to a rise of computational biology as it set a basis and foundation for it.

Computational biology, therefore, developed from studies that were centered on protein by observing a protein and getting to know more about the protein.

The scientists and the researchers found a way to use the computers indispensable for performing analysis and collecting data and information and by these, they were able to know more about the dimensions of the protein where they were able to discover that the proteins exist in three dimensions using the computational biology (Figure 8.3).

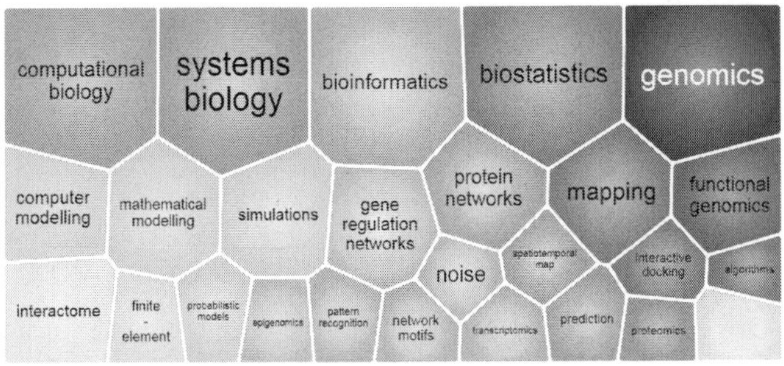

Figure 8.3. Role of computational biology.

Source: *https://erc.europa.eu/projects-figures/stories/computational-biology-spotlight-erc-projects (accessed on 3 April 2020).*

In the begging of 1950 taxonomists began using computers in carrying out their work. Taxonomists are individuals who are scientists whose main duty is to arrange living organisms into groups that are called taxa that all the organisms in a given taxon are individuals that have the same characteristics and they react the same towards different conditions. The taxonomists used the computers to help them to group the organisms by keeping the organisms that share the same characteristics in one group and separating those with different characteristics in different groups. It is way advantageous when using the computers to group the organisms rather than putting one by one because it is way easier hence causing less exhaustion to the taxonomists and it is also way faster hence it can work faster than before (Singh, 2014).

The usefulness of grouping living organisms into groups where the same organisms share the same characteristic is that they can study and have knowledge of how the organisms evolve with time; for example, they can know how human beings evolved from the Australopithecus to the homo sapiens to the homo sapiens which is the modern man. In the year of 1960, the techniques that were initially used were now introduced in DNA sequences and the amino acids sequences. the DNA sequences deal with how the DNA is shaped and the DNA is the part of the proteins that are used in showing the parents or relative of the individuals. The use of the computers was brought about by the computational methods to offer its support in molecular phylogenetics. These computational methods showed and involved using techniques that are fast rowing that has been of great benefit from and by using the algorithms which are calculations that are set to solve a given problem. It has also benefitted greatly from the study of dynammic programming where the programming languages have been used to come up with the complicated system of computation. This, therefore, means that algorithms have been used widely and their application in computational biology has been of great benefit and us with the basis that a large amount of data is applied and biology has given out many examples given the amount of data and information that is available. This has led to deeper advanced research in CS with the use of computational biology for the researchers.

At the start of 1890s, computational biology was able to bring about further developments in CS. The number of aspects of artificial intelligence (AI). Among these were knowledge representation which led to the coming up of ontologies which is showing concepts and how they relate to one another. These show that the knowledge that is involved in biology in a way that is easily read by the computer. It also involves the processing of natural language that is used in the coming up of technological ways that are used for sourcing for information from a large amount of information that is written in a scientific language. Perhaps most times the subfield used in learning of the machine that is based on the field of biology. These are made from modeling sequences for the uses of recognizing the available patterns and analyzing high dimensional data from a large amount of gene expression studies (Singh, 2014).

The foundation of computational biology is therefore mainly based on the level of proteins then it raised with time.

8.3. APPLICATIONS OF COMPUTATIONAL BIOLOGY

8.3.1. Used in Cancer Precision Drug Discovery

The accurate and most desired therapy to cure cancer involves identifying an anticancer medicine for specific tumors molecular profiles, the features that it possesses and the individuals who are suffering from cancer in the microenvironment. The major and main target of the precision medicine is to curb the cancer tumors to heal the cancer patient and in a most applicable manner and the side effects that are associated with it is as minimal as possible. There was a report that was passed by the International Agency for research about cancer that carries out the statistics to know the number of people getting cancer in a year and the number of people that are cured of it. The report that they passed out stated that more than 18 million of people were suffering from cancer in the year 2018 and the cancer deaths that were witnessed that year were approximately 9.6 million in the whole world. With the coming of cancer, solutions had to be found to ensure that this cancer is cured and the existing cancer treatment methods that were used included the chemotherapy that is including a cancer-killing chemical to a patient through the bloodstream. Antiangiogenic agents and immunotherapy were also used by the physicians to find and provide a cure for the cancer patient and to slow down the speed of the cancer cells. Some types of cancer may offer resistance to the growth of the cancer cells and this included the carcinoma, malignancy melanoma, and renal cancer.

The only way to avoid the resistivity to cancer treatment by these types of cancers is to offer anticancer drugs before. In all the other types of cancers, they respond very well to the chemotherapy that is offered but with time they respond decreases and degrades such that it does not respond to the cancer treatment as it is required it is like it has started developing some type of resistance to the chemotherapy. There have been very many cases that have been reported about the resistivity of some types of cancer to the treatment of cancer every year that passes and this has led to the death of very many cancer patients and these deaths are not easily avoidable. In such a complicated and astonishing situation, the only solution that may be sought is designing drugs with the capability and potential of curing cancer. Designing these drugs is a tiresome and complicated process that takes a lot of time since any cancer patient has a different way in which they respond to the treatment of chemotherapy and the effects that may cause harm are not easily known (Blossey, 2006) (Figure 8.4).

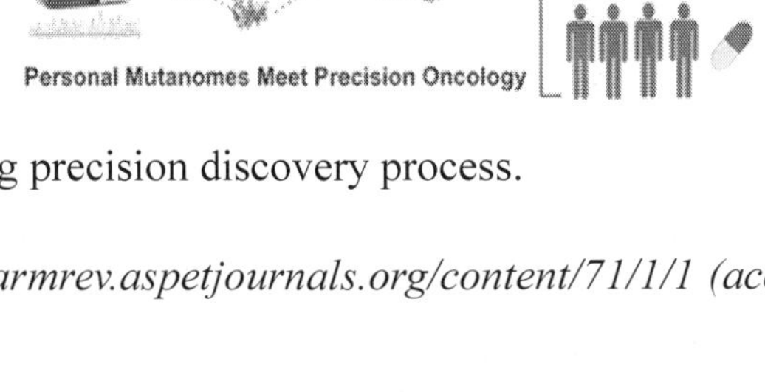

Figure 8.4. A drug precision discovery process.

Source: http://pharmrev.aspetjournals.org/content/71/1/1 (accessed on 3 April 2020).

There is an ultimate and crucial need to come up with primary mechanisms which have the capability of detecting resistance to cancer therapy.

The incorporating of tumor genetic profiling into clinical practice has enabled the knowledge that people had when it came to the complex biology of tumor initiation and progression. There is also the next generation sequencing which is a platform that scientists and researchers use to show the pattern of those people who are suffering from cancer. It is through this method that enables the cancer patients to get the kind of treatment that they require according to who the type of cancer responds in their bodies. The NGS assists as it plays a big part in curing illness but in its implementations, it faces a lot of problems that may cause it to be disadvantageous (Blossey, 2006).

Through using NGS, a lot of data is found and this has made the researchers find a lot of set of variations of the genomes. This has helped to discover other types of diseases that are harmful. With this, it means that there is a high need for using computational algorithms to be able to understand the data that is provided. Several computational tools have been incorporated to understand the data that is found and to integrate the data with genomic sequence and the data that is found in biochemical.

The use and AI are that ensure a big potential in the health sector. It can be used in finding drugs that can cure illnesses or analyzing data. the computers that are currently introduced and education using the machines can see into the data on genes.

With the evolution of computers, the modern computers that were invented could explore and see into the data that offer information about precision drugs. The main reason for using AI in carrying out analysis for data that is associated with genetic materials is to reduce workload since there are a large number of human genome projects. In the past few years the use of AI to make precision way faster in finding the type of drug that is needed to raise the performance rate of the research programs that are normally held concerning medicinal stuff. This has therefore caused a large increase in activities in the areas. In the recent years, the education and gaining of information that is related to the field of biomedical is way easier since a researcher has the access of a lot of data that concerns his course and therefore this is as a result of extended techniques which have a lot of information on the different genes that are present. With this, many other precision drugs are used for the treatment of cancer (Blossey, 2006).

The patients' needs can be catered by identifying the right drug this is because the primary intelligence does make use of the genetic profile for each and every patient. Besides, the key information can be refined by the AI system in a short period. in this context, our motive is to talk about the integration of recent biological and computers like methods to come up with a more effective solution or treatment. This will enable the making of a precision drug for an identification platform using the application of AI hence it is very beneficial.

Other applications of computational biology include they are used in laboratories and industries to carry out research. There are very many other types of applications which require and use the knowledge on computational biology and therefore computational biology is an important factor in very many fields as discovered and discussed by various scientists and researchers in the world (Blossey, 2006).

8.3.2. Computational Biology Algorithms

Computational biology algorithms are those complex calculations which are used in computational biology that enable a computational biologist to understand more and to carry out his experiments in a more simplified way that is more understandable and way easier.

8.3.3. Global Matching (SGM)

Semi-global matching (SGM) is a type of a computer vision algorithm that is used to calculate the approximate estimation from a stereo image pair which is rectified. Due to its predictable run time, its trade-off which is favorable between the quality of the results and the time taken to be computed and its availability for very quick parallel application in a field-programmable gate array, it has developed a wide adoption in actual time stereo vision appliance such as mechanics robotics and advanced driver assistance system. Therefore, computational biology is important in global matching.

8.3.4. Local Sequence Alignment

Local sequence alignment is another type of a computational biology algorithm which is majorly used in bioinformatics that enables the scientists to be able to arrange the DNA, RNA, or protein sequences so that they can find an area or region that is of similar characteristics and their functions may cause a resulting consequence. The consequence that can be caused can either be a consequence of a function or a consequence of the structure of the consequence of how the relationship evolves. How the sequences are arranged in the form of a nucleotide or an amino acid residue are normally shown in the form of rows which are located in the matric. Still, within the matrix, several gaps are put in between the residues to ensure that characters that have the same characteristics are identical put themselves in the same columns that are following each other. Sequence alignment is not only used in biological sequences but they are also used in the noon biological ones to perform the key function of calculating the distance cost that is found when the distance between two strings is calculated in a natural language or the financial data language (Blossey, 2006).

8.3.5. Hidden Markov Models

Hidden Markov Model (HMM) is a model which was invented by a scientist who was known as Markov and this model was mainly statistical meaning it was used for the recording of data and keeping of statistics. It is another type of computational biology algorithm and it was a model that was created and taken as a Markov process with the hidden states. It was therefore referred to as the HMM and was shown as the easiest dynamic Bayesian network. The type of math that was used in the creation of HMMs was one that a scientist known as L. E. Baum came up within association with his fellow workers who helped him in the process. HMM has a very close relation to the work that was being carried out previously concerning optimal nonlinear filtering condition that was done by a scientist who was known as Ruslan L. Stratonovich who was among the first scientists to discover and tell more about the forward-backwards reaction (Figure 8.5).

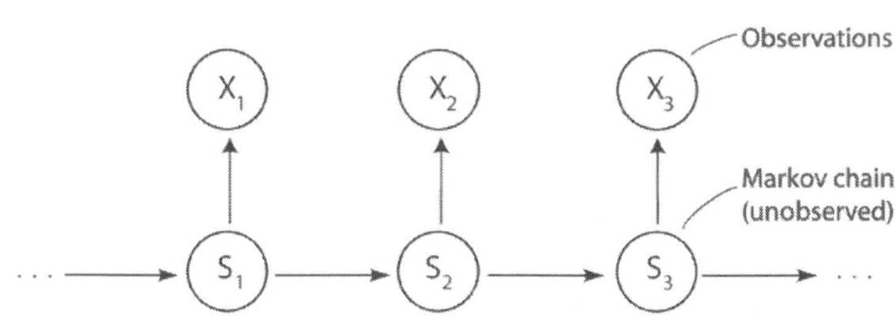

Figure 8.5. Hidden Markov model.

Source: *https://www.researchgate.net/figure/Basic-structure-of-a-Hidden-Markov-Model_fig2_24115579 (accessed on 3 April 2020)*

It is more easily understood that the Markov models, for example, the

Markov chain is applied and seen directly by the individual carrying out the analysis and hence it is observed that the changing state possibilities which are seen as mare parameters whereas the HMM the state cannot be viewed directly but it should be noted that the what comes out as the result is normally one that does depend on the state and it can be seen directly. The output is normally in the form of data or token. Every state is normally.

Every state has a probability distribution over the possible output tokens. Hence, the order of tokens generated by hmm gives more information about the order of states; this is also called pattern theory, a grammar induction topic. Hidden which is an adjective means the state order in which the model goes through, not to the parameters of the model; and the model is still known as a HMM even if the parameters are exactly known (Blossey, 2006).

The models of Hidden Markov are popular because they are used to make learning easier and for temporal pattern recognition. By temporal pattern recognition, it is expressed in speech, how one writes, recognizing the facial movements of a person, part of speech and tagging. On the other hand, the musical score follows discharges that are not complete and bioinformatics.

An HMM is normally seen as normally as a mixture model where it possesses variables that are hidden. By variables that are hidden, it means latent variables. These hidden or latent variables which possess the lead of the mixture component that is chosen to take part in the visual observation and they, therefore, have a close relationship to the Markov process rather than standing and working on its own. In recent years, HMM has been put together as pairs between the Markov models and triplet Markov models which enable complicated data structures to be taken into consideration and the modeling of nonstationary data. Therefore, HMM is just a type of computational biology algorithm which was invented by the great scientist Markov and was taken as Markov process with the states which were hidden and this brought about to its name being HMM which was shown as the simplest dynamic Bayesian networks. It is also noted that the kind of mathematics that was used in the making of the HMM was a great invention of a scientist who went by the name L. E and he did not do this alone but with the help of other great scientists.

The HMM is therefore used as an algorithm in making the computational biology complete in association with the other algorithms and therefore it is a key part and should not be ignored. By studying this, we notice that algorithms are important for the formation of computational biology and by this, we can get to see and understand the relationship between algorithms and computational biology. There are other computational biology algorithms which include the population genetics, evolution tress, gene regulation networks, and chemical equations. These are discussed further to get a better understanding of computational biology algorithms (Blossey, 2006).

8.3.6. Population Genetics

The population is the number of people living in a particular place for a particular period. This, therefore, means that population genetics is the genes of people living in a particular place at a certain given time. Population genetics is the intensive study on how genes vary in a population and factors that concern the evolution of how these genes change with time to explain this variation. It was discovered and laid down by Hardy-Weinberg law which is kept as population size is big and there is mating between the populations at several occasions and there is mutation selection and therefore the population does not go out of where they live to live in another new environment. In case this is not possible, the allele frequencies and the frequencies of the genotype can vary between different generations such that the previous generation does not have the same allele and genotype as the current population. The variations that occur due to ethnicity in the frequencies of the alleles are seen in the whole genome and finding this genetic diversity, patterns that evolve and can be tagged and variations that lead to illnesses can be found. This will, therefore, lead to international initiatives and a lot of databases that are in depth that shows many variations of a gene that are present (Blossey, 2006) (Figure 8.6).

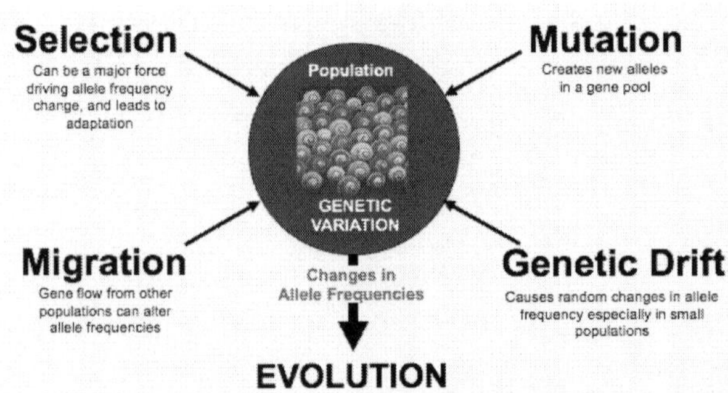

Figure 8.6. Population genetics.

Source: https://www.easynotecards.com/print_list/95021 (accessed on 3 April 2020).

By using population genetics to how genes diverse to try and show how the allele changes with time and the genotype frequencies. The genetic studies or the study of the genes aim to show how alleles are associated with the probability of an illness occurring and how it affects the sector of medicine and how it also affects how the population is affected by the illness. Genes and alleles frequency only occur when there is mating models, the size of the people living in a particular place at a certain time and distribution, the changing in the structure of the genes with time and the shifting of people from one area to another and therefore these frequencies depend on this factors. When we assume that the factors which are stated in Hardy Weinberg law as an important principle of genes in a given number of people living in an area it shows the model for finding the frequencies of the alleles and random mating population in an area at a given time.

8.4. JOBS OF A COMPUTATIONAL BIOLOGIST

A Computational Biologist can perform a lot of functions and has a lot of work that he can do. The jobs that an individual who has studied computational biology can perform include the following jobs; Computational biologist algorithm, computational biologist, data scientist, a computational biologist and bacterial genetic, computational biology image analyst, computational biologist microscopy and computational biology lecturer. These careers are performed well by individuals who have the knowledge of computational biology and they all require specific skills that they can acquire easily when they study computational biology as a course in their school life.

Computational biology algorithm is an individual who knows computational biology such that they can understand the algorithms that are associated with computational biology. Algorithms are complex calculations that are used by computational biologists to find and understand more about the gene and allele variations between groups of people living in a specific place in a certain given period. Computational biologist algorithm as a career is an individual who performs the work of researching and discovering the algorithms that are needed to carry out the computational biology and they came out with the required results eventually in the end (Blossey, 2006).

The computational biologist is also another individual who has the skills of computational biology is required. Just as the name states, a computational biologist has the work of understanding all the computational biology progresses such that they can interpret the data that is collected. The computational biologists use the idea of algorithms which are formed to come up with an appropriate interpretation of their data and information.

They can use the computers to explain more about the variations of the alleles and genes in a given population and they, therefore, are skilled in this sector.

Computational biologist's data analyst is another job that a computational biologist can undertake in the course of his work time. Just as the name states, a computational biologist data analyst is an individual who is skilled in the way they can interpret a large amount of data that is found from the research and findings of the computational biologist. Computational biology work involves a lot of activities and from this, a lot of data is normally collected and from this data, it may be complex and complicated such that it may prove hard to interpret but when an individual who is skilled in interpreting the data that is acquired is found, then the work will be way easier and they can also work as a team in ensuring that the results come out as desired (Blossey, 2006).

Computational biologist and bacterial genetic is another job that a computational biologist can perform. Computational biologist and bacterial genetic is an individual who is not only skilled in the sector of computational biologist but they are also skilled with the skills to identify the genes of bacteria and interpret data that they acquire from it. There is a relation between computational biology and bacterial genetic because both of them deal with the evolution of genes and therefore these two can be combined to come up with one major job sector and therefore they can save more by just employing one individual to perform both jobs instead of employing different individuals. Most individuals are therefore advised to study both computational biology and bacterial genetic so that they can be able to find a wide market once they begin working since the individuals who studied both are more advantaged to get a job than one who studied computational biology only.

Computational biology image analyst is another job in the computational biology job sector. It is characterized by individuals who have the skill on computational biology meaning that they studied computational biology yet they can still interpret and analyze an image when it appears. Computational biology image analysts are important individuals in computational biology since they interpret the images of the genes and they assist the computational biologists to understand the images and to interpret the data that they acquire from their research. Computational image analysts, therefore, work hand in hand with the computational biologists in the course of their career.

Computational biologists lecturer is an individual who teaches students who have taken up the course of computational biology. Computational biologist lecturer is also another job in the computational biology sector as the individuals who lecture students have the skill in computational biology. A computational biology lecturer, therefore, has a lot of knowledge on computational biology that they need to pass them to the students so that their students can also be a perfect in computational biology as they are. Most computational biology lecturers receive a large amount of pay just like all other carriers in the computational biology job sector (Blossey, 2006).

8.4.1. Skills Needed by Computational Biologists

The skills that are needed by computational biologists to perform their work in the most effective way possible include the following skills that range from programming and software skills, bioinformatics tools skills, bioinformatics resource and database skills, sub domain software skills, understanding the basics of life science skills to soft skills which include the flexibility, patience, communication, and teamwork. These skills are key skills to every computational biologist and they are needed to be understood more so that they can be interpreted in the best way possible. The following are some of the skills discussed further below.

Programming and software skills are some of the skills that are needed by a computational biologist to perform his work. Programming is an important skill since it enables the computational biologists to come up with new software that is needed for their workflow in computational biology. The skills that the computational biologist needs in programming states that the computational biologists must know the programming languages and they apply them in coming up within the software and therefore their work is more interesting and more easy to operate than it was before (Singh, 2014).

Understanding the basis of life science is also another skill that computational biologists require because computational biology deals in organisms that are living and these organisms fall in the sector of life sciences. This, therefore, means that in the course of computational biology there is also a unit that deals in life sciences. By understanding the life sciences, it enables the computational biologists to face an easier time in discovering the genes and studying the variations of these genes and how they are related to each other. They can also study the variations of the alleles that are found in living organisms and they can study their variations.

Flexibility is another major and key skill that computational biologists need because their work and study comes across a lot of variations and therefore an individual who lacks flexibility may fail to perform the work as desired and they are therefore not suitable for this course and job. Flexibility is also needed when the individuals have to go to a different environment and learn from there about a whole different population. If the individuals are not able to fit in into this environment, they will have caused a large disappointment since they will not be flexible enough to fit into the new environment and perform their duties just they will (Singh, 2014).

Patience is another skill that is required by computational biologists. Patience is the ability of an individual to wait for something without complaining or to wait. Most of the computational biologists lack patience when they are carrying out their research as they expect the results to reveal themselves as fast as possible as soon as they begin their projects but they end up giving up before the results come out. The computational biologists need to understand that computational biology is not an easy process and therefore it needs a lot of time to reveal and before the results can come out. They are therefore advised to take time to understand and wait for the results patiently.

Communication is another skill that is required in computational biology since communication is key for the passing of information to the other computational biologists. Communication is the passing of information from one individual to another in a way that is not distorted and in a way that will be interpreted most appropriately without distortion. Computational biologists, therefore, need to have the skill of communication so that they can tell the other individuals what they found in their study and research and through this, the other individuals can carry out further research.

Lately is the skill of teamwork which is the ability of computational biologists to work together without any quarrels or fights between the individuals such that the can operate more effectively and they can give out information in a friendly and nice way. The advantage of teamwork is that all the individuals can perform their work in a nice way and to the best of their ability but when, there is no teamwork in an organization then the individuals will perform their duties with a lot of hate and disagreements which can lead to the fall of the organization (Singh, 2014).

Chapter 9

Computational Astrophysics

CONTENTS

9.1. INTRODUCTION

Computational astrophysics refers to the application of numerical systems to solve research issues in astrophysics from a computer. Numerical techniques are applied whenever the arithmetical model defining an astrophysical structure is too complicated to solve manually. Nowadays, it's hard to find good examples of research projects that don't apply computation (Figure 9.1).

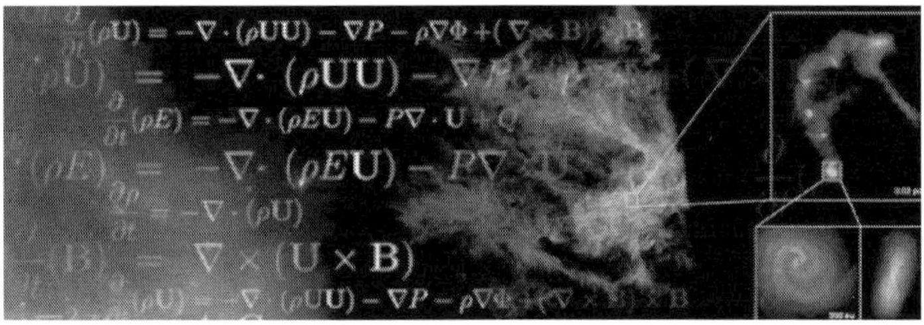

Figure 9.1. Computational astrophysics explains various elements of the universe through numerical equations.

Source: *https://starplan.dk/about/research/astrophysics (accessed on 4 April 2020).*

This field has come quite a long way coming from the initial days when astronomers started to use support instruments for their calculations. There have been key advances in this sector, mostly embracing the relatively fresh models of multi-scale and multi-physics models, apart from introducing the Python coding system that is essential to computing.

The sector of computational astrophysics unlocks new windows in how we understand and research the heavens. This swiftly growing new field of astronomy merges modern computational systems, novel firmware design, progressive algorithms for both prototypes and data analysis, including original software applications and related technologies to discover fresh phenomena, and making projections in cosmology, astronomy as well as planetary sciences.

Moreover, the combination of Computational Astrophysics together with Cosmology inspires a wide variety of topics which, coming from an astronomical viewpoint cover different scales and a wide collection of statistics, physics as well as chemistry.

As for computing, it can be understood in the broader sense and may comprise of hardware, algorithms, application, networking, compression, and managing of big data coming from massive telescopes and surveys, molding, simulation, conception, high-capacity computing, complex data computing, and even machine (ML) learning (Koberlein and Meisel, 2013).

Additionally, computational astrophysics fills the gap existing between observation and hypothesis. The enhanced quality of observations plus the need for profound understanding of the fundamental physics has drove demand for greater resolution and improved physical realism in arithmetic simulations. With quickly growing firmware performance, it's estimated that the significance of large-scale simulations shall only grow going forward; therefore, software systems must also develop to keep ahead with computational astrophysics observations and theory.

9.2. BRIEF HISTORY OF ASTROPHYSICAL SIMULATIONS

The first ever records of theoretic astronomy have been traced back to ancient Egypt, in particular the 18th recorded dynasty (1550–1292 BC) where Pharaoh Hatshepsut's kingdom architect, Senmut, came up with the first theories explaining this concept.

His calculations later allowed astronomers to identify structure and define patterns in heavenly bodies, a phenomenal of astronomy which is still applicable today. Present day astronomy; nevertheless, began with the invention of the original refracting telescope, developed by Hans Lippershey during the year 1608, and with a collecting scope of roughly 1 cm2.

A year later Galileo Galilei recorded the first astronomical implementation in 1609, applying a telescope of same design. Around 400 years following that momentous original implementation of the new technology, collection zones of the biggest research telescopes today have risen by a ratio of roughly 106, therefore becoming among the most popular 10-m group of telescopes widely used today.

Digital workstations were first introduced during the late 30s and have helped a lot in enhancing computational astrophysics. By 1945, the first popular programmable model, known as ENIAC, accomplished a computational speed similar to around 200 modern float points (double precision) processing per second (flops).

Nowadays, the quickest supercomputers reach speeds above 1017 flops, which is an improvement to the factor of nearly 1015 in sheer performance in only a matter of seven decades. Therefore, while observation technology has grown significantly—though relatively slowly—throughout the last four centuries, scientists have observed a major technological breakthrough in living memory (Irwin, 2007).

Continuing revolution in the accessibility of digital processors has triggered a totally new aspect of research, where key astronomy facilities aren't limited to the mountain tops of Hawaii or Chilean Andes. Even from the home, computers are able to record, process, analyze, and retrieve the large quantities of data obtained from observing campaigns. Nevertheless, arguably the largest impact on how astronomers pursue their research questions has been achieved through numerical recreations of astrophysical content.

Some scholars believe computational astrophysics dates back to the mathematical estimations of the movement of the moon or planets, so as to calculate ephemerides for tidal shifts and navigation. Originally, the word computer meant an individual hired to calculate certain amounts or levels of arithmetical accuracy.

When electronic virtual computers were introduced following World War II, for breaking encryption programs as well as compute artillery assortment tables, nevertheless, they were rapidly adopted to other reasons following the end of this war. For astrophysics, this also included preparing the original stellar structure systems in the 50s, including development of mathematical approaches for liquid flow and shock-catchment at roughly the same period (Irwin, 2007).

Significant improvements through the years that followed consisted of the application of transistor systems, rather than vacuum tubes, developing of compiled languages, implementation of IEEE principles for the illustration of float point integers and arithmetic (formerly manufacturers used their individual pattern for bits) in addition to the creation of massive integrated circuits, which permit for complexity of processing design which is experienced today.

New trends in computers are leading towards dispersed memory parallel processors, through different cores which are capable of vector handling. Similarly, as developments in hardware improve, advancements in numerical analysis, computing, and application engineering have prompted consistent procedures for inter-process contact across networks, item-orientated languages like Fortran95 and C++, inferred languages like Java and Python, imagining tools like OpenGL, and application engineering tools like Subversion (SVN) and CVS.

Additionally, astronomical research naturally lends itself to computation since it's characterized by massive ratios in temporal as well as spatial scales, including complex and mutual nonlinear processes, plus the extreme circumstances present in interstellar space.

Following the emergence of digital computers, soon it became possible for researchers to study systems in inter-galactic vacuum, hot plasmas within stellar surfaces, multi-year timescale procedures, and the physics of black-hole, all which can't be studied through Earth-based laboratories. Modern restrictions to studying the universe through computation rests in software, especially with regards to the limited comprehension of algorithms which can calculate multiscale, Multiphysics challenge (Irwin, 2007).

9.3. THE ORIGINAL SIMULATION EXPERIMENTS

Among the first astrophysical models was conducted in 1941 with the assistance Erik Holmberg, a scholar at Lund University with access to various photocells. Going by the fact this amount of radiation falls off as the reverse square of a distance, such as gravity, which he invented an experiment for simulating two merging galaxies. The advancement of computational astrophysics has been quick and progressive. Holmberg's experiment made him one of the founding members of what currently is a large amount of astronomical investigations in gravitational theories.

During his time, Holmberg didn't have any access to computers; therefore most of his calculations were done through hand. The scientific article he wrote in 1941 has also become interesting in various respects, though unclear on precisely how the elements (such as, photon counts) were applied to improve the location of particles (light bulbs) (Irwin, 2007).

9.4. INCENTIVE FOR A HOMOGENEOUS APPLICATION SETTING

Creating high-quality model software is reasonably straightforward when the tangible scope of the issue is restricted. The task becomes significantly more difficult when the application scope covers multiple physical fields, or in case the dynamic scope in temporal or dimensional scales surpasses the accuracy of the firmware.

Effective examples of composite multi-physics applications in computational astrophysics include NBODY7, FLASH, and GADGET, which all have wide user bases plus can be used to solve various issues.

A few of these codes discuss relatively narrow scopes of physics plus are restricted by the particular numerical algorithms used to solve the fundamental equations, though others, such as FLASH, are vastly modular in their interior organization—in a few ways the same as AMUSE.

In a standard temporal and spatial scale measuring astronomical phenomena, colors showcase physical domains: such as gravity (blue), hydrodynamics (yellow),), stellar evolution (red), as well as radiative procedures (green). Different domains are identified through name, like the folding of a massive molecular cloud (yellow circle), plus a variety of livable planetary orbits (blue circle).

Besides, gravity, and hydrodynamics extend a broad variety of temporal as well as spatial scales, while radiative procedures and stellar evolution display much narrower scopes. Remember that both spatial as well as temporal scales extend through a range of roughly 14 magnitude orders, ranging from galactic circuits at one point to stellar unions or complex orbital forces on the other.

Different existing simulation codes offer quality solvers within their particular physical domains, though astrophysical issues often need solvers for a vast range of domains. Case in point, comprehending the expulsion of primordial gas coming from an implanted star cluster coming from a galaxy merger needs simultaneous handling of collisional stellar forces (protostellar cluster), no collision stellar dynamics (galaxy union), hydrodynamics (intergalactic gas), stellar development (entrenched protostars and stars), plus radiative procedures (observations between stars and intergalactic gas). These procedures happen on equivalent temporal and spatial measurements (Irwin, 2007).

Rather than developing new algorithms for solving all of these issues simultaneously, there's need to endorse the philosophy that every physical domain may be solved individually, then merged into a reliable solution at distinct intervals in duration and space.

Moreover, validation of this simulation may be consequently achieved through re-computing the model using a unique solver for every physical domain. Through this, it's possible to study the merger (or absence, thus) of the resolution with a series of mathematical implementations.

Besides, the Astrophysical Multipurpose Application Environment allows the user to merge existing solvers to create new applications which may then be remerged to study progressively complex problems. It allows for the development of multi-physics and multi-scale program software in a tiered fashion, plus allows for testing of every intermediate stage as the sophistication of the software increases.Computational astrophysics has a hierarchical element architecture which covers dynamically mutual libraries for mimicking stellar evolution, gravity dynamics, (magneto) hydrodynamics, as well as radiative procedures; it also has some support for astrochemistry. The applications are capable of using a few or all of the resources concurrently, plus can exchange information in a special and deterministic method. Through this hybrid simulation setting, it's possible to review multiphysics procedures operating on a wide variety of scope and timescales (Irwin, 2007).

9.5. COMPUTATIONAL ASTROPHYSICS AND PROGRAMMING LANGUAGES

Scientists have largely adopted Python as the application language for the subject's framework and top-level management features, as well as bindings for the networking interface. The choice is motivated through Python's flexibility, wide acceptance in the research community, product-oriented design, and capacity to allow quick prototyping, which reduces the software development sequence and allows for simple access to the communal code in the open module (though at the cost of marginally reduced performance) (Figure 9.2).

Figure 9.2. An astrophysicist examining data in a laboratory for computation.

Source: https://physicalsciences.uchicago.edu/academics/academic-departments/ (accessed on 4 April 2020).

Nevertheless, the whole computational astrophysics setting is structured so that fairly marginal computer time is actually spent within the framework itself-majority of the time is spent for the community code. Plus, the overhead arising from Python in comparison to the compiled top-level language is mostly 10%, though sometimes much less.

The application of the communication level in computational astrophysics uses the basic Message Passing Interface (MPI) program. Typically, MPI, and SmartSockets get used for communication purposes between computing nodes on equivalent distributed-memory structures, or inside computational grids. For computational systems, nevertheless, they are applied as communication networks between different processes, no matter whether or not these are found on one node as the regulation script, or run parallel (Oberlein and Meisel, 2013).

Community codes are scripted in different languages, showing the programming backgrounds as well as preferences of the authors. Consequently, there are pair of interface functions that determine each community code. Additionally, the interface of community programming is known as the partner, plus is scripted in the native script of that code. These interfaces network through one of the text-passing protocols available.

However, the key restriction on secured languages is the need that the community encryption is scripted in a language through MPI and Smart Sockets bindings, like C, C++, Java, and elements from the FORTRAN system. It's emphasized that, right from the operator perspective, the particulars of the interface plus communication protocols remain invisible. These particulars are necessary for computational astrophysics design; however, many top-level users are quite unaware of them. For the user, Python code script resembles a conventional serial program.

9.5.1. Vocabulary

The basic system of the computational astrophysics framework can be subdivided into 3 general components. In illustrations, the top phase is (red and orange) and is mainly user-scripted, the middle level (blue) applies the networks onto the community programs, and the lowest layer (cyan) comprises of the community components and the real community source code, that's linked to the other parts of the framework through the sockets or MPI. Some main components are defined as follows:

1. ***Python User Script***: It addresses a particular physical issue or group of problems, which is in form of a system-based or user-

scripted Python commands which act as the user-interface for the framework. It's the only aspect of production scripting that must be input by the operator. The connection between community codes mainly is applied in this layer, through the assistance of support classes meant for transforming units and information structures availed by computational astrophysics models.

2. ***The Community Module***: This layer consists of three key elements which are:

- *The Manager (Orange):* It provides an item-oriented interface covering the communication layer through a protocol of system-oriented utility features. This layer covers unit conversion. Plus it comprises of the state engine including the related data repository, both of which are needed to guarantee reliability of data across different modules. The layer is generic—meaning it's not definite to any particular issue or physical domain.
- *Communication Layer (Blue):* It recognizes the bi-directional communication between a manager and communal code layer. The same is implemented through a proxy system and a related partner, which mutually provide the link to every community code.
- *Community-Code Layer (Cyan):* It comprises of vital community codes and tools control and data managing operations on them. Every part of the code in this level is domain-based, although the program may be developed to be rather general in its specific physical domain.

Many astrophysicists apply computers in their daily work, plus an increasing amount of astrophysics systems now have research departments specially meant for computational astrophysics. Key research bodies are the U.S. Energy Department which has research initiatives for astrophysics, including the now decommissioned European AstroSim collaboration. Another notable active program is the global Virgo Consortium, focusing on cosmology.Moreover, in August 2015, during the conference of Global Astronomical Union, a fresh commission C.B1 focusing on Computational Astrophysics got launched, therewith identifying the significance of astronomical discovery through computation.Some significant techniques for computational astrophysics are particle-in-cell (PIC), including the associated particle-mesh (PM), N-system simulations, Monte Carlo techniques, and grid-free (through smoothed particle hydro-dynamics (SPH) acting a significant example) plus grid-based techniques for fluids.

Additionally, procedures from mathematical analysis for resolving ODEs and PDEs equally are used. The simulation of astrophysical patterns is of particular significance since many objects and procedures of astronomical interest like stars and nebulae include gases. Fluid computer systems are usually joined with radiative transfer, including (Newton) gravity, nuclear physics as well as (general) relativity for studying highly energetic matter like supernovae, active galaxies, relativistic jets, plus gamma-ray bursts plus are also applied to develop stellar structures, planetary development, star evolution and even galaxies, plus exotic objects like pulsars, magnetars, neutron stars and black-holes (Koberlein and Meisel, 2013).

Besides, computer simulations are typically the only method for studying stellar collisions, galaxy unions, and galactic and black-hole mergers. Recently, the sector has been making more use of parallel as well as high processing computers. Plus, computational astrophysics being a scientific field makes wide use of firmware and software technologies. The systems are often vastly specialized and developed by dedicated experts; therefore generally find partial popularity in the broader (computational) physics society.

9.5.2. Hardware

Same as other sectors, computational astrophysics utilizes super-computers and processor clusters. Up to the scope of a regular desktop, it's possible to fast-track the hardware. Possibly, the most notable of these computer architecture made particularly for astrophysics is GRAPE or (gravity pipe) from Japan. By 2010, the largest N-body simulations, like DEGIMA, could perform all-purpose computing on photo processing units.

Various codes and software systems exist alongside different researchers and consortia that preserve them. Many codes seem to work as fluid solvers or n-body bundles of some kind. Some common examples of n-body encryptions are ChaNGa, Starlab, MODEST, and nbodylab.org.

As for hydrodynamics, there's usually some coupling between the codes, since the fluid motion typically has some different effect (like gravity, or radiation) as it applies to astrophysical situations. Case in point, for SPH/N-body there's GADGET and SWIFT, and grid-style/N-body RAMSES. There are also systems that provide an interface structure for large amounts of publicly accessible astronomical codes applicable in addressing stellar dynamics, cosmic evolution, hydrodynamics, as well as radiative transport.

9.6. COMPUTATIONAL VS. ANALYTIC TECHNIQUES

Solutions produced through numerical approaches are usually just approximations to the precise solution of the fundamental equations. Nevertheless, much more complicated systems of equations may be solved mathematically than may be solved analytically.

Therefore, estimate solutions to the particular equations present in numerical methods typically provide way more insight, in comparison to specific solutions for approximating equations which can be solved mathematically. For instance, time-dependent arithmetical solutions of liquid flow in 3D can display behavior that's not expected from a single-dimension analytic service to the solid-state (time based) equations.

Improvement in computing power within the past few decades has led to a progressively greater share of issues in astrophysics which can be solved from a desktop computer. Nevertheless, the most computationally demanding problems in astrophysics continue to be limited by memory as well as floating-point tempo of the biggest high-performing computer (HPC) systems accessible. Besides, the use of HPC becomes necessary in maximizing the spatial, temporal, and frequency range of solutions, to cover more physics, or even when big parameter surveys are needed for understanding the statistics (Koberlein and Meisel, 2013).

Conventionally, the most significant applications of computational astrophysics have covered the fields and are discussed in subsections.

9.6.1. Stellar Structure and Evolution

The inner configuration and development of stars with varying masses and chemical structure was originally determined during the 60s utilizing numerical techniques to resolve the calculations of stellar structure. Nowadays, the frontlines of research comprise of calculating multi-dimensional stellar systems of quickly rotating stars, molding the effects of hydro-dynamical procedures like convection from original principles, apart from understanding how stars produce magnetic fields via dynamo processes (Figure 9.3).

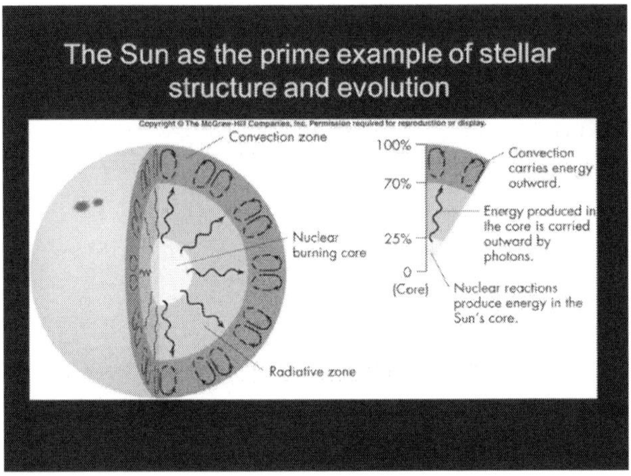

Figure 9.3. Stellar evolution studies the birth and development of stars from a computational astrophysics perspective.

Source: *https://slideplayer.com/slide/8711865/ (accessed on 4 April 2020).*

Most stars, in their different evolutionary stages, right from conception to super-compact remnants following an energetic explosion, comprise very wide aspect in astrophysics. Besides, their understanding is vital for most other sectors of astrophysical research, since stars are a main source of data from nearby and distant parts of the cosmos (Koberlein and Meisel, 2013).

The physics defining their structure, evolution, plus final fate covers all aspects of physics including; fluid dynamics, thermodynamic, particle physics, nuclear or atomic physics and general relativity, plus more needs to be performed. Scholars also work on many of these features theoretically, handling the astrophysical issues almost exclusively with mathematical programs and define computational procedures. The complexity of most of these issues needs the use of powerful computers at the technical forefront. Presently, studies on stellar items at research units can be subdivided roughly into cosmic evolution of individual stars, binary structures and accretion disks, compact remnants and supernova explosions.

9.6.2. Structure and Development of Single Stars

The context of stellar physics involves the hydrostatic progression of single stars. This can be investigated through a highly developed arithmetical code (known as GARSTEC, or Garching Star Evolution Code), developed in the 60s but since underwent continuous development and updated regularly.

The code may be used on stars of different masses and original chemical composition, though is also adequately suited for very precise calculations of the solar inner parts, and for reasons of astero-seismology. The primary emphasis rests on the structure as well as evolution of small and middle-size mass stars. The first option is present mostly in cosmic halo plus in globular clusters, apart from serving as watchers of the galactic-chemical evolution, midsize stars are also a significant nucleosynthesis platform.

Even though the code is a conventional hydrostatic single-dimensional one, still investigations are being done on stellar structures, which need a dynamical technique, with both 2-and 3D hydro-codes. These problems comprise of key convections in large and developed stars, covering convection within in the Sun as well as red giants, atomic flashes, and revolution in stars (Koberlein and Meisel, 2013).

The goal is extracting essential properties of these effects and including them in an accurate method within the 1-d protocol, which remains to be the only means of following stars through their whole lifetime.

1. ***Binary Stellar Systems and Accretion Disks*:** The makeup and development of stars reveals extra features in binary star systems. In case two stars get so adjacent that they affect one another through gravitational effect, then radiation and matter may overflow the physical procedures brought about by the interactions because various interesting phenomena present in the observations.

Besides, this evolution causes binaries with a dense star, which may either be a white dwarf like in cataclysmic variables, AM Herculis stars, novae, or even neutron stars and a black-hole like in the transitory X-ray-binaries.

Additionally, the 'living' catalogue developed by Ritter and Kolb mentions data for cataclysmic ratios, minimal-mass X-ray binaries as well as other related objects, including more than 2000 items with recognized or suspect orbital phases. Accretion disks are equally important for short-term and long-term evolution of binaries, they are developed around the dense star to the greater angular motion of matter abundant and coming from the nearby companion star (Koberlein and Meisel, 2013).

The heat-viscous instability of the accretion disk triggers cyclic disparities of luminosity, particularly the disparities in cataclysmic variables, plus various X-ray transients. Because of the fact accretion, physics processes are similar for stars, it can be applied for studying supermassive black-holes, instabilities, and development of accretion disks, and can also be applied to understanding Active galactic nuclei through the cataclysmic variables acting as a laboratory.

Additionally, during the end of stars' life cycles, the event is typically marked by cataclysmic processes: powerful explosions which disturb the fading star and eject most of the star's material. Because of the massive energy release that accompanies these explosions, they may briefly become as bright as their own galaxies allowing people to observe them through vast distances (Koberlein and Meisel, 2013).

Computation astrophysics seeks to understand the nature of celestial and transient objects, looking at the problem in two angles: on one side, scientists characterize the detected properties and variety of objects through applying modern statistical tools, therefore deriving constraints for hypothetical explosion models.

Consequently, they may assume a forward-molding approach, beginning from explosion models then simulating the observation exhibition using radiative transference or radiation hydro-dynamical calculations. Presently, the main focus rests on thermonuclear supernovae (Type Ia), as well as hydrogen-rich supernovae explosion (Type IIP). These two classes are applied as cosmological distance meters, researching the universe's expansion history. The investigations assist with minimizing the systematic uncertainties that are inherent to these calculations (Koberlein and Meisel, 2013).

2. ***Radiation Transmission and Stellar Atmospheres*:** Without oversimplification of assumptions, usually computational techniques are needed to evaluate the transmission of light across the outer levels of the star, as well as its contact with matter via absorption, emission, as well as dispersal of photons. Generally, the calculation of multi-sections for the contact of light together with matter for the astrophysically appropriate ions is by itself a puzzling computational challenge.

The development of these stellar atmosphere structures shares different challenges together with radiation transfer issues in other systems like planets, interstellar mediums (ISM) and accretion-disks. Modern calculations can enhance the frequency resolution, cover a better treatment for opacities, plus treating for non-hydrostatic atmospheres.

Oftentimes, radiative transfer is necessary for getting information from the range of astrophysical bodies available for research. Computational astrophysics provides a greater understanding of the physical as well as mathematical context of radiative transfer, including its applications to both cosmic and planetary atmospheres. The field covers both the phenomenological and physics of early-form and late-form stars, and super-cool dwarf stars plus extrasolar planets (Irwin, 2007).

Notably, it presents a bridge between standard radiative transfer as well as stellar atmosphere molding and novel techniques, from both hypothetical and computational viewpoints. With emerging fields of application, including a drastic enhancement in both perceivable and computational amenities, it also covers the impending perspective for the field. Assuming turbulence exists in a celestial body, it means assumption of justification for the collision-less plasma, and one probable explanation covering the outflows means that magnetic re-connection is improved by the turbulence via anomalous resistivity.

Besides, atomic spectral lines may be broadened through different effects, such as radiation, Stark effect, opacity, and even Van-der Waals damping, even though the dominant expansion effect in coronal systems are because of thermal waves of the hot, planetary plasma. The Gaussian profile may reflect the field-of-sight velocity dispersal of a wholly Maxwellian ion population, though more often, this is measured in order to be wider than what may be qualified for thermal motions, depending on the highest ionization temperature (Irwin, 2007).

Additionally, stellar spectra offer the primary means for quantifying stellar constitution as well as stellar physics, really "the astronomer's valuable chest." The background of astronomical spectroscopy has been fairly brief, comprising of no more than two centuries, though it's quite rich. Astrophysicist William Wollaston became the first one to detect spectral lines, back in 1802. The scientist noticed some dark spaces in solar spectrum witnessed through a prism that's fed through a narrow split in the window-shade, apart from marking the gaps between various colors. They comprised of elements like Na (I) D lines.

Taking from Wollaston's ideas, Joseph Fraunhofer who is a glass-maker by profession, used the solar scale to test for quality and achro-maticity of various optical products he created. Fraunhofer also re-discovered the shadow lines in 1814. He describes that in a shuttered-room, he permitted sunlight to move through the narrow slits in the shutters. He wanted to determine whether for the color-image of sunrays, the same bright stripe could be seen, just like the color photo of lamplight.

However, instead of this he discovered with the telescope nearly countless solid and fragile vertical lines, which nevertheless are darker compared to the rest of the color-photo; some look to be almost wholly black and branded the darkest structure alphabetically (Irwin, 2007).

Nowadays, we still refer to spectral lines found in the stellar spectra as "Fraunhofer lines," using D for the Na I D, and H and K to mark Ca II H. Other lines available in the segment show that he noted 100s of other fainter lines also qualified for measuring wavelengths for lots of objects, applying a neutral diffraction grating consisting of parallel thin lines. The technology was also applicable for spectrometry and measurement of Sirius, Venus, and different star systems having an objective prism.

Through his research, William Herschel discovered that spectra cover measurable data concerning the source, plus tried to determine how and what it entailed from flame spectroscopy. The colors hence communicated through the various bases for flame afford, and in some cases, a complete and neat way for detecting rather small ratios of them.

Nevertheless, the flames always comprised of sodium-impurities and therefore created the yellowish Na (I) D lines; plus for years, the bright lines prevented spectroscopists from detecting other fainter lines being uniquely determined through other elements. Additionally, Brewster, and others believe that the sunlight colors were because of interference, regionally, from the three primary shades of yellow, red, and blue, therefore leaving no solid solar reason for lines (Irwin, 2007).

Additionally, Becquerel became successful in photographing the entire solar continuum in 1842, capturing multiple lines in the ultra-violet which can't be witnessed by plain eyes. Others have also followed the example. The quantitative solar spectroscopy became of age through Kirchhoff. He discovered first that luminous flame emission lines can be seen as the dark-lines against a light continuum background plus then, with Bunsen, who discovered that wavelength concurrence between bright flame outlines and dark solar contours imply that flame as well as sun share a common line-causing substance, no matter if it's emitting or absorbing.

Both Kirchhoff and Bunsen detailed flame as well as spark spectra for multiple elements. The tale goes that they further determined the quantity of sodium in fire produced by the Mannheim flame, witnessed from their Heidelberg lab window, plus that they, while deliberating that measurement-at-the-distance during a short walk the evening after, recognized that they demonstrated that spectral-line programming is dependent of distance plus thus allows quantitative inquiry of sources far much distant than Mannheim. Besides Kirchhoff then determined that iron, magnesium, calcium, chromium, and sodium-nickel are definitely present within the sun, plus cobalt, barium, zinc, and copper probably (Irwin, 2007).

Stellar spectroscopy persisted after Fraunhofer though at no greater pace until later when Father Secchi began a Jesuit observatory center in Rome. The scholar wrote a total 700 papers including two books (The Stars and Sun), all done in three decades, plus began spectral classification.

Furthermore, Pickering equipped a series of telescopes with minimal-dispersion objective prisms, gaining spectra of different bright stars within the field concurrently on one plate (on 5-minute exposure for even up to 6th magnitude stars per 10th-degree square field through the 8-inch Bache telescope). Henry Draper's niece Antonia Maury became the next in line to successfully use Pickering. She applied the technique to examine roughly 5000-plates of bright stars through much greater dispersion.

Maury developed a fresh classification model, covering 22 classes and 5 orthogonal divisions with line sharpness being among the deciding criteria. The Doppler broadening strategy had been recommended as a mechanism though wasn't yet widely accepted. The wider amount of classes was widely criticized, particularly from Potsdam. However, some a number of Maury's subsets now make lots of sense in hindsight, defining high luminosity star giants and super-giants which are sharp-lined because of small collisional expansion.

Another scientist, Miss Cannon, developed the O-B-A-F-G-K-M series with decimal sub-divisions which are still being used today. After participating in classifying around 5000 bright stars, the scientist began investigating the Henry Draper Directory, the subsequent system of Henry Draper Memorial, during the year 1911 and successfully finished classifying 225,300 stars in only four years.

While Miss Cannon indeed had assistants, she must have worked industriously. The researcher's lifetime work amounts to roughly 395,000 classifications. It's fascinating to know that this massive industry was firmly morphological. The classification process was believed to be evolutionary, thus the words early- and late-forming stars (Irwin, 2007).

Following Hertzsprung and Russell's plotting, still the nature of spectrum classification was uncertain. This puzzle was resolved following the pressure influence that was identified by Saha and Pannekoek, where they produced their equation for equilibria ionization, while Fowler and Milne effectively connected stellar shades with ionization variances. The issue was resolved during the year 1925 in a thesis written by Cecilia Payne, considered the first woman in history to get an astronomy PhD from Harvard that was later known as the "most brilliant PhD thesis in astronomy" according to Struve.

She demonstrated that stars for the most part share a similar composition, though display varying line strengths in comparison to Saha-Boltzmann sensitivities for temperature and mass. Stellar spectroscopy grew from basic morphology to astrophysics. Ultimately, quantitative spectrometry grew from the works by Russell and Adams to include others such as Pannekoek, Struve, Uns¨old, Minnaert, Menzel, Allen, and Charlotte Moore among others.

They built upon the pioneering efforts of their predecessors in gaining better comprehension about stellar line developments, apart from turning spectral lines into effective tools for stellar quantity determination. Computational astrophysics took off during the preliminary half of 20-th century; where the concepts of "equivalence width" of the spectral line plus the "growth curve" for measuring its reliance on the ratio of extinction were presented by Minnaert as well as his co-workers at Utrecht. Measuring the equivalence widths of spectrum lines became an industry on its own following these discoveries.

The benefit of Spectral line expansion Spectral lines mapping the line extinction system through a source feature, both height reliant, into the emerging spectrum. Now it's possible to specify the form of the curve extinction coefficient. There's massive literature available on stellar-line expansion. The key features are: regular broadening or "radioactive damping," because of reduced lifetimes of active states; impact broadening, because of collisions with or distresses by other particles (Angela and Shiflet, 2014).

In addition, Doppler broadening through non-thermal motions; typically split between micro-turbulence and macro-turbulence for balances that are minute or large in comparison to photons which mean free paths; rotating Doppler widening, of outlines in the flux scale of the non-resolved star; part-time frequency redistribution, the situation between the borders of clear scattering and full redistribution.

Furthermore, Radiation widening Spontaneous de-excitation restricts the lifetime of motivated states through a statistical distribution feature, and thus causes ambiguity in the power of any evolutions out of them depending on the uncertainty relation. The line broadening is known as natural broadening, or radioactive damping; "natural" here means that the line is widened even in the nonexistence of other elements and "damping" arrives from the classical definition of a spectral streak as an inhibited driven harmonic oscillator. For a dual-level atom, one transition has the command γrad = γrad (u = Aul 3.43) since the lower ratio of the dual-level atom contains an infinite lifetime, plus doesn't contribute in any way to existential uncertainty (Angela and Shiflet, 2014).

9.7. ASTROPHYSICAL FLUID DYNAMICS

Most of the dynamics that determine visible matter present in the universe may be considered to be a form of compressible fluid. Besides, time-reliant, and multidimensional solutions for fluid equations, plus the outcomes of magnetic, gravitational, and radiative fields, need numerical techniques. A wide range of issues are addressed through this way, ranging from convection to dynamo activity in cosmic and planetary interiors, and even development of galaxies plus the wide scale arrangement of the universe (Figure 9.4).

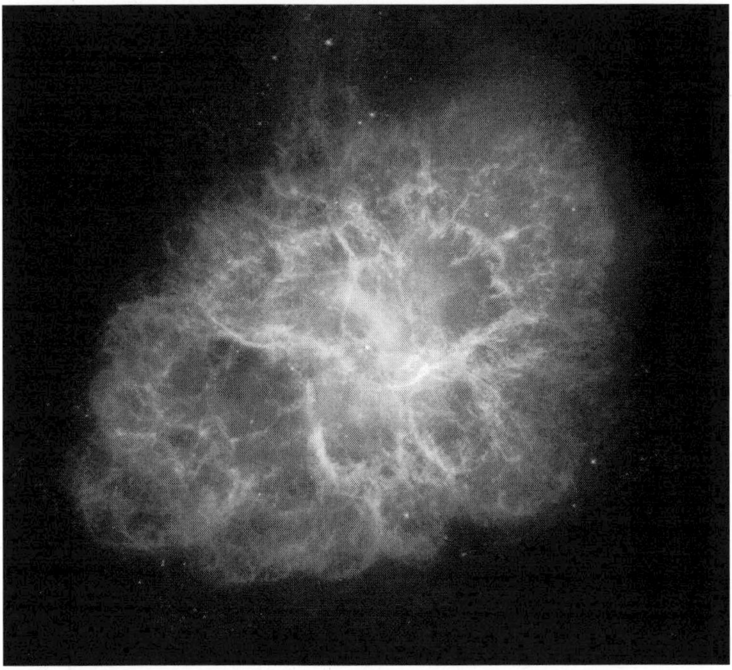

Figure 9.4. The fluid content of stellar objects can be measured through modern computation techniques.

Source: *https://staff.fnwi.uva.nl/o.j.g.porth/post.php?id=5 (accessed on 4 April 2020).*

The discipline of astrophysics fluid dynamics (AFD) can be defined as an emergent discipline that stems historically from the systems of stellar evolution, as well as space plasma physics. Among the fundamental physical suppositions behind AFD theory is that liquid equations of motion precisely define the progress of plasmas on balances, which are massive in comparison to particle contact length scales (Holder and Eichholz, 2019).

Specific attention is provided to wholly fluid prototypes of top-grade astrophysical plasmas. The function of computer modeling in AFD research has further been highlighted, plus a set of all-purpose application encryptions for AFD studies is discussed.

Codes are known as ZEUS-3D and ZEUS-2D, apart from solving the calculations of AFD in 3D or 2D, respectively, in various coordinate geometries for broad primary and boundary situations. The subjects of bipolar outflows coming from galactic super bubbles, super shells or protostars are also captured in computational astrophysics.

Furthermore, astrophysical fluid dynamics refers to a modern class of astronomy that involves fluid mechanics that deal with the movement of fluids, such as the gases consisting of the stars which consist of, or any fluid that's present in outer space. This discipline covers the basics of mechanics of liquids through different equations, varying from the continuity model to Euler's calculations of collisional liquids and so on.

This is a broad study of physical jurisdictions of astral bodies including their motions in space. A detailed understanding of this topic needs more knowledge of the general equations determining fluid mechanics. Many of the programs for calculating astrophysical liquid dynamics comprise of models of stellar bodies, accretion disks and Astrophysical jets, including the molten dynamics of galaxies (Holder and Eichholz, 2019).

9.7.1. Theory Concepts

Astrophysical fluid is completely different from what people usually study on earth, since all of this occurs in a vacuum having zero or low gravity. Majority of the Interstellar bodies aren't at rest, instead they operate in ultrasonic motion under the activity of supernova explosions, radiation fields and stellar winds, including the time-based gravitational field because of spiral density motions in the cosmic disc of galaxies. Considering that supersonic motions nearly always create shock waves, these have a crucial role to play. Galaxies also have a dynamically substantial magnetic field, meaning their dynamics is determined by the calculations of compact magneto-hydrodynamics.

For some situations, electrical conductivity becomes massive enough for the perfect magneto-hydrodynamics to be a decent approximation, though this isn't true in star formation regions in which the gas mass is high plus the amount of ionization remains to be low. Among the most fascinating processes involves star formation. It's understood that stars develop from the ISM, plus that this mainly happens in Large Molecular Clouds like the Rosette Nebula, for instance (Holder and Eichholz, 2019).

It's further been known that for some times the inter-stellar cloud may collapse upon its own gravity, in case the gravity is big enough, though in the regular ISM, it could only happen in case the cloud carries a mass of many thousand sun masses-way greater than the mass of any particular star.

As such, there should be a process which divides the cloud into much smaller and high capacity clouds, whereby the masses fall within the same category as the stars. Generally, self-gravity can't achieve this, though as it seems there are procedures which do this, just in case the magnetic pressure becomes way greater than thermal pressure, like in the case of Large Molecular Clouds. These procedures depend on the contact between magneto-hydrodynamic lines with a thermal variability.

The magneto-hydrodynamic wave within a medium where the magnetic force is much greater than the thermal force can generate dense regions, though they can't by themselves ensure the density is high enough in order for self-gravity systems to work. Nevertheless, the gas present in star forming areas is usually heated by intergalactic rays and is chilled by radiative activities.

The final result is that gases reaching a thermal equilibrium status, where heating balances cooling may exist in a total of three distinct phases with a similar pressure range: I) warm stage with a lowered density, II) the unstable level with intermediary density, and III) a cold stage at lowered temperature (Holder and Eichholz, 2019).

A rise in pressure, caused by a supernova or even spiral density wave may change the gas from a warmer phase into an unstable stage, plus the Magneto-hydrodynamic wave may then generate thicker fragments during the cold phase where self-gravity is powerful enough for the gases to collapse and form stars.

During this process, it's possible to study the science of interstellar gas and comprehend the development process of stars. It's just but one example where computational astrophysics applies.

9.7.2. Key Concepts of Fluid Astrophysics

The calculations of fluid dynamics form the basic tools that are necessary in creating a wider understanding of the aspects of Astrophysical Fluid Dynamics. Some of the fundamental equations and their respective applications are listed below:

1. ***Mass Conservation*:** The continuity equation uses the principle of mass conservation to fluid flow. Take, for instance, a fluid moving through a static volume tank with one inlet and outlet. In case the flow remains steady, meaning, there's no buildup of fluid inside the tank, it means the ratio of fluid flow within the entry should be same as the ratio of fluid movement at exit for density conservation. If, within the entry (or exit) featuring a cross-sectional zone A (m2), the fluid parcel moves a distance of dL in an amount of time dt, it means the total volume flow rate or (V, m3/s) would be: V is equals (A. dL)/Δt.

The theory for AFD, as it applies to supersonic Flow system, shall require users to consider the Compressible flow status whereby density isn't constant. The application for molten dynamics in astrophysics can be seen in Neutron stars, consisting of ancient star remnants which have gotten at the culmination of their evolutionary path, through time and space.

Some of these fascinating objects are birthed from once-massive stars that swelled to 4 to 8 times the scope of the sun before finally blasting in a shattering supernovae. When such an explosion throws out the star's outer cover into space, the interior remains—though it no longer does nuclear fusion. Having no outward force from fusion to offset gravity's inward push, the star shrinks and falls in on itself.

Regardless of tiny diameters—roughly 12.5 miles or (20 km)—neutron stars have almost 1.5 times the density of our sun, therefore they are considerably dense. Only a sugar-cube sized neutron star's material weighs around a hundred million tons when placed on Earth. Moreover, a neutron star's nearly incomprehensible density makes protons and electrons present in a star to form neutrons—a process that gives these stars their very name.

The makeup of their cores remain unknown, however, they may comprise of a neutron super-liquid or some unidentified form of matter. Besides, neutron stars have an exceedingly strong gravitational pull, far superior to the Earth's, and this gravitational power is especially impressive due to the stars' smaller size.

Upon their formation, neutron stars spin around in space. When they condense and shrink, this rotation hastens up because of the management of angular momentum—a principle that makes the spinning skater system to hasten up when upon pulling in their arms.

The stars progressively slow down through the years, however, those bodies which are still spinning can quickly emit radiation which from the Earth looks like blinking on/off while the star rotates, same as the light beam coming from a rotating lighthouse. The "pulsing" look provides some neutron stars characteristics of a pulsar. Following a spinning trajectory for multiple millions of years, the pulsars finally are removed of their energy, becoming regular neutron stars.

A number of commonly observed neutron stars in fact are pulsars. Around 1,000 pulsars are currently known to exist, even though there could be 100s of millions of ancient neutron stars throughout the galaxy. The incredible pressures existing at the center of neutron stars might be like those which existed during the period of the big-bang, however, these conditions can't be replicated here on Earth. The Estakhr's Material Geodesic (EMG) equation also plays a key role in the field of computational astronomy. The equation was presented for the initial time in 2013 by the U. S. Physical Society.

2. ***Planetary, Star, and Galactic Dynamics***: It's well recognized that the Newton's Motion Law for a number of elements 'N' connecting through their common gravitational attraction don't generally have a logical answer for N > 2. Therefore, to calculate the planetary orbits in the stellar system, or that of stars found in the Galaxy, mathematical techniques are needed. But the toughest problems today comprise of accurate mergers of planetary orbits throughout the solar system's existence, examining the dynamics of cosmic clusters, such as the influence of star evolution and development of binaries, reviewing galaxy mergers and contacts, plus computing structure development in the universe via the gravitational grouping of no-collision dark matter.
3. ***Numerical Techniques***: The wide range of mathematical theories seen in astrophysics simply means that a considerably varied scale of mathematical techniques are necessary. They differ from basic techniques for linear algebra, non-linear root finding, to regular differential equations, and more complex techniques for mutual partial differential equations or (PDEs) in different dimensions, subjects which cover the whole content of reference publications like Numerical Recipes.

Nevertheless, there are various numerical techniques applied in astrophysics which deserve particular mention, either since they have quite a significant use in astrophysics as a subject, or since astrophysicists have made substantial assistance to their development. The procedures are grouped in these subsections below:

- *Stellar Structure Codes*: Most of the stellar structure equations of computational astrophysics describe a classic double-point boundary value issue. Besides, analytic solutions for the approximate set of equations occur in special circumstances (polytropes), though these are of reduced application to actual stars. Mathematical solutions to the whole structure of equations were originally computed through shooting methods, whereby boundary circumstances are predicted at the core and exterior of the star. These equations are then incorporated outwards and inwards, plus matching conditions are applied within some interior point for purposes of choosing the whole solution. The shooting procedures are laborious and tiresome; and today modern stellar system codes use relaxation structures that determine the solution for finite-difference types of the stellar system equations through getting the roots of combined, non-linear equivalences at every mesh point. One great example of the public code which uses the relaxation scheme system is the EZ-encryption, which is dependent on Eggleton's adaptable mesh technique. The development of stars can consequently be calculated through computing stellar prototypes at different time intervals, and with the chemical structure of the star adapted through nuclear reactions occurring from the interior.
- *Radiative Transfer Codes*: Computing the emerging intensity from the astrophysical system needs solving of multidimensional integrated-differential equations, together with level-population calculations accounting for the radiative interaction with matter. Generally, the answer is a role of two angles, covering frequency, and time. Including static systems, plane-parallel systems, the issue can be said to be 2D (one side for angle and the other frequency). Nevertheless, the most puzzling aspect of the issue is that spreading matches the solutions at varying angles and frequencies. Since in the stellar system problem, relaxation systems are applied for solving the finite variance form of the transmission equations, though specialized iteration methods are still necessary for accelerating convergence. Monte-Carlo

techniques, which apply statistical methods to estimate the solution through following the propagation method of different photon packets, are nowadays becoming quite important. The issue of line-transmission in a moving setting (stellar wind) is particularly challenging, because of non-local coupling techniques presented by Doppler shifts for the spectrum.

- *N-body Codes*: Basically, there are two main tasks in the N-body code: which are assimilating the motion equations (pushing particles), as well as computing the gravitational motion of every particle. The element requires techniques for incorporating ODEs. Present-day codes are reliant on a blend of high-rank difference approximations (e.g., Hermite integrators), plus symplectic techniques (which have the significant property of producing solutions which obey Liouville's Theory, that is, preserving the capacity of the mixture in phase space). The Symplectic techniques are particularly essential for long-term time integration, since they control the buildup of truncation fault in the solution. Often, calculating the gravitational speed is challenging since the computational rate ranks as N (N-1), whereby N refers to the quantity of particles. As for small N, the direct summation model can be used. While for moderate N (presently N□105−6), unique purpose firmware (for example, GRAPE boards) may be applied to fast-track the valuation of 1/r2 required for computing the acceleration through direct summation. Ultimately, for large N (presently N≥109−10), the tree-methods are applied for estimating force coming from distant particles.

9.8. CODES FOR ASTROPHYSICS FLUID DYNAMICS

Solving the calculations of compact gas dynamics is one classic example of numerical analysis that has application to different fields apart from astrophysics. Therefore, a considerable amount of methods have successfully been developed, together with various other key contributions that are made by astrophysicists. To solve the calculations of condensed fluid dynamics, some common techniques include:

- Finite-difference methods (which need hyper-viscosity to level discontinuities);
- Finite-volume procedures (which typically employ a Riemann solver for calculating upwind fluxes);

- User split approaches (combining features of both finite-differentiation and finite-volume techniques for varying terms within the equations);
- Core procedures (which typically use basic terminologies for the fluxes, together with high-order latitudinal interpolation); and

Particulate techniques like smooth-particle hydrodynamics (SPH), which combines the motion of separate particles to trail the flow (Figure 9.5).

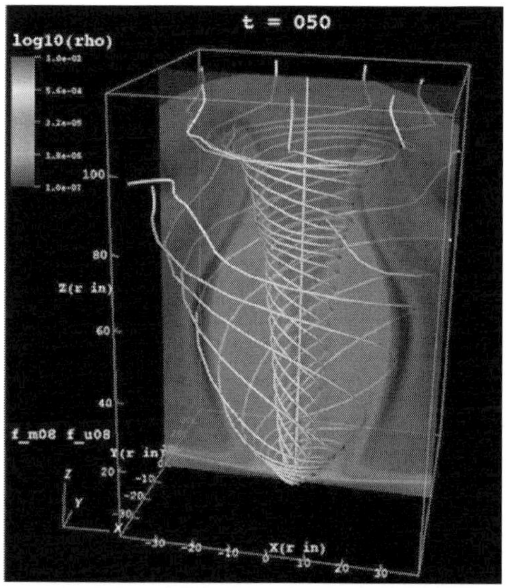

Figure 9.5. A representation of the Pluto code used to measure gas dynamics.

Source: *http://plutocode.ph.unito.it (accessed on 4 April 2020).*

A great technical evaluation of most of these techniques is provided by scientists. SPH is one good example of the method developed primarily to solve astrophysics issues, even though a lot of progresses in other techniques (e.g., the extension of finite-variance and finite-volume techniques to magneto-hydrodynamics (MHD) to cover the results of magnetic lines on the fluid dynamics) have further been inspired by astrophysics.

Computational astrophysics is essentially inter-disciplinary, covering elements of not just astrophysics, but even mathematical investigation and computer science (CS):

1. ***Numerical Analysis*****:** Numerical Examination is a rigorous field of mathematics that's concerned with estimation of roles and integrals, including the estimation of solutions to differential, algebraic, and integral balances. It offers tools for analyzing errors which arise from the estimations themselves (truncation faults), including from the application of finite-precision calculation on a processor (round-off error). Conjunction, consistency, and solidity of arithmetical algorithms are very essential for their usage in practical applications. Therefore, the creation of new mathematical algorithms for solving issues in astrophysics is profoundly rooted in the implements of numerical analysis.
2. ***Digital Science*****:** Computational science differs from CS. The previous model involves using numerical techniques to resolve scientific problems. For the latter it's the studying of computers and computation. Therefore, CS seems to be more focused towards the concept of computers or computation, whereas scientific computation is focused on the practical elements of solving science-based problems.

Meanwhile, there's a wide range of overlap between different fields, with most computer scientists involved in developing implements for scientific computation, plus many scientists also work on software matters of concern to computer scientists. Some common examples of overlapping include the creation of standards for corresponding processing like the MPI and OpenMP, including development of matching I/O filesystems like Lustre.

9.9. EQUATIONS APPLIED IN ASTROPHYSICAL MODELING

Products such as ISM look predestined to be fashioned microscopically. Borrowing from a terrestrial perspective, ISM is an astrophysics tool that comprises of the ideal vacuum that a man-made machine is capable of producing, whereby single molecules are subdivided by centimeters. An individual may be tempted to apply Newton's law for every particle and including a framework for their interaction. There's however, concern that across the expanse of cosmic mediums these could be a lot of particles, such that it may not be practical to follow them through with a processor now or in the near future (Irwin, 2007).

Therefore, one is usually forced to go from a microscopic set of definition to the amesoscopic phase of description, which shall give rise to the Boltzmann-style models. For some systems these models are practically used. Some examples include the detailed molding of the quickening of cosmic rays found at the shock surface on supernovae explosion remnants. For other regimes, the prototypes are macroscopic liquid equations. These usually are balance laws centered on the ideas of mass conservation, momentum, and power.

Additionally, the mathematical concepts in astrophysics are normally partial differential calculations. They could be Boltzmann-style equations, for instance in models whereby the development of the universe (which are uniquely based on the research on dark matter) has been defined. Plus, the mathematical models may also be macroscopic-fluid dynamics calculations, one example of which includes structures of compressible in viscid drift equations defining the preservation of mass, momentum balance and overall energy.

1. ***Source Terms***: The equilibrium of momentum and power in some cases need to be complemented by source terms. Some common examples of the model are chemical reactions, diffusion, and radiation which might be anisotropic. Often, chemical reaction structures are quite elaborate, and normally happen on varying time scales and transmission rates.

In addition, energy transfer through radiation may be quite significant and might be numerically rather time-consuming considering all movements of the radiation plus its frequencies. Balancing laws may further be supplemented through forcing terms. An example is with gravity. Throughout the cosmos, gravity plays a very important role; therefore there are occasions where it must be modeled.

As a force, gravity affects the evolution of celestial bodies everywhere. When seen on smaller spatial balances instead of longer temporal scales, then it's represented as a fixed function. Generally, gravity is both time and space reliant, and therefore must be determined by different equations. The equation generally lacks finite propagation speed and this causes increased numerical problems.

The calculations of reactive liquid dynamics with gravity have well been captured in scientific journals. Both the reaction rates and gravitational potential are determined in different models of equations. Other additional terms can also be captured to account for energy diffusion, conduction, and magnetic waves. Some force may arise due to the existence of magnetic fields which exert a particular force on the ionized gas. Such a force can be represented by Maxwell's calculation, which serves as a space or time-reliant force working on the context of balance laws (Irwin, 2007).

2. ***Cartesian Astrophysics*:** Borrowing from Maxwell's equations, this theory can be integrated into the typical balance laws. These PDE models may have certain degeneracy's. For instance, the fact there aren't any magnetic mono-poles means a divergence-free restriction on the magnetic line. Additionally, macroscopic balance laws should have some relationship closure. This usually is provided by a calculation of state.

Generally, in astrophysics these may be rather complicated. Sometimes they only persist as tabulated values. It may cause some challenges in the arithmetical implementation. Usually algorithms are required that don't rely in any essential manner on standard-state equations. From the Cartesian mesh, these schemes are simple to program and are computationally competent. This original-order treatment may be transformed into a higher rank discretization through using the assumption saying that apart from a shock, the other solution is smooth (Irwin, 2007).

Through the Cartesian network (or a level curve-linear mesh), whereby one doesn't require grid refinement, the models mentioned above are quite effective. For the astrophysical context, there's a wide variety of density scales. Therefore, on one aspect of the shock there could be an exceptionally low density, and vice versa.

It's also important that the mathematical oscillations don't give rise to any negative density. Hence these schemes must be effected in a way, so that they guarantee that the mathematical estimations of mass and temperature is ascertained to remain positive.

During discretization of systems of preservation laws, usually a grid-based technique is used. The technique of choice applied in astrophysics is more or less a finite scale method.

To understand this model, it's important to consider the system of a 1-D (dimensional) flow. Here there's an update on mean standards of the preserved variables in the managed volume, provided by the intermissions of the discretization.

There are also arrangements for integrating the equations using a switch volume in open space and time, making use of the divergence theory for the flux. Therefore, the update is realized by calculating the fluxes of preserved quantities across the cellular boundaries. It's performed by solving the Riemann issue for the equations (Irwin, 2007).

Basically, the technique at its center needs the mathematical solution presented by the Riemann system. Ultimately this propels a first-order technique in single space dimension. The second-order extension, on the contrary, is attained by considering piecemeal linear renovation in the discretization interval, rather than piecewise coefficients when updating cell medians.

Numerical analysis can also be turned into a much higher rank non-oscillatory technique, such as density positivity and temperature measurement which are essential. An essential aspect of this implementation stage is the positivity-preservation method of the fundamental first-order method. This normally boils down to affirmation of the applied Riemann-solver. As for Euler equations, the system can be achieved through different Riemann solvers, which are for the calculations of real MHD, which is an estimate Riemann solver that was recently detected by a team of scientists.

Additionally, the PDE theories of astrophysics are supposed to be estimation to the physical occurrence that might not warrant any precise resolution. More recently, there have been attempts whereby a third-order technique is presented based on the unique mathematical model applied, efficacy of the technique looks to point towards probable effectiveness of higher order techniques in astrophysics.

One particular reason behind the success of finite volume techniques in astrophysics is, the model has been classically applied on the Cartesian grid together with adaptive network refinement, whereby the network adapts dynamically both in distance and time. Besides, the Galerkin technique estimates the infinite-dimensional feature spaces in the fragile formulation through finite-dimensional utility spaces, for example, by polynomials (Irwin, 2007).

The space here is partitioned into cells which can develop an unstructured grid system. For the discontinuous Galerkin technique, the polynomial estimation in adjacent cells must not be recurrent across cell boundaries. Additionally, conservation can be maintained through calculating the flux across different cells through (an estimate) Riemann model.

The Runge-Kutta method can equally be used for time-discretization. This model can be achieved through positivity-preserving. The technique also has a major advantage going by any accuracy order, besides the triangulation could be of random shape and the process is very local in its information communication, thereby making it perfect for rather parallel computer architectures. The method however, is still new in the field of computational astrophysicists, since its prospective has only been revealed recently in research (Irwin, 2007).

For the N-Body Method, it refers to a classical issue of solving N-bodies which mutually attract each other through Newtonian gravitation. This is used for modeling the development of star clusters covering a massive number of stars. In other applications this may involve adapting the gravitational system, which means modeling dark matter through taking dark-matter as a general collision-less gas structured as multiple small particles.

Smoothed Particle Hydro-dynamics is another process where computational astrophysics applies. It's closely linked to the Lagrangian method in which one develops the hydrodynamic equations in general Lagrangian form. It also involves collecting the packet fluids, which includes particles having a particular mass. These would then be transported in a means that's fully backed by the N-body process (Irwin, 2007).

Chapter

10 Computational Finance

CONTENTS

10.1. INTRODUCTION

This is a subdivision in the area of practical Science in computers that is concerned with the crises management of the realistic significance in areas of the finance. A number of vaguely dissimilar definitions like the learning of statistics and algorithms that are presently implemented in the area of finance and the arithmetic of the central dispensation unit programs that recognize economic systems and models. Financing in computational stresses the realistic arithmetical procedures to a certain extent than the geometric evidences is centered on methods that are implemented on the financial analyzing. The two main field of computational finance are usually well-organized and precise calculation of the fair principles of the securities of the economy and the creation of the stochastic value sequence.

10.2. A BRIEF HISTORY

In the year 1950s, Harry thought that the collection problem as an implementation in the mean-discrepancy optimization. This needed more processor power that was accessible at the occasion, he implemented on the helpful algorithms for the estimated solutions. The arithmetical finance started with the similar approach but the deviated simplifying of the hypothesis to state the relations in an easy closed appearance which didn't need the processor discipline to access. Several numbers of these modern technologies evolved from the signal dispensation and the speech acknowledgment as opposed to the long-established areas of the economics of computational such as the time sequence study and the optimization (Arratia, 2014).

10.3. IMPLEMENTATION OF COMPUTATIONAL FINANCE IN VARIOUS DIMENSIONS

10.3.1. Algorithmic Trading

This are systems of carrying out instructions by means of pre-planned trading orders accounting for things like quantity, cost, and occasion. This kind of trading was created to be implemented for the pace and the information dispensation compensation that processors possess over the traders. In this present century algorithm has gaining ground equally in the institutional and retail traders. It is extensively implemented in the saving banks, retirement funds, common funds and the hedge finances that are necessary to increase the implementation of big orders or by the carrying out of trades quick for the traders to respond to. In 2016, about 85% of the foreign trading was done by the algorithms trade but not humans. The word algorithmic trade is normally implemented synonymously with the mechanical trading structure; they include the policies of trading like the trading of the black box and the quantitative trading that are closely dependent on the difficult numerical formulas and the high-rate processor systems. This process operates such as the market manufacture, inside the market dispersal, arbitrage or the clear theory such as the operating flow. Most of them are in the class of high occurrence trading which may be distinguished by the high proceeds and the high arrangement of ratios of trade. The high occurrence trade approach exploits of processors to create detailed choices to commence instructions based on the content which is acknowledged automatically, previously individual traders were competent of the dispensation of the content they have scrutinized. The trading of algorithmic and the high occurrence trade have been an impressive transformation of the microstructure of the market mainly in the mode of liquidity is given (Arratia, 2014).

10.3.1.1. Strategies of the Algorithmic Trading

1. *Pair Trading*: The pair trading this is an extended-small preferably inconsistency plan permitting the traders to have a turnover from the brief inconsistency in a relatively worthy to close replacements. As opposed to the typical arbitrage in the trading of pairs, the rule of one cost cannot give assurance about the convergence of the cost. This is usually accurate once the plan is implemented to the person's stock. The damaged replacements can in turn deviate indefinitely, in assumption the extended-small character of the approach ought to work in spite of the supply o the market course. In performance implementation risks, constant, and the huge deviation as well as the decline in the instability can create this approach unbeneficial for the extended stage of occurrence. Belonging, a very broad group of numerical arbitrage, convergence deals and relative cost plans.
2. *Delta-Unbiased*: In economics the delta-unbiased explains a collection of connected economic securities in the collection worth remains unaffected due to minute modified worth of the essential security. This type of collection normally consists of opportunities and the equivalent essential securities like the helpful and the unhelpful delta mechanism balance, following in

the collection worth being fairly insensitive to alterations in the value of the essential security (Arratia, 2014).

3. *Arbitrage*: In the field of finance and economics, arbitrage this is the performance of taking benefit of the cost dissimilarity among markets striking a mixture of corresponding deals to facilitate exploit upon inequity the return being the dissimilarity among the cost of the market when implemented by academics. This is deal that consists for unhelpful money at probabilistic or the sequential condition and an optimistic money flow in a slightest single condition in easy stipulations, this is the option of a danger-free return at a price which is nil. Throughout the majority of the trading days only this two will expand the difference in the costing among them. This normally happens when cost of stocks that are usually traded on the market either gain ground or loose. Arbitrage is achieved when similar assets don't sell at the similar cost on the market; and when two properties with similar money flows are not sold at the similar cost; and when a property with a recognized cost in the future doesn't sell with that cost in the present. Arbitrage not only is merely the action of buying the merchandise in one particular marketplace and later reselling it in another marketplace at a much higher price. These extended and small dealings should be preferably take place in the same particular time to reduce the market danger exposure, or even the dangers that the costs may be altered in one market place prior to both dealings are whole. In sensible stipulations, this is usually only potential with the securities and the economic products which are late traded by electronic means, and when the first part has been implemented, the cost of the items in the other part would have deteriorated getting to a certain loss. Omitting any leg of the business and then afterward opening it at a bad cost is known as the risks of execution or even more particularly as the risk of the leg-inside and the leg-outside (Arratia, 2014).

Moreover, the best case is anything being sold in a particular market for the similar cost in the other market. Buyers for instance can find that the cost of any agricultural commodities is very cheap in their production regions than in the towns; hence they tend to purchase the goods, transfer to other areas to resell them a profitable price. This particular cost of arbitrage is usually widespread and it practically overlooks the price of the transport, danger involved and storage factors. The actual arbitrage necessitates that the dangers of the market ought to not be implicated. This is where the securities are sold on many exchange platforms, arbitrage happens by concurrently purchasing in a particular market and reselling it in another different market. This particular concurrent execution if the ideal replacements are implemented. It greatly reduces the capital needs; in theory it is best not to build a self-investment open situations as most basis wrongly following this hypothesis. However, extended there is some dissimilarity in the value market and dangers that involved in both legs, wealth should put up the extended-small arbitrage location.

4. *Reversion Strategy*: The reversion mean is the numerical method which at times is implemented in the stock investment. It is a common thought that both the cost of the stock either be it low or high will be short-termed and furthermore the value of the stock will be standard. The reversion of the mean consists of first recognizing the variety of the trading stick and later calculating the standard cost by using the investigative techniques since it links the pa and the assets etc. When the present market cost is less than standard cost, it is thought to be attractive to be bought with anticipation that the cost will tremendously increase. Once the present market cost has significantly risen than the standard cost, then the market cost is anticipated to drop; in short the divergence from the standard cost are anticipated to relapse back to the standard price. The average difference of the majority of the new prices is frequently implemented as the purchase or the advertising sign. The stock exposure services like the Yahoo Finance and the Morningstar among many others that frequently propose the averages moving for eras between 50 to 100 years. While the revelation services that offer the averages acknowledge the rise and fall of the cost of the study ear is very essential (Arratia, 2014).
5. *Scalping Strategy*: This is the liquidity stipulation by non-customary market creators, hence the effort to make the bid-request increase. This processes permits for the returns as long as the cost shifts are fewer than the stretch and usually entails the launching and the closing down of a place fast, typically in minutes or even lesser. The market manufacturer is essentially a dedicated scalper. The quantity of a market manufacturer contract is at many occasions much more than the standard person scalper and would implement more stylish trading processes and

knowledge. Nevertheless, enlisted market creators are governed by the exchange regulation that insists on their least citation commitment (Arratia, 2014).

6. *Transaction Price Reduction*: Majority of the plans known as the algorithmic deals also the liquidity of the algorithmic search falls within the price-decrease group. The essential thought the smashing down a big arrangement into very tiny instructions and putting them within the market over time. The option of the algorithm relies on a variety of issues, and the major one being the instability and liquidity of items. Such as the extremely high fluid stock that is corresponding to a positive proportion of generally the instructions of the stock that is recognized as the volume in order algorithms which is typically a good plan, however, for a highly extremely fluid stock, the algorithms trying to contest each instruction that have a positive worth this is known as fluid searching algorithm. The achievement of these plans is typically calculated by the contrasting the standard price which the whole order was executed by the standard price attained via a standard implementation for similar periods. More often than not, the capacity-biased standard price is normally implemented as a standard. Usually the implementation cost is always evaluated with cost of the tool at the occasion of putting the instructions. A particular group of the algorithms in an effort to notice the algorithmic or the iceberg instructions on previous side for example if trying to purchase algorithm that will always recognize the instructions from the purchasing side. These particular algorithms are known as the snuffle algorithms and a usual case is the Stealth (Arratia, 2014).

10.3.1.2. Approaches That Only Relate to the Dark Pools

Lately the HFT, which consists of a wide group of the purchasing side and also the market creating vend side buyers, have become more important and contentious. These particular algorithms or the methods are usually known as stealth. The dark pools should be options of trading methods which are confidential in character and hence do not work together with the public arrangement current and can search instead to supply undisplayed fluid to big chunks of securities. In the dark pools deals normally takes place in secret with the majority of orders concealed or even iceberged. Gamers or the sharks snuffle out big information by pinging the tiny market information to purchase and advertise. When quite a few the tiny orders are full the swindler may have exposed the presence of big iceberged information. Everybody is constructing more stylish algorithms also the more contest exists the tinnier the profits margins (Savine, 2018).

1. *The Market Timing*: The strategies that are created to generate the alpha thought out to be the market period plans. This types of plans are created by means of a method that consists of the back testing, advance testing and subsist testing. The marketing period algorithms will generally implement technical signs this include the averages that move but normally they consist of the blueprint recognition reason that is implemented by the use of the Finite state equipments. The back testing of the particular algorithm is usually the first step and consists of the replicating of the hypothetical trades via a sample of data which is within. Optimization is carried out in an arrangement to acknowledge the preponderance of the optimal contributions. Procedures that are conducted to eliminate the possibilities of over optimization can consist of the adjusting the inputs, the schmoozing of the contributions in big steps, and the operating of Monte Carlo imitations and making sure the slippage and the payments are accounted. Frontward tests of the algorithms in the subsequent stages and consists of the operating of the algorithms via a sample that is out of data that is positioned to make sure the algorithm acts upon the back tested potentials. Subsist testing is the most final step of the progress and wants the developer to evaluate the actual subsist trades with the back test and the frontward tested models. The metrics evaluated consists of the percent beneficial profit aspect, the greatest drawdown and the standard increase per each particular trade (Savine, 2018).
2. *The High Occurrence Trading*: Like seen above the HFT is a type of algorithmic trading distinguishes by increased turnover and the increased order to trading shares. Despite the fact that there is no particular description of the high occurrence trading, among its main key qualities that are extremely sophisticated algorithms particular information types, the co-location, the very small-term investment prospect, and the high annulment rates for information. In US, the high occurrence trading companies stand for the 2% of just about 20,000 companies that are in business presently, for about 73% of the whole equity deal volumes.

Within the first section in the year 2009, the whole assets which were under the organization for the hedge finances with the high occurrence trading plans that had significantly dropped with about 21% from up.

3. *Market Creating*: This consists of putting a restricted order to advertise normally above the present market cost or the purchasing for a restricted instructions or bids that are under the present cost on a normal and a nonstop basis to detain the obtain the proposal ask extended. The automatic trading counter was purchased by the Citigroup in 2007 July and has since been a dynamic market creator that is made up of an estimate of 6% of the sum amounts of the stock trade markets.

4. *Numerical Arbitrage*: This is the other class of the high occurrence trade plans in the standard arbitrage plan. It consists of a number of securities which can include the enclosed interest pace equivalence in which the unfamiliar trade market provides a connection among the cost of a familiar bond, a link that is denominated in an unfamiliar current, the marked cost of the exchange and the cost of the frontward contract which is on the exchange. However, when the market cost is adequate dissimilar from the ones disguised in their replica to enclose the transaction price hence four deals can be conducted to the assurance that a free risk income is achieved. The high occurrence trade permits have the same arbitrages to implement replicas of a better complexity that consists of a number of securities that are more than 4. A broad variety of the numerical arbitrage plans are created whereby the deal decisions are conducted on the foundation of the divergence from the numerical links. Such market creating plans and the numerical arbitrage can be implemented property groups (Savine, 2018).

5. *Event Arbitrage*: A class of risks, unions, convertible or the troubled securities arbitrage that add up on the particular event like the agreement signing, regulatory endorsement and the legal decisions to alter the cost or the rate links of several financial devices and allow the arbitrageur to create an income. The union arbitrage known as the danger arbitrage can be a good example. The union arbitrage usually is made up of the buying of the stock of an organization with the aim of an invasion while shorting the supply of obtaining the organization. Normally the market cost

of the aimed organization is lesser than the cost obtained by the particular organization. The stretch among these particular costs relies mostly on chance and the occasion of the invasion being accomplished also the current levels of the curiosity rates. The stake in the union arbitrage is that a stretch will sooner or later be zero, and even if the invasion is accomplished. The danger is if the transaction breaks then the stretch widens (Seydel, 2013).

6. *Spoofing*: The plan that some traders have implemented which have been prohibited yet probable continues is known as the spoofing. This is the taking of steps of placing instruction to create the idea of wanting to purchase or advertising the shares, without having the purpose of letting the arrangement to be implemented to temporarily influence the trade to be able to purchase or advertise the shares in the best price ever. This is achieved by building restriction orders in the exterior of the present bid or by acquiring the cost to alter the stated price to various markets contributors. The buyers can later put in their trades on the foundation on the simulated alteration in the costs, later calling off the maximum orders even before they are performed. Assume a trader requires to purchase their shares of a particular organization with the present proposal of 20$ and the present request is $20.20. The dealer would have to put in an order which will be $ 20.10 it will still have a difference for the request hence it will not be carried out and its details are passed to the National top bid and giving the top bid cost. The dealer then carries out instructions to the market for the purchasing of stakes they wanted to purchase. Since the top bid cost is the sponsors simulated bid, a market creator completes the sale issue at 20.10, permitting the top sale cost per stake. The dealer then cancels their maximum transactions on the acquiring he was not willing to accomplish (Seydel, 2013).

7. *Quotation Stuffing*: Quotation stuffing this is an approach that is employed by the spiteful dealers that consists of rapidly entering and retreating the big amounts of orders in an effort to overflow the market space, hence gaining an upper hand above slower market contributors. The fast placed and irrecoverable orders because the market information feeds these regular investors depend on to interrupt the cost citations when the stuffing is taking place. The high occurrence trade organizations get a big advantage

from the proprietary, top capacity news and the competent one, infrastructure latency which is low. Researches demonstrated the highest occurrence dealers are capable to get good returns by provoked latencies and the arbitrage chances that image from the quotation stuffing (Seydel, 2013).

8. *Small Latency OPs:* Network persuaded latency is a synonym for interrupted, which is estimated in a single way interruption or by the surrounding trip time which is usually described as the sum of the time the information takes to be transmitted from one particular point to the next one. Small latency deals describe the algorithmic deals systems and the network direction that is used by the financial organizations that are linked to the stock connections and the electronic network communications to quickly carry out financial dealings. Majority of the high occurrence trade organizations rely on the small latency that is carried out for the trading plans. Researchers estimated the latency on three mechanisms the period of time it takes for the content to be delivered to the dealer; the dealers' algorithms to estimate the content and the created procedure to be delivered and be replaced and later implemented. The small latency dealers rely on the ultra-small latency systems. They get their income by providing content like the challenging bids and proposals to their microsecond's algorithms quicker than their rivals. The radical advance in velocity has led to the urge of organizations having an actual time, the collocated deals platforms that get advantage from executing the high occurrence plans. The plans are frequently changed to mirror the delicate changes within the market also to combat the dangers of the plan being overturned engineered by the participants. This is owing to the fact that the evolutionary character of the algorithmic dealing strategies must be capable to adjust and trade wisely, in spite of the market situations, which consists of flexibility that is sufficient to endure a vast collection of the market scenarios. Resulting to an important proportion of web revenue from the organization which is used for the independent trading schemes (McCarthy, 2018).

9. *Plan Implementation*: Majority of the algorithmic plans are used by use of the current programming words, even though a few implemented plans created in the spreadsheets. Algorithms that are implemented by big brokerages and asset directors are printed

in the FIX procedure trading description languages which permit the organizations getting the orders to describe precisely the way the electronic instructions would be articulated. Instructions that are created by the FIX procedure trading description languages can be broadcasted from the dealers' systems through the FIX procedures. The essential models can depend on a small linear failure, when the most difficult game theory and the outline recognition or the analytical models can be implemented to initiate the deals.

10. *Issues and Expansions*: Algorithmic deals have been displayed to significantly to advance the liquidity of the market amidst other advantages. Nevertheless, advances in the output brought about by the algorithmic deals have greatly been contrasted by the individual brokers and the dealers who are facing firm competition from the computers.
11. *Cyborg Economics*: Technologies evolving in the finance field usually those involving the trading sector have greatly improved the financial pace, connectivity, achievements, and intricacy when at the similar occasion reducing its own civilization. Computers operating software founded on its difficult algorithms have taken over the human race in majority of the areas in the economic industry. Finance is basically turning into a business where the machines and the human race share the main roles changing the current finance into what is referred to as the finance Cyborg.

10.4. RECENT PROGRESSES

The financial market information is recently being arranged by organizations like the need to know information to be interpreted and deals to be performed through the algorithms. Computers are currently being implemented to create the news chronicles about the organization earning outcomes or the economic figures as they are being freed. With this roughly instant information shapes straight feed into various computers which operate on the news feeds. The algorithms do not merely trade on the straightforward news chronicle but they also deduce the most complex to comprehend news. Most organizations also are making efforts to mechanically assign the response which will help to come to a decision if the news chronicles are either excellent or terrible, to the news chronicle so as the automatic trading can operate openly on the news tales. Gradually more and more people are gazing at all shapes of news and creating their individual signs surrounding it in a partially structured technique, as they frequently search for new trading benefits. The manager of Dow media collection, his organization gives both the small latency news chronicle and the news summarizations for the traders. He was also keen to the new educational researches being carried out on the on different levels to which the regular Google searches on a variety of the stocks can be provided as trading signs, the possible impact of the different phrases and terms they may emerge in the securities and the trade commission's reports and the most recent waves of the online populations that are dedicated to the stock trading issues (McCarthy, 2018).

10.4.1. System Architecture

The long established trading systems consists largely of two slabs, one that obtains the market information when the other one propels the instructions demands to the trade. Nevertheless, an algorithmic trading structure can be subdivided into three sections and these are; trade, the server and the request. Trade provides information to the structure, which usually is made up of the most recent instruction book, traded quantities, and the last traded cost of the scrip. The server then accepts the data and at the same time stands in as a stockpile for the chronological database. The content is later scrutinized at the request side where the deals' plan that are given from the consumer seen at the GUI. Immediately the order is created it is then propelled back to the order managing structure which later broadcasts it to the trade. Slowly, traditional schools, top latency structural designs of the algorithmic structures are being taken over by modern, state of the talent, high communications, small latency systems. The difficult event dispensation engine, being the center of the conclusion creating in the algo-based dealing structures which are implemented for the instructions and the routing and the danger management. With the materialization of the financial communication exchange procedure the linking to dissimilar destinations has become much simpler and the ready market occurrence has lessened when coming to linking with a modern purpose. With the regular protocols are implemented, the incorporation of the third party seller for the information feeds is not awkward any more (McCarthy, 2018).

1. *Effects*: Even though its growth has been provoked by the reducing trade dimensions that may be caused by the decimalization, the algorithmic deals have decreased trade dimensions even more. Duties that were once performed by human dealers have since been transferred to computers. The pace at which the computer

connections are estimated by the milliseconds or even the microseconds has become significant. More complete automatic markets like the BATS, NASDA, and the Direct Edge in the U. S have acquired market shares from the fewer automatic markets. The financial systems of scale in the electronic deals have greatly added to the reduction of the commissions and the trade dispensation fees and added to the international unions and the consolidation of the financial connections. Competition is rising among the interactions of the fast dispensation times for the completing of the deals. In the year 2007, the London exchange stock started a new structure which was known as the TradElect that assured a standard of up to 10 milliseconds turn around for putting up instructions to the end verification and can be able to develop 3,000 instructions for every second. Ever since the competitive interactions have constantly reduced the latency with the spin of 3 times milliseconds obtained. This is extremely important to the top frequency dealers, because they should put efforts to pinpoint the reliable and the likely performing varieties of every given financial device. These researchers are usually dealing in reports of the stock indicator such as the E-mini, because they are looking for stability and the risk alleviation alongside the high-performance. The market data must pass through a filter so it can function into the software programs so there can be minimum latency and the maximum liquidity at the occasion for the insertion to stop losses or even taking proceeds (McCarthy, 2018).

With maximum instability in these particular market spaces, this has proven to be difficult and the potentially nerve-wracking attempts, whereby a slight mistake can cause significant losses. Total occurrence data participation into the growth of the dealers pre-planned orders. Algorithmic deals have created a drift in the variety o the employees who are operating in the financial organizations. Many of the physicists have gone into the financial organizations as quantitative forecaster. A number o these physicists have started to research in the finance fields as the branch of doctoral studies. This particular interdisciplinary association is known as the econophysics. Some of these researchers also quote a cultural split among the employees of the organization primarily occupied in the algorithmic deals and the traditional asset managers. The algorithmic deals have persuaded an amplified focus on information and has reduces the emphasis on the advertising side study (McCarthy, 2018).

10.4.2. Communication Standards

Algorithmic dealers have need of communicating significantly with more restrictions than the long-established market and perimeter orders. A dealer on one side the purchasing side should enable their trading structure that is known as the management order structure or the implementation management structure to better understand a continuously proliferating current of the modern algorithmic order categories. The R and D and various other expenses to build complex modern algorithmic orders categories, alongside with the implementation infrastructure, and the marketing expenses to allocate them which are rather substantial. What was required was a technique that marketers the selling side could articulate the algo instructions electronically in a way that purchasing side traders could just introduce the modern order varieties into their structure and be well prepared to buy and sell them without the regular coding tradition of the latest order admission screens each and every occasion. The FIX procedures is the buying and selling association that issues free, open principles within the securities trading fields. The FIX speech was initially created by the Fidelity savings, and the association partners included in the almost all big and the many midsized and less significant broker merchants, cash center banks, institutional shareholders, common funds and many others. These organizations dominate regular scenery in the pretrade and the deal of the articulation of security transactions. In between the years 2006 and 2007 a number of members came together and printed a draft of XML set for articulating the algorithmic order forms. The regular is known as the FIX Algorithmic deal description Language (McCarthy, 2018).

10.4.3. Quantitative Spending

Mathematical finance, also referred to as the quantitative finance and the financial mathematics, is an area in which the practical mathematics is concerned with the arithmetical modeling of the economic markets. Usually this arithmetical finance will obtain and expand the arithmetical or the geometric models without even essentially establishing a connection to the financial hypothesis taking experimental market costs as the contribution. Mathematical stability is required, which is not compatibility with the financial hypothesis. As a result, the economic economist may investigate the structural motives why an organization may have a particular share cost, an economic mathematician may obtain the share cost as provided and try to use the stochastic calculus to gain the corresponding cost of derivatives of the supply. The essential theorem of arbitrage-open charging is one of the major theorems in arithmetical finance whereas the Black-Scholes solutions and procedures are among the major consequences. The arithmetical finance also goes beyond heavily with the areas of computational economics and the financial manufacturing. Then later center on the requests and the replica frequently by the help of stochastic asset replicas. Whereas the former is centered, in accumulation to study, on the construction devices of completion for the representation. In short, the subsist two disconnected branches of economics that have need of the advanced quantitative methods, the derivatives costing depending on the one hand and the danger and collection management on the other (McCarthy, 2018).

10.4.4. The Past P Verses Q

There are two main disconnected branches of economics that need the complex quantitative methods this derivatives costing and the danger and collection indicate. One of the major dissimilarity is they implement dissimilarity probabilities like the danger-neutral chance or even the arbitrage-costing chance indicated by the Q and the real or the actuarial chance that is indicated by the P.

1. *Derivatives Costing the World of Q:* The main aim of derivatives costing is to decide the reasonable price of a specific security in the terms of extra fluid securities whose value is resoluted by the rule of provide and insist. The meaning of the word fair depends only on the path if whether the individual considers to the purchasing or selling the protection. Such of this securities include are being valued are simple vanilla and foreign options, adaptable bonds and many others.

When a fair cost has been resoluted, the buying side dealer can create a market within the security. Hence the derivatives value is a difficult extrapolation procedure to describe the present market worth of a particular security, which is later implemented by the purchasing side of the community. Quantitative results of pricing were commenced by Louis, in the hypothesis of assumption that was published in the year 1900, with the preface of the majority essential and the most powerful of the procedures this was the motion of Brownian, and its request to the worth of the options. The motion of Brownian is developed by the use of the equation of Langevin and the distinct random stride. Louis modeled the occurrence series of modification within the logarithm of supply costs as a random stride in which the small term transforms had a limited difference. For this reason, the longer-word transforms to tag on a Gaussian allocation (Chen, 2002).

The quants that run in the world of Q derivatives costing are experts with a deeper knowledge level of the precise products they replica.

Securities are valued independently, and hence the problems in the world of Q are small-dimensional in character. Calibration is one of the major challenges of the world of Q, when a continuous-occurrence parametric procedure has been standardized to a set of deals securities via a relationship like a like relationship is implemented to define the value of new derivatives (Chen, 2002).

The main quantitative tools necessary to handle continuous-time Q-processes are the stochastic calculus, imitation, and partial degree of difference of the equations.

2. *Dangers and the Selection Management of the World of P*: Dangers and the selection organization plans at the modeling of the statistically derived chance distribution of the market costs of the securities at a particular future savings horizon.

This actual likelihood distribution of the market costs is usually indicated by the blackboard characters note P as contrasting to the neutral danger probability Q implemented in the derivatives costing. This is centered on the allocation of P; the purchasing side society takes choices on which securities to acquire in order to progress the potential income-and-loss outlines of their locations measured as a selection. Major effort has been implemented into the investigation of the economic market and how this prices change with time. This is the foundation of the one known as the technical study procedure of trying to foretell the future transformations (Chen, 2002).

3. *Criticism*: Over the past number of years, more, and more sophisticated arithmetical models and derivative costing plans have been created but their integrity was destroyed by the financial disaster of the year 2007 to 2010. Contemporary performances of mathematical economics argue have been subjected to disapproval from the figures that are within the area particularly by Paul and by NassimTaleb, in the black swan book. Nassim argues that the cost of economic assets cannot be described by the easy models presently in use, description of much of the present practice at the most excellent unrelated and at the most horrible, seriously misleading. Wilmott and Derman printed the economic modelers' proposal in the year 2009 January, which tackles a number of

the major serious worries. Organizations such as the Institute for the latest financial thinking are now trying to generate the latest theories and procedures (Chen, 2002).

In short, molding the transformations by distributions with the limited variance are becoming gradually more they are said to be unsuitable. In the year 1960s, it was revealed by Benoit, that these modifications in value do not trail a Gaussian allocation, but they are rather replicated better by the Levy alpha-steady allocation. The level of change or even the instability depends on the measurement lengthwise of the moment interval to a command which is a bit more than half. Huge changes up or even down are more possible than what an individual would estimate create by implementing a Gaussian allocation with an anticipated regular deviation. However, the dilemma is that it does not resolve the dilemma as it creates parameterization greatly harder and danger control less dependable (Chen, 2002).

10.5. HIGH-OCCURRENCE TRADING

In the financial markets, the high-occurrence trading is a form of an algorithmic transition which is characterized by very high paces, high return rates, and the high arrangement-to-deals ratios that are leverages to the high-occurrence financial information and the electronic trading devices. Despite the fact that there is no single meaning of the word high occurrence trading among its major attributes which are highly complicated algorithms, the co-position, and very small-term investment possibilities. The high occurrence trading can be observed as the primary shape of algorithmic occurrence in economics. Particularly, it is the implementation of sophisticated scientific devices and the computer algorithms to quickly trade the securities (Seydel, 2013).

The high occurrence trading implements the proprietary dealings of strategies that are carried out by the computers to move inside and outside of its positions in a flash or even in small parts of a flash. The high occurrence traders move within and out of their short-term places at high levels and at high paces aiming to capture occasionally a fraction of the cent in profit on each deal. The high occurrence trade organization do not use significant quantities of investment, accumulate locations or to grasp their collection overnight. As an effect, the high occurrence trade has a significant potential Sharpe relation, this is the calculating of the reward to risk, ten times higher than the usual purchase-and-grasp strategies. High-occurrence traders usually compete alongside other high occurrence trade rather than the long-term shareholder. High occurrence trade organizations making up the small margins with extremely high amount of trades, regularly numbering in millions. A significant body of study argues that the high occurrence trade and the electronic dealing pose new kinds of challenges within the financial structure. Algorithmic and the high occurrence traders were seen to have added to the instability in the Flash collapsing on the 6th May 2010, when the high-occurrence liquidity suppliers rapidly withdrawing from the market space. A number of these European states have proposed restricting or the banning of the high occurrence trade due to worries about its instability (Seydel, 2013).

10.5.1. Strategies

The high-occurrence trading is the quantitative dealings that are described by the short selection of holding phases. All the portfolio-distribution of decisions is prepared by computerized quantitative representations. The achievement of this high occurrence trading plans which are largely motivated by their capability to simultaneously process these large sizes of information, amazingly the average human dealers cannot do. The precise algorithms are strictly guarded via their proprietors. A lot of this practical algorithms are actually quite straightforward arbitrages which would previously have been executed at lower occurrence competition be likely to occur in the course of who can implement them the quickest rather than the one who could establish new burst through algorithms. The ordinary types of the high-occurrence trading comprise of several kinds of market-creation, occasion arbitrage, arithmetical arbitrage, and latency of arbitrage. Majority of this high-occurrence trading plans are not counterfeit, but in its place exploit tiny deviations from the market stability (Seydel, 2013).

These particular strategies become visible closely related to their admission of the modern electronic sites. The academic investigation of Chi-X's admission into the fairness of the European market exposes that its commencing coincided with a big high occurrence trade that prepared markets by means of both the current market, NYSE-Euronext, and the latest market, Chi-X. The investigation showed that the latest market supplied the ideal conditions for the high occurrence trade market-creation, small fees like the rebates of quotes that directed to the execution and a quick system; however, the high occurrence trade was equally dynamic in the present market to relieve of the nonzero situations. The latest market entries and the high occurrence trade onset are further exposed to correspond with an important improvement in liquidity contribution (Seydel, 2013).

1. *Ticker Tape Taping*: Much this information takes place to be unintentionally embedded in market statistics for example quotes and the amounts. By the scrutinizing a current of quotes, computers are able of the extracting content that has not so far as crossed the news broadcast screens. Ever since the entire quote and the amounts of information are public, such like plans are fully submissive with all the appropriate laws. Filter trading is the major one of the more ancient high-occurrence trading plans that involves the monitoring of big amounts of supplies for important or the unusual cost changes or the volume action. This comprises of the trading on of announcements, information, or even other occasion criteria. The software would later create a buying or selling plan depending on the character of the occasion being searched for. Tick dealings often aims at the distinguishing the beginnings of the big orders that are being put in the market space. Such as, a big order from a retirement fund to purchasing will obtain place more than some hours or even years, and will give an increase in value due to the increased commands. An arbitrageur can attempt to mark this happening and later purchasing up the security, later the profit from the selling backside to the annuity fund. This plan has turned out to be more complex because the introduction of devoted trade implemented organizations in the year of 2000s, which provided the optimal deal for the annuity and the other finances, exclusively designed to get rid of the arbitrage chance (Arratia, 2014).
2. *Occasion Arbitrage*: Certain recurring proceedings create a predictable small-term reply in a chosen set of securities. The high-occurrence dealers normally take benefit of such inevitability to create the short-period incomes.
3. *Arithmetical Arbitrage*: One more set of the high-occurrence trading plans are plans that are taken advantage of the predictable brief deviations from the stable numerical relationships in the center of the securities. Arithmetical arbitrages at very high occurrence are actively implemented in all the fluid securities, which are the equities, links, futures, overseas exchange and many others. Such plans may also engage classical arbitrage plans, like the covered interest speed parity in the overseas exchange market space, which provides a link between the costs of a domestic link, a connection denominated in an overseas currency,

the marked price of the exchange, and the cost of an advanced bond on the exchange. The high-occurrence trading permits the similar arbitrages by means of the replica of the greater difficulty involving various others more than four securities.

4. *Indicator Arbitrage*: This exploits the index tail funds which are bounded to the purchasing and the selling of large amounts of the securities in amounts to their changing weights in index. However, if a high occurrence trade organization is able to contact and develop information which forecasts these modifications before the trailer fund to follow, they can purchase the securities before the followers and later sell them on a return (Arratia, 2014).
5. *Information-Based Trading*: The company news in the electronic content arrangement is available from various sources which including the commercial contributes like the Bloomberg, the open news websites, and the Twitter news. The automatic systems can recognize the company names, the keywords and at times semantics to create the news-based deals before the human dealers can develop the news.
6. *Low Latency Plans:* A disconnected naive group of the high-occurrence trading plans relies completely on the ultra-small latency straight market accessing the know-how. In these plans, the computer researchers rely on pace to gain very small advantages in the arbitraging value discrepancies in a number of particular security dealing simultaneously on distinct markets spaces.

Another feature of the small latency plan has been the change from the fiber optic to the microwave knowledge for the extended distance networking. Particularly since the year 2011, there has occurred a tendency to implement the microwaves to broadcast the data across major connections like the one connecting the city of New York and the Chicago. This is mainly because the microwaves moving in the air suffer a smaller amount than 1% pace reduction is compared to the light moving in a vacuum, while with the conventional thread optics light moving over 30% slower (Arratia, 2014).

7. *Order Assets Plans*: The high-occurrence trading plans may implement the properties resulting from the market information feeds to recognize the instructions that are placed at the sub-optimal values. Such instructions may give a return to their counterparties the high-occurrence dealers can attempt to

acquire. Such examples of these particular features comprise of the era of an order or even the dimensions of the displayed orders. Following is important to the order assets and may also permit the trading plans to having a more accurate prediction of the future value of the security.

8. *Granularity and Correctness*: In the year 2015, the Paris-headquarters regulator of the nation 28th European merger, the European Securities and Markets power, planned the time standards to the duration of the European merger that could be more precisely synchronize trading watches, to inside a nanosecond, or even the one-billionth of a fraction to refine the rules of a entry-to another gateway latency occasion, the pace at which the deals venues recognize the order after getting a trade application. By implementing these more comprehensive time-stamps, controllers would be improved able to differentiate the arrangement in which trade requirements are established and then executed.

Bibliography

1. Allen, H., & Joseph, E., (2019). *An Introduction to Computational Science* (p. 470). Berlin: Springer.
2. Andreas B. J., Jens, G., François, A., & Henrik, A., (2012). *Guide to Computational Geometry Processing: Foundations, Algorithms, and Methods* (pp. 2–82). Berlin: Springer Science & Business Media.
3. Angela, B. S., & George, W. S., (2014). Introduction to computational science. *Modeling and Simulation for the Sciences* (2nd edn., p. 857).
4. Arratia, A., (2014). *Computational Finance: An Introductory Course with R. Berlin* (pp. 1–71). Springer Science & Business Media.
5. Blazek, J., (2005). *Computational Fluid Dynamics: Principles and Applications* (pp. 1–77). London: Elsevier.
6. Blossey, R., (2006). *Computational Biology: A Statistical Mechanics Perspective* (p. 276). Florida: CRC Press.
7. Brian, K., & David, M., (2013). *Astrophysics through Computation: With Mathematica ® Support.* London: Cambridge University Press.
8. Charles, D. H., & Chris, R. J., (2011). *Visualization Handbook* (pp. 39–97). London: Elsevier.
9. Chen, S. H., (2002). *Genetic Algorithms and Genetic Programming in Computational Finance* (pp. 1–79). Berlin: Springer Science & Business Media.

10. Davidson, D. B., (2010). *Computational Electromagnetics for RF and Microwave Engineering* (pp. 1–74). London: Cambridge University Press.
11. Eijkhout, V., (2013). *Introduction to High Performance Scientific Computing* (pp. 12–64.). New York: Lulu.com.
12. Irwin, J. A., (2007). *Astrophysics: Decoding the Cosmos* (pp. 1–63). New Jersey: John Wiley & Sons.
13. Kaveh, A., (2013). *Computational Structural Analysis and Finite Element Methods* (pp. 1–101). Berlin: Springer Science & Business Media.
14. Ladeveze, P., (2012). *Nonlinear Computational Structural Mechanics: New Approaches and Non-Incremental Methods of Calculation* (pp. 1–55). Berlin: Springer Science & Business Media.
15. Langtangen, H. P., (2013). *Python Scripting for Computational Science* (pp. 1–70). Berlin: Springer Science & Business Media.
16. Leszczynski, J., (2012). *Handbook of Computational Chemistry* (p. 1430). Berlin: Springer Science & Business Media.
17. Lewars, E. G., (2010). *Computational Chemistry: Introduction to the Theory and Applications of Molecular and Quantum Mechanics* (pp. 1–85). Berlin: Springer Science & Business Media.
18. Liseikin, V. D., (2009). *Grid Generation Methods.* Berlin: Springer Science & Business Media, 1–67.
19. Liseikin, V. D., (2013). *A Computational Differential Geometry Approach to Grid Generation* (pp. 4–59). Berlin: Springer Science & Business Media.
20. Magoules, F., (2011). *Computational Fluid Dynamics* (pp. 1–63). Florida: CRC Press.
21. McCarthy, E., (2018). *Foundations of Computational Finance with MATLAB* (pp. 3–81). New Jersey: John Wiley & Sons.
22. Miller, R. N., (2007). *Numerical Modeling of Ocean Circulation* (pp. 3–87). London: Cambridge University Press.
23. Mittra, R., (2012). *Computational Electromagnetics: Recent Advances and Engineering Applications* (pp. 1–75). Berlin: Springer Science & Business Media.
24. Rae Earnshaw & Norman Wiseman. (2012). *An Introductory Guide to Scientific Visualization* (pp. 3–53). Berlin: Springer Science &

Business Media.

25. Savine, A., (2018). *Modern Computational Finance: AAD and Parallel Simulations* (pp. 13–47). New Jersey: John Wiley & Sons.
26. Seydel, R. U., (2013). *Tools for Computational Finance* (pp. 57–84). Berlin: Springer Science & Business Media.
27. Simona, P., & Luca, F., (2015). *New Challenges in Grid Generation and Adaptivity for Scientific Computing* (pp. 1–91). Berlin: Springer.
28. Singh, G. B., (2014). *Fundamentals of Bioinformatics and Computational Biology: Methods and Exercises in MATLAB* (p. 339). Berlin: Springer.
29. Spellmeyer, D. C., (2005). *Annual Reports in Computational Chemistry* (pp. 19–91). London: Elsevier.
30. Wendt, J., (2008). *Computational Fluid Dynamics: An Introduction.* Berlin: Springer Science & Business Media, 3–87.
31. Wilson, S., (2013). *Methods in Computational Chemistry,* (Vol. 5, pp. 1–84). Berlin: Springer Science & Business Media.
32. Wright, H., (2007). *Introduction to Scientific Visualization* (p. 147). Berlin: Springer Science & Business Media.
33. Wünschiers, R., (2012). *Computational Biology: Unix/Linux, Data Processing and Programming* (pp. 4–80). Berlin: Springer Science & Business Media.
34. Xin-Qing, S., & Wei, S., (2012). *Essentials of Computational Electromagnetics* (pp. 1–29). New Jersey: John Wiley & Sons.
35. Young, D., (2004). *Computational Chemistry: A Practical Guide for Applying Techniques to Real World Problems* (pp. 1–5). New Jersey: John Wiley & Sons.
36. Zingoni, A., (2010). *Advances and Trends in Structural Engineering, Mechanics, and Computation* (pp. 9–59). Florida: CRC Press.

INDEX

F

G

H